Bradley Willis

The Development of Naturalist Legal Theory

The
Development of
NATURALIST
LEGAL
THEORY

H. McCoubrey

CROOM HELM
London • New York • Sydney

© 1987 H. McCoubrey
Croom Helm Ltd, Provident House, Burrell Row,
Beckenham, Kent BR3 1AT
Croom Helm Australia, 44–50 Waterloo Road,
North Ryde, 2113, New South Wales

British Library Cataloguing in Publication Data

McCoubrey, H.
    The development of naturalist legal theory.
    1. Jurisprudence — History
    I. Title
    340'.1   K230

    ISBN 0–7099–4669–4

Published in the USA by
Croom Helm
in association with Methuen, Inc.
29 West 35th Street
New York, NY 10001

Library of Congress Cataloging-in-Publication Data

McCoubrey, H., 1953-
    The development of naturalist legal theory.

    1. Natural law — History. I. Title.
KF415.M35   1987   171'.2   86-32803
ISBN 0-7099-4669-4

Phototypeset by Pat and Anne Murphy
10 Bracken Way, Highcliffe-on-Sea, Dorset

Printed and bound in Great Britain
by Billing & Sons Limited, Worcester.

Contents

Acknowledgements

The author wishes to acknowledge the encouragement which he has received from colleagues in the Department of Law at Nottingham University in the preparation of this book. Thanks are due in particular to Mr M. J. Gunn who has read and commented upon some of the chapters in draft, also to Mr D. R. Halson and Mr M. J. Sterling who have both endured with fortitude the views of the author upon legal theory in the course of conversation. All of these persons, however, are entirely innocent of complicity in the author's views which are his responsibility alone.

Thanks are also expressed to those who have kindly granted their permission for quotation to be made from certain copyright material. In particular, to Butterworths Law Publishers Ltd in respect of the All England Law Reports. To Mr H. Collins in respect of *Marxism and Law*. To Professor R. M. Dworkin in respect of *Taking Rights Seriously*. Extracts from the Authorised King James Version of the Bible, which is Crown copyright in the United Kingdom, are reproduced by permission of Eyre and Spottiswoode (Publishers) Ltd, Her Majesty's Printers, London. To the Keter Publishing House of Jerusalem Ltd in respect of the *Encyclopaedia Judaica*. To the Oxford University Press in respect of H. L. A. Hart's *The Concept of Law* (1961).

Last, but by no means least, thanks are expressed to those of the author's personal and professional acquaintance who have assisted with the tedious but vital task of typing the manuscript.

Preface

Legal theory, like many other subjects, can be approached in a number of different ways, each emphasising different aspects of the phenomenon of 'law'. The differences between such approaches tend to generate controversies which may have value in so far as they may generate debate upon real questions but may also stultify debate by imposing false categorisations and raising debate upon artificial 'issues'. Modern Western jurisprudence has developed from a number of strands of thought among which one of the oldest and most fully developed is that known as 'naturalism'.

The essence of a 'naturalist' legal theory is a central concern with the moral nature of law and its claim to be obeyed. Naturalist theory in its various forms is concerned with both ends of the moral spectrum of legal assessment, with the ideal of what will constitute morally 'good' law, but also with the minimum moral standards which law-makers must observe if their laws are to have any claim to obedience in the conscience of their subjects. This is quite a different emphasis from that, for example, of positivist jurisprudence, which is centrally concerned with the formal nature of laws and law-making — by what processes rules and standards may be enunciated in such a way that they will be recognised by courts and other formal or applicatory institutions. Unfortunately this distinction in theoretical approach has generated a rather specious 'debate' founded upon the premiss that laws are defined either by reference to moral criteria or by reference to formal criteria, and much energy has been expended upon the advocation of each position upon this supposed issue. In fact laws may properly be defined by reference to both moral and formal criteria of identification depending upon the purpose for which the definition is being made. Each type of approach in legal theory has its role to play and to suggest that any particular form of theory may be exclusively 'right' or 'wrong' is greatly to over-simplify the very complex issues involved in the study of law and the way in which it functions.

The issues raised by naturalist legal theories are of immense importance, going to the root of the nature of the moral claim of laws. This book is intended to provide a description of the development of this aspect of Western legal theory from its ancient origins to the major issues of modern debate. In doing so it is intended to set naturalist ideas in their context and to discuss the continuing relevance of naturalist ideas in the modern world. It is hoped that this book may serve to outline not only the importance but also the essential interest of the naturalist tradition in the development of legal theory.

H. McCoubrey
Nottingham

Introduction

A society, whether it be a stamp club or the political society which we term a state, can be seen to depend upon some structure of norms accepted by the generality of its members. There is of course a great difference between the rules of a club and the laws of a state in terms of significance, generality, volume and complexity of administration, but in each case the same basic function is served. Such a formal normative structure is not necessary for two broad reasons: firstly, to define what forms of conduct are prescribed or proscribed for the members of the society and, secondly, to set out a convenient framework for the conduct of day-to-day transactions and thus to avoid needless disruption occasioned by avoidable disputes and to resolve such disputes as do arise by peaceable means. The administration of such norms calls also for a set of rules governing the practical opposition of the system. Within any given society there are of course many other normative influences than those categorised as 'legal'. They include religious and ethical teaching, moral perceptions, convention, personal relationships and such apparently 'trivial' influences as fashion. From all of these, however, law is distinguished in a developed society by formal enunciation, generality of application and mandatory quality. Laws may in fact be described as mandatory human ordinances representing the most formal type of social regulation and prescribing at least those minimum standards of conduct and necessary formal procedures upon which the continuance of social order is taken to depend. Of these qualities the most immediately notable is that law is mandatory. Legal prescription does not offer a choice of compliance or non-compliance; by legal statement the pattern of conduct described is rendered in some manner a matter of 'obligation' for those subject to the system concerned.

This idea of the 'obligation' to obey laws is one of the most fundamental and controversial issues in the theory of law. The question in its most basic form is simply this — why do people obey 'laws' and why should they? Upon this issue there has been much debate but little apparent consensus. The central issue of debate is the effect of the quality, in particular the moral quality, of laws upon their claim to obedience, or, to put it another way, the relation of morality to validity in the assessment of laws. Are laws simply orders coercively imposed by the state and therefore claiming obedience ultimately by virtue of the application or threat of application of force? Alternatively do laws have a moral dimension which imposes some form of obligation to obey upon its subjects irrespective of the application or potential application of coercive measures? In the latter case the further problem arises of the effect upon the status of a purported 'law' of the absence or defectiveness of such a moral component.

It is generally said that there are two schools of thought upon these issues which broadly represent the two propositions outlined above: these are the 'Positivist' and 'Naturalist' schools of jurisprudence. In fact this simple demarcation line is much too simple but as a conventional wisdom must be accepted as a starting point. The Positivist school is the more recent in origin and dates from the turn of the eighteenth and nineteenth centuries. It has remained the dominant form of legal theory, at least in Anglo/American jurisprudence, through the post-war years, although the modern position of theory has more recently become much more fluid again. The identifying feature of a positivist legal theory is a concentration upon the formal identification of law as it *is* rather than upon law as it morally, or otherwise, *ought* to be. Thus upon positivist perceptions, once a means has been found of identifying formally binding rules, the requirements of legal theory are satisfied. The moral quality of laws, while obviously a matter of importance in its own right, is then seen as having no relevance to their status as 'laws'. This is what the founding father of legal positivism, Jeremy Bentham, termed 'expository jurisprudence'.[1] The analytical positivism of Bentham and his disciple John Austin is at first sight an attractively simple form of legal theory. Law is presented as essentially the command of a political sovereign, the ultimate political superior in a given society, backed by the threat of a sanction in the event of non-compliance. On this view it is the threatened sanction which is the cause of obedience. Bentham himself was prepared to treat the concept of sanction as embracing the promise of reward as well as the threat of punishment. Austin, however, took the simpler line of treating sanction as the threat of an unpleasant consequence.

Such an explanation may account fairly effectively for the operation of the criminal law so far as those of criminal inclination are concerned; it is much less satisfactory, however, as an explanation of the working of civil law. Much of civil law is not in reality essentially coercive but rather facilitative. The law of contract is designed to enable people to carry out their business in a convenient and known format, not to 'punish' them for breaches of contract. In another instance the law of succession and testamentation is designed to facilitate the transfer of property upon death and so far as possible to obviate damaging post-mortem disputes among the potential heirs. It is true that the law of tort is in many ways the civil equivalent of criminal law but even here the basic aim is to provide a forum for the peaceful resolution of major private disputes which might otherwise be settled in more socially dangerous ways. These major aspects of law lend themselves much less readily to a simple coercive model of law. Austin sought an explanation in a sanction of nullity, meaning, for example, that wills are made in accordance with the Wills Act, 1837, and succeeding legislation because the testator 'fears' that otherwise his or her wishes will not be implemented. This seems a strangely contorted view of what are in reality a set of instructions for the transaction of a piece of formal business. If the will does prove to be ineffective that is the inevitable product of incompetence upon the part of the testator or his solicitor and is surely no more to be seen as 'punishment' than the collapse of a badly assembled piece of self-assembly furniture. Viewed thus the purely coercive model of law becomes problematic. There is also the question of the derivation of sovereign power. Bentham explained sovereign power in terms of a general 'habit of obedience', which has a certain evident relevance. However, the insistence upon law as a simple command necessarily involves a concept of *authority* which cannot readily be explained in terms of the mere application of power.

H. L. A. Hart undertook a reworking of the 'command' theory of law taking account of these problems. He replaced the simple command model with a double classification of legal rules as 'primary', or duty imposing, and 'secondary', or power conferring. The latter classification takes account much more satisfactorily of the phenomenon of constitutional law and thus permits a more subtle analysis of sovereignty. Here Hart distinguishes between 'obligation' and 'being obliged' — the one being a concept of duty and the other merely the practical effect of coercion, law importing the former. At the end of the day, however, the aim of positivist theories is the identification of the formally valid law, which properly describes obligation in the sense of a formally imposed duty. Positivism does not and has no need to consider the alternative aspect of legal obligation — that is to say the moral claim of the positive[2] law to be obeyed irrespective of formal definition or processes. Hart properly attributes the sense of legal obligation to the recognition of 'authority' rather than the mere fear of force but the ultimate claim of authority is a matter falling somewhat outside the scope of positivist enquiry since it is a claim based upon moral as well as formal or political assumptions.

The attempt to incorporate moral factors into the definition of 'law' is the hallmark of the other broad school of legal theory, that collectively termed 'Naturalism'. This is a very much older and more diverse body of theory than is the relatively more recent body of positivist theory. The principal concern of naturalist theory is the moral quality of law and the status of a formally enacted or otherwise made law and the effect of moral defect upon its status. This branch of theory concerns a different aspect of 'obligation' — the moral claim to obedience. The naturalist enquiry is not an easy one to pursue since two apparently intractable difficulties immediately manifest themselves. The first is the external criterion upon which the moral authority of law is to be based, the second is the practical implication of any such criterion for the claim of laws to obedience. The nature of this type of theory is often misrepresented as a crude claim that a morally defective 'law' is not effective, literally, 'lex iniusta non est lex'. Since all too many examples of morally dubious laws which have indeed been enforced may be brought to mind upon even the most scanty of historical reviews, any such proposition would be patently absurd. The actual form of naturalist concern was expressed more usefully by the great Dominican thinker St Thomas Aquinas in the form: 'les tyrannica, cum non sit secundum rationem, non est simpliciter lex, sed magis es quaedam perversitas legis',[3] which is to say that a tyrannical law which is contrary to reason is not absolutely and straightforwardly law but a perversion of law. This implies not that 'bad' laws cannot be made and imposed but that such laws are defective in being wrongly made and are thus limited or even entirely lacking in their claim to be obeyed as a matter of conscience. This is in fact a concern with the moral nature of the power to make laws rather than with the formal identification of state prescription. The two basic issues call for separate discussion.

The moral criterion of identification

A moral assessment of law must be made upon some exterior

standard. Various possibilities have been and are advanced. All involve, however, some pattern of expectation to which the reality of legal provision can be compared. Crudely these may be categorised as the absolute and the deduced. The one is derived from a perception of an externally created moral order such as the will of God, the other from an evaluation of human nature. These categories are of course no more than descriptive and are certainly not mutually exclusive in that many theories have elements of both. For example, there is no reason why expectation should not be derived from observation of human nature while attributing that nature to the Divine will. In such a case one may call the method deductive but the rationale absolute. On the other hand there are many supposedly objective theories which actually include a considerable element of doctrinal choice, whether or not the choice is perceived or admitted. In fact, the distinction is one of order rather than type. In either case a superior order is argued and set up as a criterion of moral assessment by which the quality of positive law may be considered. It is in the perception of the origin of the higher order, and in the effect of derivation from it, that the distinction emerges.

The perceived relationship between law and morality is a very ancient one but the common assumption of a very simplified perception in early times is somewhat mistaken. Law develops from custom but it is a controversial question whether or not custom *is* law or merely pre-law which, as suggested by Hart, awaits the addition of an administrative and rule-making 'superstructure' to become 'true' law. Whatever the status of customary rules as 'law', such rules are closely related to moral ideas. They are in effect enshrined traditions of 'proper' social behaviour. Customary rules are further commonly associated with tribal or 'national' ancestral spirits and by extension therefrom with divine command. The resulting quasi-'sanctity' of established habit is a common feature of most societies. Problems of a jurisprudential nature arise when law-making institutions are developed, as opposed to mere acceptance of inherited static rules. The problem is to transfer the apparent 'authority' of customary rules to newly made rules which are obviously not the work of gods or ancestral spirits, nor indeed sanctified by long traditional usage. The obvious solution to this difficulty is to relate the power to make laws *de novo* to the same higher power from which customary rules were seen as deriving their authority. Thus law-making comes to be seen as a power granted upon terms through some mechanism which transcends the machinations of human politics. This in turn means that new rules are related to a conceptual scheme which sets limits to the proper scope of their operation. This is not of course to say that a powerful ruler could not step beyond such bounds, merely that he would encounter difficulty in doing so to an increasing extent as he moved beyond the conceptual limits. It has been established that most 'primitive' rulers were very powerful within a known tribal tradition but would have found it virtually impossible to effect major changes in the tradition. Examples may be found in societies that were very far from 'primitive' also. An extreme instance of this may be seen in the case of the Egyptian Pharaoh Amenophis IV. This ruler, who was seen not merely as a servant of the gods but as a god in his own right, attempted to overthrow the established, and chaotic, polytheism of ancient Egypt and to replace it with a monotheistic solar cult of his own devising based upon the worship of the sun disc, Aten. As a symbol of the new order the Pharaoh changed his name to Akhetaten. Even Pharaonic power could not achieve such a change, however, and upon the death of Akhetaten the new order collapsed. His successor but one, the youthful Tutankhaten, changed his name to Tutankhamun to symbolise the restoration of the traditional polytheistic religion headed by the priesthood of Amun–Ra at Thebes.

The codes of laws promulgated by ancient near-eastern civilisations clearly indicate the derivation of law-making power from a higher authority. One of the best known of such codes, that of King Hammurabi of Babylon, is headed by a relief carving of the king standing before the god Shamesh whose approval of the king's work is clearly implied. It would be possible to view this development as a cynical manipulation of religious belief by powerful rulers but cynicism would be both misplaced and rather naïve here: it was in essence a recognition of the moral nature of law and government. This type of perception lies at the root of most naturalist legal theory and amounts to the idea of governmental power as a power which is not unlimited but held upon terms that it should be exercised for the good of the community. The many and very apparent divergences of opinion derive from the varying forms attributed to the perceived resulting 'trust'.

To judge from the evidence of the Code Hammurabi, the Babylonian idea was of a divine commission to the king to do justice. The actual modes of the king's doing so were perceived in a very secular and surprisingly 'modern' way. The code was really a secular code presented in the form of royal edicts or judgements dealing with particular problems and recorded both as specific decisions and as exemplars. However, it would appear from the curses called down upon anyone who might seek to set aside the code or to traduce its principles that to step outside the divine commission to do justice might have been seen as some form of denial of the basic role of kingship. It must of course be admitted that attempts to protect inscription from defacement by ritual curses upon prospective vandals was a common enough practice in the ancient world, perhaps a parallel with modern attempts to cow defacers of notices with threats of legal proceedings and roughly as effective. It may even be possible, while admitting the dangers of reading too much into such ancient records, to discern in the ancient Babylonian conception of law a naturalist and religion-based theory of the authority of law linked with a quasi-positivist view of the actual making of laws.

Other ancient legal theories took a variety of views upon the nature and detail of the relationship of the higher order to human prescription. In ancient Judaic theory the 'law' was seen overtly as the will of God enshrined in the scriptures as a divinely ordained way of life for the faithful. This code, which is much more detailed than the Code Hammurabi, is found in the Pentateuch (the first five books of the Old Testament). However, if the Torah was not to become a frozen Holy Law some means of taking account of new situations not originally contemplated had to be found — in other words the familiar problem of conferring authority upon new prescription. The solution was found in a process of interpretative accretion through the unwritten tradition of the Halakah. The divine authority of the Torah was extended to the Halakah by the elegant device of an assumption that an accepted interpretation was a 'discovery' of something necessarily inherent in the original prescription and thus sharing in its authority. This of course is a very rigorous form of naturalism in which the higher authorisation is identified with the specific details of prescription as well as with the general purpose of prescription.

Judaic naturalism contributed one of the two major strands to the development of Western naturalist legal theory. The other, and contrasting, strand of development was derived from classical Hellenistic thought. The Hellenistic tradition was based upon rational enquiry into the nature of man and his social life. Whether based, as in the case of Plato, upon a rational but abstract idealism, or, as in the case Aristotle, upon consideration of human nature as such, the basic perception was similar in outlook. The ideas resulting were presented as the product of enquiries into the nature of things with the aim of setting up a rational standard for consideration and criticism rather than a doctrine. The role, if any, of divine intervention was seen as a separate and very much vaguer issue.

These widely variant approaches were fused eventually in the development of the Christian tradition of legal theory. The early church took a Judaic absolutist view with the further point that law was necessitated only by sin and would, in the eventual abandonment of sin through redemption by Divine grace, in due course cease to have a role to play. A law which was itself sinful or an inducement to sin was naturally seen as an abomination. This simple view was gradually modified over the centuries, especially after the Christianisation of the Roman Empire under Constantine the Great (AD 306–37). St Augustine of Hippo believed that law was both the penalty and the remedy of sin and that the ideal life according to the will of God would have no place for it. However, in the fallen state of man law was 'good' in so far as it curbed sin according to the Divine will and 'bad' in so far as it did otherwise. In that this view posits an ideal prescription to which law is very much a 'second best', it is really a form of Christian Platonism. St Thomas Aquinas (1225–77) carried the process of synthesis further, having the benefit of the rediscovery of the works of Aristotle since the time of St Augustine. For Aquinas, as for Aristotle, law was the natural product of the life of man as a social animal and not a temporary aberration. Aquinas considered that the 'good' positive law would accord with the *Lex Aeterna*, the will of God, as known to man through the *Lex Divina* (revelation through scripture) or the *Lex Naturalis* (perception of the Divine will made manifest in the natural order through the operation of human reason). However, he thought also that law had no necessary connection with sin — it was its coercive nature rather than its prescriptive function which was the product of the Fall. This view is maintained to the present day, the work of the Thomist writer John C. H. Wu being a very clear example.

The Age of Reason naturally sought its inspiration in less spiritual forms and favoured Social Contractarianism which appeared in the seventeenth century and developed over the course of the eighteenth century. The chosen method of this form of theory was to enquire into the basic social needs which law evolved to satisfy. The model for law is then one which is perceived as most adequately fulfilling these requirements. The 'contract' itself was, at least for the later theorists of this school, a rhetorical device rather than an assertion of a historical reality. It was in fact the direct ancestor of John Rawls's 'original position' with the initial contractors behind their 'veil of ignorance'. On this view the moral suasion of law is seen to depend upon the extent to which it fulfils its designated social purpose.

Within the historical tradition of Western naturalism there is thus a wide range of opinion upon the source of the moral authority of law although a closer investigation shows much less conflict in reality than is prima facie apparent.

Outside the European tradition, legal theory has also tended to take a naturalist form, again with a range of types of approach. Two examples from opposite ends of the spectrum sufficiently illustrate the point. Islamic legal theory is the product of one of the most legalistic of societies but also one which most directly identifies its theory and practice of law with religious doctrine. In its fundamentalist form, Islamic legal theory argues that mankind, and most especially the faithful, is already governed by a direct divine prescription superior to and superseding positive law in the form of the Sha'ria, the Holy Law of Islam. The Sha'ria is seen as having been given directly by Allah to the prophet Mahomet as an immutable law for the faithful. In fact and inevitably the Sha'ria, like the Torah, is associated with many accretions of tradition in the form of Haddith. The Hadditha are recognised traditions which have themselves become authoritative. There are in fact considerable divergences of interpretation and disputes as to application, which are resolved partly by internal mutual toleration.

Upon the orthodox Islamic view the Sha'ria is not the ideal model for positive law — it is itself the *only* true law. After some years of secular dilution in many parts of the Islamic world the impact of modern Islamic fundamentalism has led to a massive resurgence in the influence of Sha'riat law in many jurisdictions.

At the opposite extreme stood classical Chinese legal theory. This theory was the product of the union of two sharply conflicting philosophies, Legalism and Confucianism. The legalists believed that man is inherently inclined to vice and must therefore be coerced into proper conduct by the rigorous application of minutely detailed, positive laws. The Confucians in contrast believed that man is basically inclined towards virtue and will follow a virtuous example when one is set before him. The legalists triumphed initially under the first Imperial dynasty, the Chin, but their overthrow by Liu Pang and the foundation of the Han dynasty led to the establishment of Confucianism as the state ideology of Imperial China. The result was that the role of law was severely limited to what we would call the criminal sphere. Civil disputes were made a matter for non-official (but nevertheless clearly understood) procedures dependent upon convention and social pressure. Within its defined arena the law was highly legalist in tone and seen as a means of coercing into the appearance of virtue those who were not otherwise inclined to it. Virtue itself was seen as residing in a universal natural order which prescribed the proper life of man as well as natural phenomena in general. This natural order was seen as founded upon the dictates of Heaven (Tien), but the Confucian sages considered that the nature of the powers of Heaven were unknown and that speculation upon the point was therefore idle. Confucian theory therefore depended upon a certain perception of human nature which was recognised as having a higher origin along with the rest of the natural universe, the nature of the originator being unclear, however.

Naturalist strains may also be discerned in realms of theory where they would not at first sight be anticipated. Marxists would not willingly accept the label of naturalism since Marxist theory is conceived as pre-eminently scientific and objective as an exposition of the processes of social development through the medium of 'class struggle'. However, the Marxist view of law does have some distinctively naturalist features. In the classical Marxist exposition law is seen as an instrument of class repression used by a ruling class to maintain its economic dominance and especially associated with the 'bourgeois' phase of development, that is to say with the capitalist economy. The end of social development through class struggle is seen as occurring with the 'proletarian revolution' after which the process of successive overthrow of dominant classes ceases for lack of further repressed economic groupings. This ultimate revolution is said to be followed by a re-educative period of 'dictatorship of the proletariat' which is to usher in the era of genuine communism. In the communist society the bourgeois legal order is seen as having withered away to be replaced by a communal 'ordering of things'. However, during the 'dictatorship of the proletariat' positive law would remain with the twin function of protecting the interim socialist state against 'counter-revolutionary' elements and supplying a mechanism of ideological re-education. Lenin himself took a very positivist, almost Benthamite, view of positive law and regarded it as a strictly temporary and regrettable phenomenon, as did the leading Russian theorist of the day, E. B. Pashukanis. Subsequently, however, in the era of Vyshinski the doctrine of 'socialist legality' developed, in which the making and application of positive law is subjected to ideological considerations thereby producing a 'socialist' law free from 'bourgeois' taint. The earlier view which disdains law has something vaguely in common with Platonic theory and the later idea clearly subjects positive law-making to an alternative prescription, albeit in this instance a man-made alternative. This is not of course conventional naturalism but the affinities with naturalism appear upon study to be much closer than would otherwise be expected prima facie.

The effect of the moral criterion

Having made a decision as to what moral criterion of assessment is to be applied in the consideration of the quality of positive law, the naturalist must next ask what is to be the effect of application of the criterion. In particular, what is the status of the positive enactment which falls short of the moral standard set? Few, if any, naturalist theories fall into the fatuity of claiming that an iniquitous enactment is devoid of effect. Sadly, simple observation of world events suffices to disprove any such idea. The range of possible opinion is none the less broad. At one extreme it might be argued that a morally 'bad' law has no claim to be called a true 'law' being rather the coercive demand of a tyrant without moral claim to obedience. At the other extreme it might be argued that an assessment of moral defect in a law is a useful tool of criticism, and an argument for appropriate change, but does not in itself have any effect upon the enactment or its status. Whichever side is leaned towards, there is mingled with the first question the problem of social stability and the issue of what 'price' in bad law ought properly to be paid for its continuance.

It is commonly assumed that religion-based theories incline to the former view and rational theories to the latter. In fact few theories reach either extreme and the expectation that many would involve a misunderstanding of the nature of the enquiry being made. The error commonly made is to seek for a moral effect upon the way a law actually 'works', that is, has effect. On this basis of course no law is directly invalidated by moral defectiveness, as John Austin correctly asserted, believing himself thereby to have refuted naturalism. As the positivists assert, laws are made formally and abrogated formally whether their content be moral, immoral or merely amoral. What is in question from the naturalist viewpoint is not the formal status of 'laws' from the positivist position but the extent to which laws have a claim to obedience operating upon the conscience of their subjects in the absence of immediate coercion. In short the question is the authority of a law and not the extent to which it can successfully be imposed through naked coercion. Much can be done which should not be, which is not to say that such things should be accepted or encouraged.

It is not enough to say, however, that a law which does not meet the selected criterion lacks moral suasion; some guide to propriety of action — whether mere argument or active resistance — is called for together with some provision for the making of the determination in the first place.

In the first place a certain, though limited, degree of bad law is preferable to the anarchy which a frivolous disregard for law would bring about. The great issue is how much and how 'bad' the level of tolerability is — in short that point at which morality and good conscience dictate that positive prescription cannot be followed — notwithstanding issues of social stability. The comfortable assumption of those of us reared in a well meaning legal order that such a point is practically inconceivable is unfortunately a dangerous misconception. The present century discloses all too many instances in which men and women have been faced with exactly that dilemma and have chosen the path of conscientious disobedience. Many of them died for their beliefs as martyrs in concentration camps, some survived to pose their questions anew. Issues of such drama are spared to most but such remains the end of the road of denial of the relevance of morality in the consideration of law-making.

Again a range of types of approach is available. The simplest option is to regard actual or potential immorality as a political rather than a jurisprudential fact and to await its effects upon that level. The mainstream of classical Hellenistic legal theory was upon those lines. Plato, in *The Last Days of Socrates*, argued, or rather imputed the argument to Socrates, that it is the duty of a good citizen to argue for changes to bad law but, if his fellow citizens reject his advice, then he should abide by their decision or move to another state. This was of course more practical advice in the era of small Greek city-states than in the modern world. The view is that laws *should* be moral and that their failure to be so is ground for criticism and change but not a denial of any element of 'law' quality.

The detail of the Christian view of the matter has shifted over the centuries in matters of detail but the fundamental conception of the transcendence of the will of God over positive ordinance has not. The view of all theorists who considered the matter up to and including St Thomas Aquinas was that a law defying the will of God would be an abomination. St Augustine denied such an ordinance the status of 'law', comparing it with the tyrannical demands of a brigand or a pirate which might of course secure compliance but which had no power to command the Christian conscience. St Thomas Aquinas also denied immoral or ungodly moral authority but referred to them as laws which were spoilt. His essential point was that the power to make law is granted by God for the benefit of mankind in accordance with His will; abuse of that power for other purposes is an evil which can only be imposed through coercion since it has no inherent authority. St Thomas recognised the dangers in a purely subjective and random selection of 'good' laws by the individual and sought systematic assessment. This was readily available in medieval Europe in the form of the centralised power of the Papacy which could and did bring considerable pressure to bear upon secular governments. In theory the ultimate sanction lay in the secular powers of the Holy Roman Emperor but that was more theory than fact in practice. In modern times, indeed since the late sixteenth century, that approach has hardly been a viable option although doctrinal pronouncement remains far from without influence in many countries. Despite the lack of direct effect the moral position of the Churches can be effective even though now, as in a sense perhaps always, a particular crisis must be resolved by the person facing it and not by an institution.

Legal theory cannot supply a dogmatic answer to such particular questions of conscience but it can provide a framework of reference against which such issues may be judged, It is true that law in general has a claim to the obedience of its subjects in that it represents the basic formal structure of the society in which they live. However, the law and the makers of laws do not anywhere have an unlimited power to demand whatever they will. The dividing line between what may properly be demanded and what may not is the boundary drawn between the rule of law and tyranny.

Even in the most virtuous of societies not all laws are 'good' and even in the most morally reprehensible not all are 'bad'. The distinction between 'good' and 'bad' laws and the proper reaction to the latter are difficult issues, as the historical multiplicity of answers given clearly demonstrates. The fact that the answers may be obscure does not rob the question of importance, however. There are in fact many common strands of thoughts to be discerned in the various naturalist theories, especially once some of them have been extracted from their archaic historical settings. The aim of the present study is to present some of the more important ideas and to seek in them some general naturalist principles of value to the modern study of law in a world which has no less need to understand the moral nature and proper limitations of lawmaking than any previous age.

Notes

1. Bentham, *A Fragment on Government*, Preface: 13.
2. Positive law is that which is formally enacted or made by human institutions of state as binding prescription within a particular society, in distinction from, for example, the law of God, the laws of Nature or scientific laws.
3. St Thomas Aquinas, *Summa Theologica*, 1a 2ae, 92:1.

1

Early Beginnings

There is no real consensus upon the point of social development at which 'law' as a formal institution may be said to have appeared. To some extent the question is one of form rather than substance in that the answer obviously depends upon the selection of definition of positive law. A customary society evidently has a system of prescription which may well be mandatory and can be very elaborate. The suggested distinction between a 'customary' and a 'legal' society made by many commentators is that the former is necessarily static whereas the latter is, at least potentially, dynamic — the functional distinction being that in a 'legal' as opposed to customary society new rules can be made and old ones changed or abrogated as developing social needs may dictate, the new or altered rules having immediately effective authority. Upon this view it is the making of rules which defines a 'legal' society and not the mere existence of prescriptive rules. This question of 'authority' is of supreme importance. A prescriptive or proscriptive rule which has authority imposes an obligation upon those to whom it is addressed which exists irrespective of the application of, or even potential for, coercion. Coercive mechanisms may, and almost certainly will, exist but they reinforce an independently existing obligation in appropriate cases of derogation; they are not the source of the obligation in the first place. This is essentially the distinction drawn by the positivist theorist M. L. A. Hart between being 'obliged' and being 'under obligation'.[1] A person may be 'obliged', in the sense of being compelled, by anyone possessing superior force (Hart takes the example of a gunman) whereas he can be put under obligation only by someone having known authority.

1

Obligation of course exists outside the formal framework of law. Religious and ethical belief creates obligation, so too does tradition. On a more personal level people feel obligation generated by ties of family and friendship. Law is not the only social prescription by any means; it is, however, the most formal and in terms of social cohesion a very important one.

There have been many attempts to define 'law'. It is doubtful whether this could ever be done satisfactorily since the range of factors to be included or considered is vast. The question of the moral component, if any, in law goes to the root of the issue under consideration, yet some description of the phenomenon of law in general must be essayed — if only to delimit as a preliminary exercise that which is *not* under consideration. There may be no consensus upon the point of social development at which law may be said to have come into existence but there are certain generally accepted points which may be made. It seems to be generally agreed that some form of 'constitutional' structure is required for 'law' to be said to exist, even if this is no more than the enunciation of the will of a known autocrat. This basic idea can be found in various definitions of law which are otherwise very different in both form and intention. Thus, St Thomas Aquinas defined 'law' in the following terms: '. . . nihil est aliud quaedam rationis ordinatio ad bonum commune, ab eo qui curam communitatis habet promulgata',[2] that is to say, that law is a rational ordinance made for the good of the community and promulgated. In the Thomist view 'law' encompasses the laws of God as well as those of men and, bearing this in mind, the immediate constitutional point should not perhaps here be pushed too closely. H. L. A. Hart, unsurprisingly, emphasised constitutionality much more strongly in his 'positivist' definition of 'law' as involving a union of primary (duty-imposing) rules with secondary (power-conferring) rules.[3]

Whatever the view taken of detailed arguments upon the matter of definition, it may perhaps be accepted for purposes of discussion that 'law', at the minimum, involves the formal prescription of conduct for a given society which is communicated according to some known process, even if this be only the expression of the decisions of an autocrat. In general such prescription would be expected also to be mandatory rather than merely suggestive or exhortatory. In practice, 'legal' ideas, and with them legal theory, seem to develop when custom, the enshrined practice of the community, ceases to be adequate for the regulation of a more complex society and the need is felt for mechanisms for the creation of new rules and the amendment of old ones as the circumstances may from time to time require.

The origins of law lie in the more static customary prescription which preceded it. In modern jurisprudence custom is regarded more as a possible source material for legal rules than as a source of law *per se*. Thus it may be argued that a customary practice may attain recognition by the courts and thus become law through enshrinement in precedent. Moreover, in the formative years of English law, custom was very much a primary source of law. In societies of a 'primitive' type custom is indeed often the principal, if not the only, form of prescription. It would thus appear that 'rules' in the form which may fairly be called 'proto-law' predate the formal mechanisms of a legal system in the historical pattern of social development. The authority of such rules is not derived from legal institutions, there being none at the time, nor is it actually derived from coercion. 'Primitive' societies are not necessarily without coercive mechanisms,[4] but the level and effect of such mechanisms vary enormously. Often 'enforcement' occurs through social pressure more than coercion *per se*.[5] The operation of such customary rules necessarily depends upon the sense of obligation of their subjects and that sense of obligation is essentially the product of long habit. The custom of a 'primitive' society in fact commands obedience by virtue of the awe with which it becomes invested through years of practice. When formal law-making processes develop, the new rules must somehow take on something of the same mantle if they are to command the same respect and obedience.

Contrary to popular impression, rulers in 'primitive' societies were not usually unrestricted despots in the manner of some modern totalitarian dictators. On the contrary, such rulers tended to be seen as living embodiments of the tradition of the tribe or, later, the nation. Within that tradition their power might, although it was not so of necessity, be absolute but it was difficult, if not impossible, for them to step outside that tradition. The tradition might evolve, but to change it by order was very difficult even if possible at all. As societies become more complex and develop to a 'civilised'[6] state, more formal and sophisticated legal techniques become necessary in order to facilitate adequate responses to new questions and problems. Amendment of enshrined customary norms needs association with the same or a similar perceived higher order with which the customary order

3

itself has become associated.

This need to associate new 'laws' with the semi-divine ascription of custom is the basis of the idea that laws 'ought' to accord with moral precept. This may in fact be seen as an inherited idea of limitation upon government traceable back to the inability of 'primitive' rules to defy tribal mores. The ancient association of law-making[7] with moral authority lies at the root of subsequent naturalist thought and can indeed be said to be as old as legal theory itself. Perhaps as a result of this very ambiguity, such ideas have of course been worked out in many different ways in different cultures.

In most ancient civilisations religion, morality and positive law were not really seen as separate phenomena with some coincidence of action as they tend to be today, but rather as different aspects of the same thing. Even if the ruler was not regarded as personally divine, as was for example the Pharaoh of Egypt, law-making itself was generally felt to be a sacred or quasi-sacred function. This can be seen in the common ascription of law-making power to some divine conference of authority. With the increasing sophistication of secular law-making, this tended progressively to develop into something more closely approaching the modern idea of a relationship between human law and a higher moral order.

This process may readily be observed. In the Louvre in Paris there may be seen a carved and inscribed pillar of black diorite, standing some seven feet and four inches high and two feet in diameter. This monument was discovered in a fragmented state at Susa in modern Iran by French archaeologists in December 1901. It transpired, however, that it had been removed there by an Elamite conqueror from its original location in a temple at Sippara (near Baghdad) in present-day Iraq. Upon translation[8] the inscription was discovered to be a code of laws promulgated by the Babylonian King Hammurabi who reigned approximately 1790 – 1750 BC. The code itself appears to consist of a series of judgements and orders made by the King. Hammurabi seems, upon the available evidence, actually to have taken a personal interest in such matters rather than merely having the outcome formally ascribed to his wisdom. It is very clear, however, that these laws were seen as depending upon something more than the power of the king himself and were in fact related both to moral duty and to religious command. At the top of the front face of the pillar is a carving which appears to show the king standing before the enthroned god of Justice, Shamash. The apparent, and presumably intended,

4

implication of this is that Hammurabi's laws have at least the approval of the gods. This impression is confirmed by the preamble and concluding comments of the text of the code itself. The preamble states, *inter alia*, 'Then Anu and Bel delighted the flesh of mankind by calling me, the renowned prince, the god-fearing Hammurabi, to establish justice in the earth.'[9] This clearly suggests an idea of the derivation of the authority of law from the command of the gods and this motif is repeated in the final words of the preamble, as follows: 'When Merodach had instituted me governor of men, to conduct and to direct, Law and Justice I established in the land for the good of the people.'[10]

It is clear from such statements as these that the authority of the Code Hammurabi was seen as deriving from the will, indeed the command, of the gods — what is more, a command set for a definite purpose going to the root of the nature of law-making. The idea of 'the good of the people' is highly significant in this context. Some commentators have argued from the evidence of the text of the code itself that these laws are devoid of metaphysical implication and were in fact seen by their maker and subjects as simply a set of positive regulations. This appears to be quite true, so far as it goes. Indeed the first words of the concluding section of the text appear to support that position in stating that the laws are 'The judgements of justice which Hammurabi, the mighty King has established.'[11] This is, however, to ignore the point that the authority of the king to make these positive laws was seen as being derived from a higher authority than that of the king himself. This point is also made explicit in the text of the section that follows the description quoted above, in these terms: 'By command of Shamash, the great judge of heaven and earth, my justice shall glisten in the land.'[12] The nature of this claim is made clear later in the text by the assertion that 'Hammurabi, the King of justice, am I, to whom Shammash has granted rectitude.'[13] In some ways this is a surprisingly 'modern' conception of law-making. The king is presented as making laws in a modern positivist sense, not as a mere mouthpiece of the gods but upon his own rational volition. However, his power to do so is perceived as deriving from a divine mandate which imposes a clear purpose upon law-making, which is essentially one of public benefit.

The idea of laws made by men for men, albeit upon a divine authorisation, is supported by the relative absence of legal 'magic' in the Code Hammurabi. It is clear that in general legal issues and disputes were determined by a more or less rational judicial process, including rules of evidence.[14] Resort to the 'magic' of oaths and ordeals seems to have been made only in cases not amenable to rational modes of proof.[15] The picture of Babylonian legal ideas which emerges from the Code Hammurabi is that of a king and a legal system which operated as a structure of human prescription but none the less upon a commission attributed to the gods. The code, in common with many other early legal codes, concludes with a lengthy curse upon any subsequent ruler who might seek to derogate from the code. This type of curse attached to persons defacing or abrogating Royal edicts is commonly met with in ancient examples,[16] and in part they emphasise the high nature of the legal authority but they are also admittedly assertions of pre-eminence on the part of the ruler concerned. Such ancient injunctions should not be overemphasised or taken too seriously. It would be an unsafe proceeding to attempt to impose modern juris-prudential concepts upon so ancient a text which was moreover conceived in a cultural and intellectual climate vastly different from our own. However, certain conclusions may fairly be drawn from the text itself. The outline given above is at least strongly suggestive of a fairly sophisticated perception of law-making, or more accurately rule-adducing through dispute resolution, as, in itself, a rational human action satisfying positivist criteria of identification but also as the exercise of a power limited in its proper usage by a clear moral framework defined by justice and the public good.

The Code Hammurabi is not the earliest code which has come down to us in whole or part from Babylonia and Sumeria but it is one of the most complete and important. These early legal codes are of great interest in their own right. They are also of signifi-cance in the very considerable influence they appear to have upon the development of Judaic legal theory, which remains vital to the present time and has wielded an immense influence upon the development of the wide spectrum of modern legal thought.

Jewish law has existed and developed for the best part of 3,000 years. Its survival not merely as a theory but also as an operative prescription, over such a long period, is the more remarkable when it is considered that for substantial parts of that time there was no Jewish national state. There are, and have been, other systems of law which have functioned without national bases. The canon law of the Roman Catholic Church and the Islamic Sha'ria spring to mind in this context. These examples, however, were and are spiritually-based systems conceived as supra-national structures applicable to the whole body of the faithful. Admittedly both at present and in the past many Islamic states have adopted Islamic law as their national law but none the less the Sha'ria is not actually set out as a national law. The unique feature of Jewish law is its combination of religious and national characteristics and its survival in both capacities even in the absence of a supporting national state. It is this combination of characteristics which has enabled Jewish law to remain and survive as a living system of law. The significance of this is concisely summarised in the words of the *Encyclopaedia Judaica*:

> Notwithstanding its dispersion, the Jewish people continued to exist as a nation — not only as a religious sect — and constantly sought recourse to Jewish law, which it regarded as a part of its national assets through which to give expression to its essential being . . .[17]

The early origins of Judaic law lie in the period of nomadic wandering reflected in Exodus. In the Biblical description of the evolution of the law some evidence can be seen of the type of kin-based system of legal obligation commonly encountered in such societies. Such a system emphasises kin and clan cohesion, joint obligation, the importance of tradition and, often, group liability expressed through the medium of blood-feud. This may be seen in some of the more sanguinary assertions to be found in Exodus. The best-known instance is the statement that God will visit '. . . the iniquity of the fathers upon the children, and upon the children's children, unto the third and to the fourth generation'.[18] Even here, however, this vengeful pronouncement is qualified by a preceding statement that God is 'The LORD God, merciful and gracious . . . keeping mercy for thousands, forgiving iniquity and transgression, and that will by no means clear the guilty.'[19] 'Guilty' must here be taken to refer to obduracy in sin rather than necessarily the commission of sin *per se*.

The main statement of law in the Old Testament, however, reflects a later stage of development in main part. The basic statement of this law is to be found in the first five books of the Old Testament, that is to say the Pentateuch. The law, the Torah, commences with the Ten Commandments in Exodus 20. The Commandments themselves include matters of both religious and secular significance. Broadly speaking the first four Commandments are 'religious' in nature whereas the latter six are 'secular'.

Thus the Third Commandment provides that 'Thou shalt not take the name of the LORD thy God in vain . . .'[20] which is obviously a 'religious' provision, whereas the Ninth Commandment provides that 'Thou shalt not bear false witness against thy neighbour . . .'[21] which, while clearly a moral ordinance, has much more secular implications. The immediately following chapters contain a mass of detailed prescription covering secular provisions of civil and criminal law as well as matters of ritual and religious regulation. In particular Exodus 21:1 to 22:17 may fairly be seen as a code of laws in a thoroughly secular sense which is directly comparable to such texts as the Code Hammurabi. Indeed the Semitic legal tradition in which the Code Hammurabi stands had a clear formative influence upon the Pentateuch code. Quite obviously the legal provisions of the Pentateuch, both religious and secular, have not come down to us in their present form as a result of a single act of enunciation, but have rather been relayed to us through a lengthy process of transmission and development. The extent to which the appearance of the rules has been affected by the process of transmission, and in particular through their recording by the priesthood, is difficult to say but may well have been considerable.

The authority upon which this elaborate structure of prescription rests is perceived as being absolute in nature and Divine in origin. Jewish law is seen as being in the most direct sense a Holy Law which to a considerable extent was not merely formulated upon a Divine authorisation but actually ordained in content by God Himself. The Mosaic law is expressly stated to be the word and command of God, thus in connection with the enunciation of the law it is written: 'And God spake all these words, saying, I am the LORD thy God, which . . . brought thee out of the land of Egypt, out of the house of bondage.'[22]

The provisions of the Judaic code are clearly set out as the product of a Divine ordinance for the benefit of the people and so vested with moral authority and imposing a moral obligation. At the same time the establishment of the law is described in the following highly significant terms: 'And Moses came and told the people all the words of the LORD, and all the judgements: and all the people answered with one voice, and said, All the words which the LORD hath said will do.'[23] This is an interesting formulation. The moral and legal order is perceived not only as a unitary Divine prescription but also as one chosen by its subjects. It may, in this sense, be said that the Jews consider themselves to be a people who have themselves chosen as well as one which has been chosen.

Judaic theory necessarily sees the law as sanctioned by the command of God and thus perceives a fundamental linkage between the categories of religious, moral and legal obligation. This is implied by the statement in the *Encyclopaedia Judaica* that '. . . both the laws applicable between man and man the precepts concerning man and God have a single and common source, namely the written and oral law'.[24] Judaic theory firmly enjoins obedience to the law as a matter both of social and religious duty, but this proceeds from a perception of the law as derived from Divine ordinance and therefore necessarily just and true. In making this very point Stone quotes Isaiah 33:22 in which it is written that: 'For the LORD *is* our judge; the LORD *is* our lawgiver; the LORD *is* our king . . .'[25]

Human law is thus seen in Jewish thought as deriving its ultimate authority from Divine ordinance. It was not claimed, however, that the two were conterminous. Logically this could not be so. The Divine will is necessarily seen as both higher and wider than human needs and so the Divine prescription in respect of law is understood to be a partial revelation only.[26] A passage from Deuteronomy makes this clear in stating that

> The secret things belong unto the LORD our God, but those things which are revealed belong unto us and to our children for ever, that we may do all the words of this law.[27]

The passage continues to evaluate the Divine intention in the following terms:

> For this commandment which I command thee this day, it is not hidden from thee, neither is it far off. It is not in heaven, that thou shouldst say, Who shall go up for us to heaven, and bring it unto us, that we may hear it and do it? But the word is very nigh unto thee, in thy mouth, and in thy heart, that thou mayest do it.[28]

Thus the law is presented as a code grounded in Divinely prescribed moral ordinance and covering matters pertinent to the social needs of its subjects. It is not, and is not represented to be, a codification of total morality. It is seen as a moral law and thus one which imposes a moral obligation to obey upon its subjects. The claims of morality in general may nevertheless be both wider and less specific than those of legal prescription.

The ascription of the source of law-making power, and even the specific content of laws, to Divine authority is by no means uncommon and is certainly not limited to the Jewish example. However, whatever the source of moral authority for law-making, human institutions, which may have less than Divine standards of operation, are needed for the practical implementation and working of legal rules. It is in the maintenance of the relationship between a claimed moral source of law-making authority and the behaviour of human law-makers and administrators that the practical value of any theory of naturalism lies. The issue is simply that of the ways in which institutions of state can be restrained from acting in a manner which goes beyond their moral or ethical authority when formal positive definitions of the scope of their power would not suffice to that end. The solution to this problem cannot lie simply in the provisions of a code ascribed to Divine intervention, since the inherent rigidity of such a code can in time become a fertile source of injustice in application other than in the case of the simplest and most basic commands and prohibitions. However, once the need for an interpretative and/or adaptive mechanism is admitted it might seem that the original claim to transcendent authority must be lost. Upon such gloomy reasoning it might be considered to follow that such a theory of law is bound to fail through processes of social change and the effluxion of time.

A simple but effective answer to these problems was found in Judaic legal theory. The basic danger of fossilisation and consequent redundancy of the code has been avoided through a system of rational interpretation and adaption. The Written Law, the Torah, has come to be supplemented and developed by a formally unwritten tradition, the Halakah. This is not perceived as an accretion to the Written Law but rather as having been given by God to Moses upon Mount Sinai at the same time as the giving of the Torah. Granted that the Halakah is the work of scholars, there is here on the face of it a contradiction. How could subsequent scholarly elucidation possibly have been given at the same time as the Torah in the remote past at Mount Sinai? Again the Judaic solution is both simple and elegant. It is found in the idea that the scholarly interpretation of the Torah, which is found in the Halakah, is necessarily rooted in the Torah itself and was therefore inherent in the Written Law as originally given — and thus partakes of the same Divine authority. In effect the Halakah is presented as being 'discovered' rather than made. Notwithstanding this perception, the discovery of the Oral Law is a rational and scholarly process and is seen as such.

Within this perception no conflict between the God-given law, the Torah, and the humanly discovered elucidation, the Halakah, is possible. The Torah and the Halakah stem from and share the same authority and can therefore hardly diverge. It must of course be conceded that in practice and inevitably some Rabbinical law-elucidation was in fact quite clearly law-making in the normal sense which significantly changed former practices, albeit within a continuing tradition of moral authority. Interestingly a similar pattern can be seen in the case of the Islamic Hadith. Quite distinct from the Halakah, Jewish Courts also reserved and exercised a power to vary the effects of the law where justice in a particular case demanded it. However, all these means of balancing the implementation of the law hark back to a definition of 'law' which depends upon a perception of the Divine authorisation of the Torah and the inherency of the Halakah.

There remains the problem posed by a ruler who attempts to make positive rules contrary to the spirit of the Torah or the Halakah. The Old Testament supplies a simple answer to this question. The first King of Israel was Saul, who appears to have been appointed as a response to popular demand in succession to various more or less charismatic forms of leadership. The account in Samuel makes it clear that this was an appointment upon terms with an answerability to God for the exercise of the kingship. Thus it is written: 'Then Samuel told the people the manner of the kingdom, and wrote it in a book, and laid it up before the LORD . . .'[29] This is as clear a formulation of the Judaic attitude as one could wish for. What was in effect a 'constitution' is enunciated and preserved in a thoroughly 'positivist' manner, but is derived from and referred back to Divine precept. Unfortunately these 'constitutional' provisions did not wait long to be put to the test, for Saul himself defied the Divine precept. In consequence it was predicted that Saul would forfeit the kingship which would then vest not in his descendents but in one more worthy. Thus Samuel is described as warning Saul that

> . . . the LORD [would] have established thy kingdom upon Israel for ever. But now thy kingdom shall not continue: the LORD hath sought . . . a man after his own heart, and the LORD hath commended him to be captain over his people,

because thou hast not kept that which the LORD commanded thee.[30]

In due course indeed Saul and his sons died in battle and were replaced by the House of David. It is significant, however, that this is not presented as a precedent for the overthrow of erring kings, rather the replacement of Saul is put down to Divine agency. Indeed human action against Saul is specifically denounced as sinful.[31] The operation and effect of the higher order in the Judaic perception thus appears as an autonomous consequence of Divine wrath without human intervention. To put this in more neutral terms, the image is one of backsliding from 'natural' order, leading to its own nemesis. This is not to say by any means, however, that naturalism was conceived as an entirely passive system from the human viewpoint in Judaic theory. The Old Testament is replete with accounts of the denunciation of kings and rulers by prophets and other charismatic leaders such as Samuel and Elijah; in the New Testament John the Baptist stands in much the same tradition in his denunciation of Herod. A notable example of this can be seen in Nathan's criticism and warning of David for his guilty passion for Bathsheba, the wife of Uriah the Hittite.[32] Elijah's denunciation of Ahab is a yet more powerful example[33] and it is significant that here, as in the case of David, the urging to improvement was, to an extent, successful.

The theory of ancient Judaic naturalism may be seen as one of a legal order which rests upon a perception of Divine ordinance but within which human interpretation and rule-making have a proper and important role to play. In this perception 'law' as such means the Divinely given or inspired prescription. Attempts to move fundamentally away from this received moral law, as opposed to its adaption to new circumstances, are thus seen as abominations which are 'naturally' doomed to failure by their inherent moral defects. The attempts of Ahab to introduce the worship of Ba'al into Israel fell very much into this category. The notion of a rigorous and wholly inflexible code revolving around concepts of the *lex talionis* which some Christian thinkers impute to Jewish legal theory is very far from the truth, however. Judaic legal theory was and is a great deal more subtle than that. In fact the absence of any real perceived distinction between natural and positive law in Judaic theory essentially avoided the issue of the 'bad' law since such an enactment could not be part of the Jewish conception of 'law' in the sense of a prescription imposing a moral obligation to obey upon its addressees. A purported 'law' contrary to the perceived will of God, such as a command to commit adultery or to worship a false God, would be seen as a temptation involving both the commander and the obedient in sin for their disavowal of the true law. Of course rulers might seek to impose iniquitous rules but such an attempt would be an exercise not of authority but of power.

Such a naturalism is absolute. The application of the prescription may make allowance for changing needs and for humanity but the dangers of rigidity remain. It is precisely this point that is brought out in Christ's attack upon the inflexibility of the Pharisaic outlook. It must of course be conceded that Christian naturalism has proved far from immune from the same danger in the hands of some of its exponents.[34]

Judaic naturalism has proved to be a singularly fertile source of development in legal theory. Jewish law itself of course continues as a living system. In modern Israel the legal system is secular and the influence of Jewish law is therefore indirect but significant as a moral overview. This leads to a certain tension between the secular and religious aspects of modern Israel. In this context it must be wondered whether the centuries of preservation of Judaic tradition have not been obtained at the price of loss of flexibility in practice which has brought about a modern separation between religious and positive law in modern Israel of a type which would have been far outside the legal or social concepts of ancient Israel.

The impact of Judaic legal theory upon the development of Christian legal thought was inevitably massive. However, it has often been much misunderstood. It is frequently asserted that Christian doctrine represents the abrogation of the law of the Old Testament through the operation of Divine grace. If this were so, Judaic legal theory could not be more than an interesting pre-history from the viewpoint of a Christian legal theory. Actually such a view is a gross over-simplification taking little account of either doctrine or history. The early Church certainly saw the law as being ultimately superseded when all had reached a state of grace. However, in the meantime the law was perceived as necessary for those who might otherwise tend to err and stray. The linkage of law with sin was much ameliorated with the subsequent development of theory.[35] When in due course the rationalist Hellenistic theories of law and obligation were joined into the later development of theory as the other basic tradition of Western naturalism, further elaboration took place but the Judaic tradition of an absolute and Divinely ordained natural law remains one of the streams of thought which has contributed fundamentally to the development of modern Western jurisprudence. A similarly close relationship to the Judaic idea of law can also be found in Islamic jurisprudence.

In the consideration of the origins of naturalist legal theory there remains an important distinction to be made: that is the separation of ideas about the moral nature and authority of law from what may crudely be called legal 'magic'. These two may be confused upon superficial inspection but are in fact readily separable. By legal 'magic' is meant that ritual of legal practice which is used to clothe what are in fact perfectly mundane transactions with the solemnity considered appropriate in the light of their social significance. It may also be that such ritual has a real importance in imparting psychological efficacy to rules of law. These issues are the particular field of interest of the Scandinavian Realist school of jurisprudence. The founding father of this school of thought, Axel Hägerström (1868–1939), devoted a considerable amount of attention to this question of legal 'magic'.[36] It was Hägerström's thesis that law, religion and magic were originally closely related and that for law to act as an effective prescription it must elicit the appropriate psychological responses in its subjects. He argued that these responses are secured largely through the practice of quasi-'magical' rituals. Hägerström chose Roman Law as his principal field of study in the making of this point. He pointed out that much legal ritual is designed to impress upon the minds of its participants the special solemnity of the transaction entered into in order to give it an efficacy in the minds of those directly concerned with it and also the community at large which it might otherwise lack. Thus the solemn rituals involved in the transfer of land from one owner to another in Roman (or indeed English) law are, according to Hägerström, intended to suggest that a transfer of some 'real' power over the land is taking place — the point being that law operates through psychological effects which depend in considerable measure upon rituals and formal procedures which generate belief in the efficacy of the system.

Whatever the merits or demerits of this idea, the 'magical' elements in law can take two basic forms. One is the procedural ritual which Hägerström considered. The other is the resort to 'magical' means of operation within the prescription itself, such as trials by ordeal. This element varies enormously as between different times and places. Ordeal was almost absent in the ancient

14

Semitic codes; it was, in contrast, very prevalent in Europe during the Dark Ages. Rather to everyone's surprise it was found that trial by battle remained a legal possibility in England in 1818[37] and indeed the procedure was formally abolished by statute only in the following year,[38] although it had long been in practical desuetude. In this form legal 'magic' is virtually a negation of law since it seeks to throw decision-making onto entirely random and arbitrary processes which are by their nature quite incapable of acting as a uniform or rationally ordered prescription.

These are not aspects of legal development germane to the origins of naturalism. Naturalist legal theory has deep roots in religious thought, as indeed do most moral concepts, but it is not tied to the aberration of 'magical' irrationality. On the contrary, the central concern of naturalism is to define the moral framework within which a rational prescriptive order can operate and to define the moral limitations of its proper exercise. This character of naturalist thought can be seen from the earliest elaborated legal ideas, which is the particular interest of ancient Babylon and Jewish legal thought in this context. The roots of naturalism are ancient in the extreme but the development of ideas in this context has been wide ranging and highly various. The Judaic tradition is an absolute naturalism referring to Divine sanction. The obvious alternative is an overtly rationalist type of theory and it is to such theory that the discussion must now turn.

Notes

1. H. L. A. Hart, *The Concept of Law*, Chs I and II.
2. Aquinas, *Summa Theologica*, 1a 2ae, Quaestio 90, Art. 4.
3. H. L. A. Hart, *The Concept of Law*. It is worth adding that Bentham and Austin, in the notion of Sovereignty as a coercive power derived from a habit of obedience, did not deny constitutionality, they merely chose to define it as falling in large part into a sphere other than that of 'positive law'.
4. See, for example, the discussion of the late developing role of the 'Warrior Societies' in *The Cheyenne Way*, Llewellyn and Hoebel.
5. See, for example, S. Roberts, *Order and Dispute*, for examples.
6. Perhaps in the very narrow sense of developing an urban-based economy.
7. In early stages of development this tended to be seen more as 'law-discovering'.
8. The first translation was made into French by Father V. Scheil, and published as Tome IV, *Textes Elamites-Semitiques of the Memoirs de la Délégation en Perse* (Paris, 1902). The first English translation was published

by C. H. W. Johns (Edinburgh, 1903).

9. Code Hammurabi, Preamble (Front, col. 1). This and other sections are taken from the translations set out by Chilperic Edwards in *The World's Earliest Laws* (London, 1934).

10. Ibid., Preamble (Front, col. V).

11. Code Hammurabi, Conclusion (Rear, col. XXIV).

12. Ibid.

13. Ibid. (Rear. col. XXV).

14. See, for example, Code Hammurabi, arts. 9–13 (Front, cols. VI–VIII).

15. Ordeal generally took the form of putting a suspect onto the river to see if he floated or not, thus submitting the case to the river god. See, for example, Code Hammurabi, art. 2 (Front, col. V) in relation to charges of sorcery.

16. Examples may be seen in the British Museum in London.

17. *Encyclopaedia Judaica, The Principles of Jewish Law*, ed. Menachem Elon, Introduction: 19.

18. Exodus 34:7.

19. Exodus 34:6 and 7.

20. Exodus 20:7.

21. Exodus 20:16.

22. Exodus 10:1–2.

23. Exodus 24:3.

24. *Encyclopaedia Judaica, The Principles of Jewish Law*, ed. Menachem Elon, Introduction: 5.

25. Julius Stone, *Human Law and Human Justice*, p. 23.

26. The implications of this same point are elaborated in detail in the context of Christian thought by St Thomas Aquinas, see Ch. 3, this volume.

27. Deuteronomy 19:29.

28. Deuteronomy 30:11–14.

29. I Samuel 10:25.

30. I Samuel 13:13–14.

31. II Samuel 26:8–12.

32. II Samuel 12:7–15.

33. I Kings 21:17–29.

34. St Thomas Aquinas made careful provision for the absolute nature of Divine ordinance and the mutability of human society in his theory of law. See Ch. 3, this volume.

35. The later view linked the coercive form of law to sin rather than the existence of law as a system of prescription. See Ch. 3, this volume.

36. Hägerström's principal written work was *Der Römische Obligationsbegriff*. However, the best approach to Scandinavian Realist thought for the English reader is Olivecrona's *Law as Fact* (2nd edn).

37. See *Ashford* v *Thornton* (1818), 1 B. & Ald. 405.

38. 59 Geo. 3, c.46.

2

Classical Hellenistic Theory

Developed Western naturalism is the fruit of the fusion of two quite different jurisprudential traditions — one of the absolute naturalism of the Judaic tradition, the other the rationalistic tradition which originated in ancient Greece. In the fifth century BC Greece was divided up into a number of small city-states, the political structure of which ranged from the autocratic and military state of Sparta to the 'democracy', in the limited context of the free male citizenry, of Athens, with many intermediate positions in other states. This diversity of political background naturally engendered a relativist tendency in political thought. This was furthered by the fact that Greek and, later, Roman religion was an elaborate pagan polytheism which was inevitably taken in a rather allegorical spirit by the educated and cannot be said to have contained much in the way of high ethical teaching. The consequence was that spirit of scepticism and enquiry which generated the wide spectrum of Greek thought which has so much influenced the development of Western civilisation.

The fifth and fourth centuries BC in Greece were times of intense philosophical and political debate against a troubled political background. The defeat of the Persian invasion was followed by a time of Athenian ascendency particularly associated with the name of Pericles, the principal political figure in the city for a period of some 30 years and the architect of a political confederation which was in all but an Athenian empire. Athenian ascendency was brought to an end by the prolonged Peloponnesian war, the turmoils of which formed the significant background to the later years of Socrates and the youth and young manhood of Plato. Pericles died in 429 BC and the leaders of the citizen-democracy which succeeded him made serious misjudgements, in part[1] at least due to a need to placate uninformed mob pressure. Following a disastrous military expedition to Sicily there was a revolution in Athens in 411 BC in which an oligarchic faction seized power. This, too, was shortly overthrown in a violent uprising by the democratic faction who instituted a reign of terror over their opponents. Athens was finally defeated by Sparta in 404 BC and, with Spartan aid, a restoration of oligarchy followed in the form of the rule of the Thirty Tyrants. They themselves were overthrown, however, after less than a year to be replaced by a more moderate and longer-lasting democracy which besmirched its reputation, however, by the judicial murder of Socrates in 399 BC in circumstances partly derived from the political instability of the time.

The dominant thinkers of the earlier part of this era were the Sophists. Sophist theory was highly relativist and saw no necessary connection between nature or morality and law-making. Law was seen as a pragmatic expression of power embodying the interest of the law-making, and obedience to law was seen as being secured through the self-interest of the subject, if only through the avoidance of coercive measures. As a theory this was not so much immoral as amoral in that the relevance of morality to practical human affairs was in effect denied. In modern terms Sophism was a theory concerned with the successful use of power which denied any limiting idea of a moral 'authority' in law-making. This type of theory was countered by a classical naturalism with the development of which the names of Socrates, Plato and Aristotle are especially associated.

Socrates (469–399 BC) was a controversial Athenian philosopher and teacher. His career is known only in outline although some scattered matters of detail have come down to us. He clearly believed that there exists a settled moral order, but at the same time it may reasonably be assumed that the fanciful mythology of the Greek gods did not attract his literal adherence. It may be that, like many classical thinkers, he treated Hellenistic religion as an allegory of greater truths. There is certainly some support in accounts of his thought and teaching for the idea that he may in practice have tended towards some form of monotheistic perception. As a thinker and a moralist he attracted a great many followers and disciples and this ultimately proved to be his downfall. His doctrines proved uncomfortable to the Athenian establishment and his questioning of attitudes and practices came to be considered subversive in influential circles. Finally, his influence among the young men of the upper classes in Athens led his enemies to bring charges against him of sedition and impiety upon which he was convicted and executed, although the real aim may have been to drive Socrates into exile and thus relieve the Athenians of their embarrassment.

Our knowledge of Socrates's teaching comes to us mainly through the writing of his greatest follower, Plato (*c.* 429 – 347 BC), since Socrates himself was a teacher and lecturer rather than a writer. Socratic thought about the authority of law is set out by Plato in the four conversations comprising *The Last Days of Socrates*,[2] particularly in *The Apology* and *Crito*. The work is set out as an account of Socrates's trial and death but is not so much a description *simpliciter* as conclusions of Socratic thought presented in the context of those events. The trial resulted from charges of heresy or impiety and corruption of youth amounting to sedition brought against Socrates by three leading members of the Athenian establishment, Meletus, Lycon and Anytus. The trial procedure involved debate between prosecutors and defendant before a 'jury' of 501 free citizens which then reached a majority verdict. In the event of a finding of 'guilty', sentence was then similarly determined by a process of debate followed by majority vote. In *The Last Days*, *The Apology* is a representation of Socrates's arguments to the Court, although it is in no sense a transcript of anything like a speech *per se*, and the *Crito* is an argument between Socrates and his friend Crito upon the nature of Socrates's duty to accept the death penalty imposed upon him, which Socrates asserts and Crito denies.

In the course of his counter to the accusations brought against him, Socrates makes the point that the exercise of power by the state is not necessarily 'right' nor morally justified; he cites examples from the period of the rule of the Thirty Tyrants in Athens to support this proposition and indeed goes so far as to assert that a just man can hardly expect to survive in public life.[3] Socrates was in the end condemned to death, mainly perhaps because he refused to concede the propriety of the jury decision or to plead for mercy in circumstances in which he sought not the 'mercy' of the corrupt but the justice of the wise. Sentence was not carried out immediately as would normally have been the practice in Athens because the annual ceremony of the 'Mission to Delos' was in progress during which capital penalties could not be carried out. It may have been the desire of the Athenian authorities that Socrates should rid them of obloquy by escaping during the period of delay; certainly his friends urged him to do so. Socrates refused and was in due course executed by the process of drinking a cup of hemlock. The reasons for his refusal to escape are examined in the most jurisprudentially significant of the four conversations of *The Last Days*, *Crito*. The form of *Crito* is an argument between Socrates and Crito upon the necessity for Socrates's death which Crito denies. Crito argues that the condemnation was unjust and that Socrates ought to escape its implementation if only for the benefit of his friends and family by fleeing to some other city while he has the opportunity to do so.[4] This is an issue which goes to the root of the question of legal obligation. Socrates argues[5] that the existence of the state rests upon its laws and although a citizen should argue for changes where laws are bad he is none the less bound to accept the laws so long as he remains a citizen. For Socrates not to effect an escape would be a denial of the Athenian legal order and a subversion of the state more harmful in its general consequences than any individual injustice suffered by Socrates.

In Socrates's view a citizen who objects to a law has alternative options; he may quit the state for one with more congenial prescription or he may seek to persuade his fellows to change the laws. If he neither persuades nor leaves he has no option but obedience because otherwise he will subvert the state by setting its laws at nought. Socrates rests his duty to obey the law upon three grounds[6] which are, that he would in escaping act in an unfilial manner by refusing obedience to the state which raised and nurtured him, secondly that he would subvert the social order of the state by denying the validity of its prescription, and thirdly that he would break an agreement to obey the laws of the city implied by his continued residence when he had been free to leave and dwell elsewhere. There is thus advanced an argument that obligation rests upon the benefits of quasi-parental protection given by the state and upon the assumption that a person who remains in the state must be taken to agree to abide by its laws because if he does not and cannot change the opinion of the state he has the option of going elsewhere. This is an approach with obvious 'social contractarian' elements[7] but it does not in fact lead to the conclusions which might be anticipated. But Socrates's argument is capable of dangerous over-simplification. Socrates does not advance the sweeping proposition that all positive demands of the state must be complied with unless it can be persuaded to amend the prescription concerned. Such an argument would imply a duty to do evil where the state so demands. unless the state can be persuaded by the citizen to alter or abrogate its demands. One could then reasonably ask what would be the position of the moral individual confronted with the demands of the Nazi genocide laws; should he merely seek to persuade the Nazis to change their minds and if, as seems likely, he fails to aid them in the implementation of persecution? Such a conclusion would be extraordinary and is not in fact that reached by Socrates. On the contrary he is represented as asserting that no man should ever do such a thing which is unjust which means that no one is ever justified in *doing* evil at the behest of the state. Socrates argues that wrongdoing must always be avoided even if, as in his own case, the result might be escape from an unjust infliction.[8]

In *The Apology* a number of specific examples is given from Socrates's own career in which on a number of occasions he refused to undertake offices of state which would involve him in injustice — indeed he argues that his principles would have led him to condemnation long before had he not by and large eschewed public office.[9] He describes an occasion when as a member of the executive council, his only holding of public office, he opposed the illegal mass trial of certain naval commanders for their conduct in the Athenian victory at Arginusae in 406 BC under the democracy. Later under the rule of the Thirty Tyrants he and three others were instructed to bring Leon of Salamis to an unjust execution. The three complied but Socrates did not, escaping condemnation himself only through the fall of the oligarchy. Socrates is here denigrating active compliance with 'bad' laws and at the end of *The Apology* he turns the argument back upon the court in his assertion that no evil can occur to a just man[10] upon the premiss that evil is a quality of the wrongdoer and not of the victim.[11]

Thus Socrates considered that a man should never do wrong, even at the behest of the state, whatever the personal consequences of such a course might be and cited his own behaviour and general eschewal of office as examples. His own immediate case, however, differed in that he was not being pressed to do wrong but was himself the victim of wrongdoing by the state. He had sought to persuade the Athenians and had failed; he had remained in Athens when he could have left and in so doing he had submitted himself to Athenian law which had now reached an adverse conclusion. To refuse obedience at that stage, by escape, would not be to avoid evildoing, for the victim of injustice does no evil, but to deny the obligation impliedly accepted by continued residence under the aegis of Athenian law.

The duty to obey set forth by Socrates is thus neither the caricature of blind obedience as it is sometimes represented, nor the charter for civil disobedience which it is sometimes claimed to be. His view was that a citizen cannot be placed under a duty to do evil by the state, and indeed in so doing evil the citizen would be as much a wrongdoer as the state which caused his action. To this extent Socratic theory forces the citizen to make a moral judgement upon what is demanded of him; thus the citizen in Nazi Germany who betrayed others to persecution in accordance with the laws of the time may be seen as one who shared in the evildoing of the Nazi regime.[12] This is readily comprehensible in a modern context. The difficulty with the Socratic position arises precisely in the immediate context of the *Crito*. What happens where the individual, possibly through refusal to comply with an unjust demand of the state, is himself made the victim of wrongdoing? Here Socrates is uncompromising and once the options of departure or persausion have been exhausted, as *ex hypothesi* here they have, no alternative to obedience is admitted. The basis for this is partly one of social obligation derived from voluntary residence and partly a pragmatic dictum for the avoidance of social disruption and anarchy. In the modern world such a view would prevent resistance to unjust infliction although, paradoxically, not refusal to inflict injustice. It must be borne in mind, however, that Socrates's duty of obedience rests upon the prior options of departure or persuasion and the relative availability of these options must be considered before Socratic thought can be translated into a modern context.

The possibility of persuasion varies widely in modern states and the more iniquitous the state the less it is likely to be. The same applies also to departure to a more congenial place: in a world of large nations this is by no means so open an option as it might be, for a free citizen, in an agglomeration of small city-states. What then if the options of departure or persuasion are to a greater or lesser extent denied? It must seem that the arguments of voluntarily accepted obligation through residence advanced by the personified laws of Athens to Socrates in the *Crito*[13] must be weakened to an appropriate extent. Although Socrates takes no account of such a view, the relevant circumstances being outside his consideration, it is perhaps arguable that, granted the denial to the state of the capacity to demand evildoing, the denial of the posited options of departure or persuasion might justify moral resistance to unjust inflictions since the root of obligation, the voluntary acceptance of order, is cut away. This form of argument must seem to be applicable to modern totalitarianism where otherwise the Socratic prescription leads simply to a dumb obedience of a type directly condemned by Socrates himself in *The Apology*.

It has been remarked that our knowledge of Socrates's thought comes to us through the writings of his most brilliant pupil, Plato. Plato (*c.* 427–347 BC) was a scion of an ancient and aristocratic Athenian family and a pupil of Socrates. As a young man he was disgusted both by the tyranny of the Athenian oligarchs and what he saw as the undue susceptibility to the mob mentality of the Athenian democracy. He was, naturally, in particular revolted by the trial and execution of Socrates in 399 BC. Plato himself made detailed consideration of the nature of the state and its laws in order that they might be relieved of the defects which he perceived all too abundantly in the practical realities of his time. The answers which he gave to these problems were rooted in a philosophy of idealism.

Plato considered that the physical realities of the actual world are a poor reflection of a 'true' reality which is perfect and morally pure. The Platonic ideal is essentially an apprehension of this 'true reality', the provision of which is an absolute formulation of the 'good' life of man. Plato considered his ideal as a philosophical insight accessible through reason to the suitably trained human intellect. That he may have considered the grand design itself to be the product of an agency higher than man is likely but for purposes of discussion the Platonic ideal is in essence perceived as a creature of reason accessible to the higher human rationality.[14] Plato was not especially optimistic about the general proclivities of human nature, in part a reflection of what he perceived as the tendency of democracy to degenerate into mob rule. He believed that mankind must be led to the 'good' life rather than merely afforded the opportunity of finding it. There is thus undeniably a strong authoritarian element in Platonic thought but that is not to concede that Plato was in any sense an apologist for naked totalitarianism or tyranny as some of his less charitable critics have suggested that he might be.

Like Socrates, and indeed in a tradition going back to Solon (*c.* 638–558 BC), Plato believed that the health of a practical state rests upon the provision of and compliance with good laws. This indeed is the basis of the practical Platonic prescription to be found in his late work, the *Laws*. However, he did not consider laws as such to be the best possible form of prescription for the 'good' life and in his more famous work, *The Republic*, he set out the form of his ideal society. *The Republic* is an Utopia in which the ideal formula for a social order is discussed in the context of Socratic conversations. The work has little to say about law *per se* since it is essentially anti-legalist in nature.

The main concept of the scheme is that the best form of society would be one which most closely conformed to the perfect reality of ideas. This is not to be achieved through democracy or oligarchy, which are inclined by their nature towards perversity, nor by tyranny which is by definition a creature of whim. The theoretical answer given by Plato is a form of genuinely 'benevolent' dictatorship. In fact the rule of 'Philosopher-kings', who are to be persons selected by a rigorous, if arguably rather impractical, process of education and training as those with the greatest insight into 'true' reality and who are therefore vested with power to direct society in such a way as to make the social reality apprehended by the senses, concords as closely as possible with the perfection of the 'true' reality of ideas. The consequence of such direction would necessarily be to make society 'good' since true knowledge can never lead to wrongdoing or injustice. The rule of a philosopher-king would not be through the medium of laws but by orders made as might be necessary from time to time in accordance with his rational insight. This form of rule is presented as the social equivalent of 'self-discipline'[15] in that within the society the guidance of the wisest will cause the better elements of the human character to be developed just as personal self-discipline involves the subjection of the baser elements of character to the more elevated. Such a government of collective 'self-discipline' naturally involves concordance upon who is in fact best fitted to rule and who is to be ruled.[16] Within this conception 'justice' in the state is given a narrow definition as the final quality of the rationally 'good' state in association with discipline, courage and wisdom and is seen as the keeping by all members of the ideal society to their own properly allotted role and their not interfering with the performance of the roles of others.[17] The analogous definition of 'justice' in the individual is the subordination of personal appetites and inclinations to the dictates of reason.[18]

The evident problem with such an Utopian vision is the difficulty in finding a philosopher-king. It may be doubted whether Plato actually expected the scheme of *The Republic* to achieve complete and literal implementation. To imagine that he did so would be to suppose Plato to be grossly naïve.[19] It is clear that he expected an improvement in political life to result from the philosophical training of statesmen. However, his experience was not by any means entirely fortunate. Plato visited Syracuse with a view to advising its ruler, Dionysius I. Unfortunately. Dionysius disliked Plato and, according to one account, may even have sold him into slavery from which condition he had to be redeemed by his associates. Following the death of this ruler, Plato's friend Dion, a member of the royal family, invited him back to Syracuse in 367 BC as an adviser to the young and newly enthroned Dionysius II, evidently with some view to elevating him into an approximation of philosopher-king. Unsurprisingly the king proved to have little time or aptitude for the academic exercises which Plato expected him to undertake. Dionysius seems actually to have had considerable regard for Plato but he was not by any means a philosopher-king and, from Plato's viewpoint, his association with Syracuse must be judged a signal failure. There is on the other hand some evidence that Hermias, the ruler of Atarneus, took some account of Platonic teaching and even modified his rule in accordance with it.[20] On a more practical level, Plato founded an Academy in Athens, which was in essence a philosophical training school for statesmen, and which aimed to elevate the theory and practice of politics with a view to producing statesmen and politicians with enhanced philosophical insight.[21]

Plato's ideas of a more practical social order and one which might in his view be attainable, even if clearly a moral 'second best', are to be found in the *Laws*. The discussion of the *Laws* occurs in relation to a hypothetical Athenian colony in Crete called Magnesia and the main part of the work is in effect a detailed code of positive laws for the city which is in large measure a form of Athenian practice improved upon rationalist lines. The laws are perceived as 'second best' in that although they are intended to be reflections of the 'true' reality they are not the direct insights of a philosopher-king but rigid positive prescriptions rooted in moral perception, a secondary statement in the form of a rigid code which may indeed call for amendment, although little if well drafted. Inevitably in the Platonic view a legal code is seen as a less moral and less sensitive instrument of government than the direct insight of a philosopher-ruler.

Although the laws of Plato are a rigid prescription which are in their way quite as totalitarian as the 'benevolent dictatorship' of *The Republic*, they were not in any sense conceived as a mere tyrannical imposition. The prescription in the *Laws* was in fact conceived as being at least as much didactic as coercive, upon the assumption that appeal to the higher human motivations can only lead to the maximisation of the quantum of individual 'goodness' since wrongdoing may be said to be the product of the baser appetites freed from constraint in consequence of moral ignorance. Thus it is stated that the legislators should seek to persuade through rational explanation and argument in preference to compulsion through force.[22] Thus the better motivated people will be persuaded to obey law; coercion would be called for only in the case of the refractory who are creatures of baser motivation. It is for this reason that Plato insists that the code as a whole and also each individual provision must be preceded by a lengthy explanatory preamble which is patently didactic in intent.[23]

In the Platonic view all laws therefore should tend to make men 'good'[24] even if they can only be a 'second best' means to that end.[25] This leads one to the issue of Plato's conception of the nature of the duty to obey laws. In general it must be taken that his views approximate to those attributed to Socrates in *The Last Days of Socrates*, of which he was after all the author. However, further elaboration is to be found in particular in *Minos*. The *Minos* is a dialogue which was anciently regarded as being of indubitable Platonic authorship but its authenticity has been regarded as more debatable in modern times. Be that as it may, the work is Platonic in form and is clearly the product of Platonic thought even if not actually written by Plato himself. In *Minos* Socrates is represented as making enquiry into the basic nature of law. His companion responds with an answer which is in essence positivist in form, saying that law is anything which is recognised as being 'legal'. Socrates dismisses this upon the basis that a phenomenon cannot be identified with a mere instance of itself. Thus if law is that which is recognised as 'legal', the question must be raised by what 'law' are laws recognised? This is not in fact an argument of formalism leading to a precursor of H. L. A. Hart's 'rule of recognition'[26] but one which raises the basic issue of the moral authority of law upon which any non-coercive suasion must ultimately rest. The interrogatee's response to this is that 'law' is a formal enunciation of popular or communal opinion upon the subject in question. This enables Socrates to open the general issue of the 'authority' of law. He argues that the opinions enshrined in law must, to have suasion, surely be 'good' opinion which is to say an opinion which is an insight into 'true' or ideal reality.[27] This is clearly the Platonic definition of 'good' law.[28] There remains the problem that positive laws can and do differ widely in form and content, among ancient Greek city-states as elsewhere, and it seems unreasonable to suggest that one of these models should be treated as a clearer reflection of reality than all others. Plato conceded that particular laws, however, may indeed be variable according to time and place and yet still be 'good'.[29]

The Platonic conception of law is thus ultimately that of a dictate of reason[30] derived from an insight into a 'true' reality. Such a law has a persuasive and didactic role which should be sufficient in itself with coercion a secondary feature necessary only in the case of the morally ignorant and refractory. It obviously follows from this that the degree of required coercion will increase in direct proportion with the decreasing rationality and degree of explanation of laws. The Platonic idea of the 'good' law is clear, the 'bad' law is seen as in the *Crito*. Laws may be 'bad', immoral and unjust but a duty to obey remains in so far as unjust infliction is concerned but not in so far as an injunction to act unjustly is concerned, all this upon the supposition that the options of persuasion or flight exist and have been exhausted or rejected. It is to be noticed that the Platonic idea of the 'good' law is essentially authoritarian. It explains and it guides but at the end of the day it is an imposition upon the bulk of the populace which will certainly be coercive from the viewpoint of the more or less ignorant and uninformed majority.

This ideal of patricianism was rather ameliorated in the views of Plato's most famous pupil, Aristotle (384 – 322 BC). Aristotle was born in Stagira in the kingdom of Macedon in northern Greece but as a youth he moved to Athens. There, as a young man, he became a member of Plato's Academy. When Plato died in 347 BC he moved initially to Atarneus where the ruler, Hermias, was under strong Platonic influence.[31] Hermias in fact encouraged Aristotle and other philosophers to form a sort of Platonic academy in exile in his territory, although Aristotle himself later moved on to Assus and to Mitylene. In 343 BC he returned to his native land to take up an appointment which was of major significance for the future development of Hellenistic philosophy. King Philip of Macedon invited him to become tutor to his son, the future Alexander the Great. Later Aristotle returned to Athens to set up his own school at the Lyceum where he taught from 334 BC. When Alexander the Great died at Babylon in 323 BC Aristotle left Athens fearing that he might suffer the fate of Socrates in an anti-Macedonian reaction, and fled to Chalcis where he died a few months later.

Aristotle took a rather different view of law and society from that of his teacher Plato. Plato had taken an essentially pessimistic view of mankind whom he felt to need strict guidance from above for the avoidance of error, ideally in the form of the orders of a philosopher-king or, more realistically, through rationally prepared laws. Plato had admitted the importance of explanation in law but Aristotle emphasised the purely didactic function of law much more strongly. He taught that man has a natural potential for 'good', the development of which properly made laws should aim to facilitate. Not all of Aristotle's works have survived, but for present purposes his most important thought is to be found in *The Politics*[32] and the *Nichomachean Ethics*.[33] He taught that the proper end of law is to make men 'good'[34] which is to say not merely to coerce them into the avoidance of the appearance of vice. He based his argument upon a teleological approach, that is to say, an idea of progress from the potential to the actual. In the Aristotelian view all things have an inherent potential for development, the achievement of which is the 'good' of the phenomenon concerned. Thus the potential of an acorn is to become an oak tree and growth to a tree is the achievement of the 'good' of the acorn. The acorn may of course in some way fail or be prevented from attaining that end but it cannot select some other and improper end such as developing into a sycamore tree; that option does not exist for it. Animals also have a potential for development which is essentially to become a successful adult example of their species. An infant squirrel thus has a potential to become a successful adult squirrel, it may succeed or fail in this but it does not have the option to adopt the way of life of some other creature such as a tiger. In all cases progress from the potential to the actual may be impeded or frustrated but not, except in the case of man, diverted. The case of man is made especially complicated by possession of the faculty of reason. Aristotle argued that man is distinguished from the animals by reason, which is a capacity which can be either used or abused. One of the consequences of rationality according to Aristotelian thought is that man is a *politikon zoōn*,[35] that is to say, a political animal whose natural tendency is to combine in social organisations culminating in the state.[36] It being the proper tendency of all things to develop their potential to their own particular 'good' upon the teleological principle, the state, which Aristotle saw as originating as a means of attaining security, becomes a means whereby its citizens may attain the 'good' life.[37]

In the thought of the fourth century BC there were two broad ways of organising a state, through the rule of man, meaning some form of personal or oligarchic rule, or through the rule of law. Plato had accepted law as second best, Aristotle argued strongly for the rule of law as a more efficient means of attaining the reasonable conduct which would lead mankind to the 'good' life than any likely form of despotism. He agreed, however, that in the unlikely event of the actual appearance of a Platonic philosopher-king, his rule would be superior to that of the laws.

The correct aim of laws is thus in the Aristotelian perception the guidance of the natural human potential for virtue into the achievement of the 'good' life through the inculcation of virtuous habits. How is this to be done? Aristotle did not regard law as primarily a coercive imposition, any more than had Plato, but as a means of educating for virtue and thus for the facilitation of the attainment of the 'good' life.[38] The process of legislation is thus perceived as primarily one of moral education and the induction of 'good' habits of life. The makers of such law would obviously be required themselves to be trained in the framing of moral legislation through philosophical training. Once the laws had been made Aristotle saw obedience to them as itself a matter of habit[39] which should be encouraged by the education of the citizenry in the principles of the state constitution. Upon the same principle, frequent changes in the law are deprecated as tending to weaken that habit of obedience.[40] Aristotelian emphasis upon the importance of habit in forming the pattern of obedience to law in some ways prefigures Bentham,[41] but mere habit cannot as such account for obligation. It is clear that Aristotle saw law as invested with moral quality in so far as it facilitated the attainment of the 'good' life among the citizens of the state. It would seem also that he admitted the existence of a morality higher than the laws made even by a 'good' legislator.[42] The essence of his argument is that 'justice' takes two forms which are neither functionally identical nor generically different. The one is justice in a particular instance, the other is universal justice. These may be taken as roughly analogous to the modern categories of positive and natural law in that the first is man-made and variable, the second is universal and eternal. Aristotle assumes that the positive laws will be made in a moral framework but argues that 'equity' may rectify the application of the law where a legal provision, due to its necessary generality, fails adequately to cover a particular case.[43]

Aristotle has thus made his case for the making of moral laws which may vary according to time and circumstances but which have the aim of inculcating habits which will enable men to be 'good'. The question of the law which may be erroneous or even consciously 'bad' is not given much consideration, unsurprisingly in a work mainly concerned with the description of 'good' legislation. In that Aristotle refers mainly to the development of the 'habit' of obedience and counsels against much change in the law even if such change would be morally beneficial, because of the greater deleteriousness of the effect of weakening the habit of obedience, he may be taken to share the view of Socrates and Plato upon the nature of the obligation to obey law. He seems to accept that citizens should be educated in the constitutional principles of their state even if those principles should prove to be 'bad' and this can only lead the moral citizen back to the Socratic options of departure, persuasion or obedience when faced with 'bad' law.

The thought of Socrates, Plato and Aristotle is of fundamental importance but is set against a background of small city-states in which political power and civil rights were the possession of relatively small numbers of male citizens. Slavery was justified upon the basis of inequality of moral capacity, although Aristotle's handling of the matter seems to betray some contemporary unease about this convenient conclusion. More importantly in contemporary terms these theories presuppose a small citizen body in which legislation can play an individually didactic role and the legislator's relation to subjects is much more direct than is the case in any modern state. This allows of a realistic role for rational insight and persuasion or departure to a more congenial legal regime. In short it permits of a diversity which militates against consideration of the major problems of regulation upon a larger and more impersonal scale in a modern state, of which account must be taken in considering the continuing importance of Hellenistic legal theory.

Hellenistic legal theory was compelled to take account of the wider world by the meteoric career of Aristotle's pupil, Alexander the Great. The idea of universal political structures and the widening of cultural horizons which followed upon Alexander's conquests were of fundamental significance for future development of thought. It became necessary for a philosophy rooted in small city-states and supposing the superiority of the Hellenic citizen within his own state as against foreigners, barbarians and slaves to take account of very much broader horizons. At Opis in 325 BC Alexander declared that Macedonians and Persians were kinsmen and this moment symbolises the lasting effect of his conquests in the arena of thought which set the scene for later Hellenistic theory and established the base for the later development of the legal theory of the Roman Empire. The most important fruit of this widening of perspective in the immediate context was the development of Stoicism, a school of thought originated by Zeno (350–260 BC). The Stoics taught that there is a universal and rational order (cosmopolis as compared to the polis of the city-state) which governed all men and was not merely the privileged insight of Greek citizens. Thus, by virtue of the faculty of reason, all men might have insight into the rational order which may be called 'natural law' and which embodies principles of universal application of a higher order than the positive laws of any particular state. In Stoic opinion the harmony which follows from this cosmic reason is disrupted by human perversity and 'good' law thus has as its purpose the rectification of this situation so that mankind may live 'naturally' according to his inborn moral sense which is itself an insight into cosmic reason. To this end Stoicism counsels the avoidance of irrational impulses in favour of a 'proper' mode of living moulded by the dictates of right reason. This idea of a general rationality which imposed universal standards to which particular prescriptions could be referred was to provide an appropriate intellectual setting for the development of the legal theory of the Roman Empire.

Roman law was an admirably structured example of positive prescription which was to have a major formative influence upon the legal tradition of Continental Europe.[44] It is commonly asserted, however, that despite the conceptual excellence of their positive law, the Romans were not great legal theorists and in fact took over their ideas in the field of theory from the Greeks more or less unreflectively. It is certainly true that the Romans produced little truly innovative jurisprudential thought but Roman work in this field was none the less important and here, as elsewhere, was one of major systematisation. The principal legal theorist of the pre-Christian Empire was Cicero (106–43 BC). He was both a statesman and a lawyer as well as a philosopher, and was already a highly successful 'practical' lawyer when he set out to produce a systematic theory of the nature of law related to the reality which he knew. His thought was in many ways much closer to our own age than was earlier Hellenistic theory in that he was writing in the context of a developed and systematic structure of positive law professionally administered in a way in which that of the Greek city-states was not and which dealt in more or less 'modern' legal categories. Cicero was a Stoic and this is manifest in his legal

31

theory. His method was one of categorisation. He shared the general Stoic belief in a cosmic reason which acted as a universal law applicable to all mankind. He sought, however, to relate cosmic reason to human prescription in a much more concrete way than the idealistic approach of earlier thinkers would have permitted. This he did in a manner which was vastly significant for the future development of jurisprudential thought.

Cicero regarded law as an emanation of reason which ought ultimately to be a reflection of Divine or cosmic reason in the human sphere. In the light of this approach he considered 'law' to exist upon three distinct levels. The *Lex Caelestis*,[45] Heavenly Law, is the supreme cosmic reason which Cicero saw as a Divine law and as one having a higher authority than any human prescription. This is obviously a perception of the higher morality, being in fact the 'logs'[46] or highest reason of Stoic philosophy. Cicero, however, saw Lex Caelestis in a much more concrete form than the logos of the earlier Stoics, seeing it in fact not as an ultimate ideal but as a clear supreme moral prescription prescribing virtue and proscribing vice in a direct manner. The *Lex Naturae* or Law of Nature was differentiated from the Lex Caelestis in Ciceronian thought and was perceived as the reflection in the mind of man of the cosmic rationality of the higher law. Thus the Lex Naturae is the means whereby prescription may be drafted to enable mankind in a political society to live a 'good' and natural life.[47] This introduces the significant idea that it is an inherent quality of lawmaking that it should concord with a higher rationality in the interest of the moral good of those subject to it. This is a much closer tie than is to be found in Platonic or even Aristotelian thought in that it does not merely suggest an ideal or Utopian model for law-making or government but suggests that an ordinance which does not concord with the moral law is in some sense defective and lacking in an essential aspect of 'true' law quality. This is a central concept of naturalist thought and one which calls for immediate clarification. The claim is not that an immoral 'law' has no effect but rather that it is an ordinance which lacks the inherent moral quality of 'good' law and being thus defective does not merit as a matter of theoretical appreciation the full appellation of 'law' but some other and lesser term. This distinction between 'law' and morally defective ordinances goes to the root of the naturalist conception of the obligation to obey 'law' as distinguished from mere coercive prescriptions. Cicero's final category of law in general was the *Lex Vulgus* or law as commonly understood,[48] by which he meant any positive legal or quasi-legal ordinance irrespective of its moral quality. Such law might be morally good or bad without losing its basic categorisation. This Ciceronian scheme of relationships may be crudely illustrated as follows:[49]

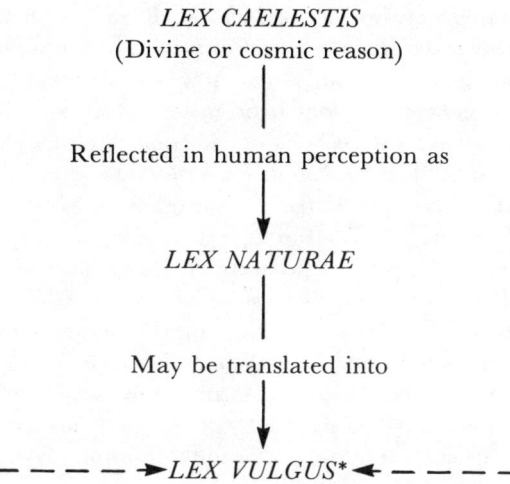

LEX CAELESTIS
(Divine or cosmic reason)

Reflected in human perception as

LEX NATURAE

May be translated into

− − − − ➤*LEX VULGUS** ◄ − − − −

(*which may also be derived from other and potentially 'bad' sources in which case it is 'lex' only in the debased and 'vulgar' sense of any formal prescription)

In so far as the Lex Vulgus conforms to the perception embodied in the Lex Naturae it will thus be 'good' law; in so far as it does not it will be morally defective law or rather pseudo-'law'.

In any such scheme it is obviously fundamentally important to devise some means of identifying the knowable portion of the Lex Caelestis applicable to human life. How then does Cicero propose that this be done? In part this is of course a matter of moral insight and teaching based upon an inherent human sense of rectitude. There was also in Roman jurisprudence, however, a more 'practical' approach to the discovery of at least some of the general principles of higher law. The Lex Naturae as a partial insight into the relevant aspects of the cosmic provision of the Lex Caelestis was seen as the common heritage of mankind and not a privileged insight of the Greek and Roman world. However, it was conceded as evident that different states and peoples have differing positive laws all of which might, in their various ways, be particular applications of the Lex Naturae. The consequence of this idea was a belief in a common fund of general legal principle which might be found among all peoples within the context of their own specific positive legal provision. The particular positive law of a given state, especially in relation to the Roman Empire, was termed the *Ius Civile*. The common fund of legal principle shared by all peoples was termed the *Ius Gentium*. In Roman practice the Ius Gentium was taken to be a sort of universal 'common law' which could be applied in cases in which either or both parties were not citizens subject to the particular provisions of the Ius Civile. This was in many ways a most enlightened concept although its actual application in the Roman Empire was no doubt the cause of some puzzlement to bemused 'barbarian' or other non-citizen litigants.

These concepts of Ciceronian legal theory were part of the general currency of Roman jurisprudence and can be found explicitly stated in the introduction to the *Institutes of Gaius*, a classical textbook of Roman law compiled in the second century AD, wherein it is stated that 'Omnes populi qui legibus et moribus reguntur suo proprio, partim communi omnium hominum iure utuntur',[50] meaning that all peoples governed by law are subject to their own particular law and partly to the common law of all mankind. Gaius goes on specifically to name the particular law of a people the *Ius Civile* and the common law of mankind the *Ius Gentium*.[51]

The same point repeating the basic statement is made at greater length with borrowings from Ulpian as well as Gaius, in the *Institutes of Justinian*. These were compiled in 533 AD well into the Christian era upon the orders of the Emperor Justinian (527–65), but drew widely upon earlier scholarship. The compilers appointed by Justinian assert that 'Ius naturale est, quod natura omnia animalia docuit. Nam ius istud non humani heneris proprium est, sed omnium animalium . . . Videmus etenim cetera quoque animalia istius iuris peritia censeri'[52] which is to say that natural law is taught by nature to all creatures and is not peculiar to mankind since all creatures perceive it. This obviously reflects the Stoic idea of cosmic reason, the Ciceronian Lex Caelestis as perceived, by man, in the Lex Naturae. The *Institutes* then proceed to make the distinction between Ius Civile and Ius Gentium indicated above and in particular distinguish the Ius Gentium by stating that 'Ius autem gentium omni humano generi commune est. Nam usu exigente et humanis necessitatibus, gentes humanae quaedam sibi constituerunt',[53] which is to say that the Ius

Gentium is common to all mankind because exigency and human necessity have led mankind to the development of certain basic rules. The *Institutes* explicitly provide also that

> . . . quod quisque populus ipse sibi ius constituit, id ipsius proprium civitatis est, vocaturque ius civile, quasi ius proprium ipsius civitatis; quod vero naturalis inter omnes homines constituit, it apud omnes populos peraeque custoditur vocaturque ius gentium, quasi quo iure omnes gentes utuntur.[54]

This is to say what a people established for its law is peculiar to that state and is called its Ius Civile, its particular law, whereas what natural reason dictates for all peoples is common to all states and called the Ius Gentium, the law of all nations. Thus again a natural reason, which is in effect the Ciceronian Lex Naturae is admitted as the common heritage of mankind and as something which stands separately from the particular local provisions of a Ius Civile.

It is clear also that practical Roman jurisprudence made the assumption that law served a moral purpose and indeed there is overt reference to the didacticism of this legal theory to be found in the opening words of the Preface to the *Institutes of Justinian*, the Christian background of which should not however be forgotten, which is of passing interest as an Imperial address to law students. It commences as follows:

IN NOMINE DOMINI NOSTRI IESU CHRISTI. IMPERATOR CAESAR FLAVIUS IUSTINIANUS . . . CUPIDAE LEGUM IUVENTUTI.

> Imperatoriam majestatem non solem armis decoratam, sed etiam legibus oportet esse armatam, ut utrumque tempus et bellorum et pacis recte possit gubernari . . .[55]

The above may be rendered as: In the name of Our Lord Jesus Christ. The Emperor Caesar Flavius Justinian . . . etc. to students of the law. The Imperial Majesty should not only be glorified by arms but also armed with laws in order that times of both war and peace *should be properly ruled.*

It may be fair to say that the practical application of theory by Roman lawyers was in some ways almost painfully literal but the theoretical groundwork of Ciceronian thought cannot simply be dismissed as a debased reworking of Hellenistic theory. On the contrary, Ciceronian legal theory, building upon the heritage of Hellenistic rationalism, provided a framework of reference within which a developed system of positive legal rules could be related by the perception of human reason to a general moral order. In this was the moral purposive idea of law-making to receive a formal concrete shape as an inherent and necessary aspect of the concept of law itself, so that an immoral 'law' failed to manifest the whole quality of the phenomenon. This was a rational conception of the moral nature of law which opened the door to the linkage of legal obligation with the idea of the proper purposes of law-making. This form of legal theory contributed the rational and systematic element to the development of Western legal theory. The arguments of obligation were to be strengthened with the Christianisation of the Roman Empire under Constantine the Great (306–37, converted AD 312), when the Hellenistic jurisprudence of the pagan Empire with its emphasis upon the proper purpose and manner of moulding obligation was fused with the Judaeo-Christian emphasis upon the role of absolute moral standards in the generation of obligation so that the unreasonable or morally repugnant law came to be seen in a stronger sense as functionally defective. To this stage of development we must now turn.

Notes

1. At least in the view of Thucydides.
2. Available in 'Penguin Classics' in the translation by M. Tredennick. The four sections are *Euthyphro, The Apology, Crito* and *Phaedo*.
3. *The Apology*, 31D – 33B.
4. The arguments of the dialogue are considered in detail by A. D. Woozley in *Law and Obedience. The Arguments of Plato's* Crito.
5. *Crito*, 50A to end.
6. Ibid., 49E to 50B.
7. See Ch. 4, this volume.
8. *Crito*, 48D.
9. See *The Apology*, 31D to 33B. There is here a parallel with the rejection by Confucius of a disciple, Jan Ch'iu, who retained office when required to collect unjust taxes.
10. *The Apology*, 41D.
11. See *Crito*, 49B.
12. This view somewhat resembles the juristic opinion reached in some of the post-war 'grudge cases', see Ch. 7, this volume.
13. *Crito*, 50B, *et seq.*
14. Cf. the Confucian perception.

15. Sir Desmond Lee's translation in the 'Penguin Classics' edition of *The Republic*.
16. See *The Republic*, 430E to 432A.
17. Ibid., 434E.
18. Ibid., 434D.
19. See T. J. Saunders, Penguin Classics edition of Plato's *Laws*, Introduction, pp. 27 – 8.
20. There are some clear parallels to be observed between Plato's ideal of a philosopher-king and the Confucian concept of the moral validation of rule by the abstract 'mandate of heaven'.
21. Plato's Academy was not the only Athenian philosophical academy; its principal rival was that of Isocrates who was of sophist persuasion and taught rhetoric rather than philosophy *per se*.
22. Plato, *Laws*, 627D – E.
23. See ibid., 718 – 19.
24. See ibid., 630C and 705E.
25. Ibid., 875D.
26. See Ch. 5, this volume.
27. *Minos*, 321a.
28. See, for example, Plato, *Laws*, 714A where law is stated to be a 'distribution of reason' (translation by T. J. Saunders, Penguin Classics edn).
29. Cairns, *Legal Philosophy from Plato to Hegel*, p. 35 usefully describes this as a distinction between 'principles' and 'rules'.
30. A point taken by St Thomas Aquinas, see Ch. 3, this volume.
31. See earlier.
32. Available in 'Penguin Classics', translated by T. A. Sinclair, revised and re-presented by T. J. Saunders.
33. Available in 'Penguin Classics' as *Ethics*, translated by J. A. K. Thomson, revised by H. Tredennick with an introduction and bibliography by J. Barnes.
34. Aristotle, *The Politics*, 1280b 12.
35. Aristotle, *The Politics*, 1253a 7.
36. It is in this aspect of his thought that Aristotle relates to St Thomas Aquinas as does Plato to St Augustine; see Ch. 3, this volume.
37. Aristotle, *The Politics*, 1252b 27.
38. See Aristotle, *Ethics*, 1103b 25.
39. See Aristotle, *The Politics*, 1269a 20.
40. See ibid., 1269a 23.
41. See Ch. 5, this volume.
42. The matter is discussed in detail in *Ethics*, Book V.
43. Aristotle, *Ethics*, Book V:x.
44. Roman law had also a considerable influence upon the development of Scots law. There was a 'Reception' of Roman law in much of Europe and even after the codifications of the late eighteenth and the nineteenth centuries the Roman influence remains obvious. In England the native Common law rooted traditions were too strongly rooted at the time of the European 'Reception' to admit of more than a peripheral Roman influence.
45. Cicero, *De Legibus*, II:8.

46. That is, 'word'.

47. See Cicero, *De Legibus*, I:56.

48. 'Vulgar Law' actually conveys the Ciceronian nuance rather well.

49. Cf. the structure advanced by St Thomas Aquinas, see Ch. 3, this volume.

50. *The Institutes of Gaius*, I:1.

51. Ibid.

52. *Institutes of Justinian*, I:2.

53. Ibid., I:2,ii.

54. Ibid., I:2,i.

55. *Institutes of Justinian*, Preface.

3

Late Roman and Medieval Legal Theory

The general form of Christian legal naturalism to this day is the product of a fusion of the theocratic Judaic tradition with the more humanistic classical Hellenistic tradition. The pattern of development of naturalist thought within the Western Church is commonly perceived as one of increasing concern with secular matters as the Church became more 'worldly' in its interests. In fact this is a rather unfair presentation of the motivation behind the progress of theoretical evolution. The shift of emphasis which occurred actually represented a subtle and inevitable accommodation to the differing problems encountered by the Church as it moved from the status of persecuted minority to that of a major public institution during the period from late Antiquity to the high Middle Ages.

Within the boundaries of the Roman Empire at the date of the adoption of Christianity as the state religion, there were to be found two principal, and contrasting, varieties of naturalism — that is to say the Judaic and Hellenistic traditions.

Within the Empire, the Hellenistic view had thus far been dominant; however, with the conversion of the Emperor Constantine the Great (reigned 306–37 AD) — the credit being assigned more properly to his mother, the Empress Helena — an accommodation between the two traditions became necessary.

The outlines of Hellenistic thought have already been examined through the theories of Socrates, Plato, Aristotle and the Stoics[1] but it remains to examine the development of naturalism from the Judaic tradition within the Church up to the time of the beginnings of the fusion of two views.

The origins of Christian naturalism lay in Judaic thought, in which 'the law' meant the Mosaic law ordained by God but with a drastically revised emphasis.[2] To Christians, the Mosaic Law of the Old Testament had, through the death and resurrection of Christ, been superseded by the operation of Divine grace at least for those amenable to its operation. 'The Law', whether the Mosaic law or human positive law, was consequently seen as an institution rendered necessary only by sin and relevant only in relation to it. Like the penances of Dante's 'Purgatorio', law was seen as becoming needless once sin is abandoned and Divine grace pursued. Thus St Paul wrote to the Corinthians that 'The sting of death is sin; and the strength of sin is the law',[3] the idea behind this being that laws are needed as a curb for sin and vice and that in the absence of sin there would be no need for any positive prescription because people would then live in accordance with the Divine scheme which plays the role of the higher law. Thus a sharp distinction was drawn between the higher 'law' (the will of God) and positive prescription which was seen as a coercive measure rendered necessary only by the fallen state of man.

It is important to realise, however, that even though at this stage law was seen as an institution born of sin, it was not itself seen as being sinful *per se*. In so far as it curbed vice and reflected Divine command, it served a Holy purpose and represented a necessary curb in the fallen world. In so far as it served ends of course it was taken to fall foul of the higher law and lacked the moral quality to command obedience as a matter of conscience. The secular state and its laws were thus seen as necessary props of social order and potential, if unwitting, agents of the Divine purpose which might perform well or badly in any given set of circumstances as the case might be.

Christ himself had said 'Render to Caesar the things that are Caesar's . . .'[4] and St Paul elaborated the point in his letter to the Romans, saying: '. . . is the law sin? God forbid. Nay, I had not known sin but by the law: for I had not known lust, except the law had said, Thou shalt not covet.' (and continuing) 'Wherefore the law is holy and the commandment holy, and just, and good.'[5]

Thus the Patristic view of 'law' in the positive sense was essentially that it defined sin and warned men off its practice and maintained social order when it was 'good' law. Even the laws of the pagan Empire were seen to that extent properly to command obedience, being needed in a fallen world in much the same way as a sick person has need of medicine. Christians, however, were supposed to avoid the institutions of the positive law as not requiring coercion to avoid vice. Civil litigation between church members in particular was viewed with especial horror as members were expedited to resolve differences in the light of mutual charity. Positive law which actually contravened the will of God was seen as an abomination to be resisted even, indeed perhaps especially, if so doing proved to be the path to martyrdom.

The overall Apostolic view of law ranged therefore from acceptance in general to indifference so far as the faithful themselves were concerned. The Christianisation of the Empire necessarily led to a reappraisal since a church which had become the Empire's spiritual partner could hardly dismiss the secular traditions and institutions of the Empire as a regrettable and temporary expedient. Consequently Christian thinkers had to take account of the Hellenistic culture of Rome and its traditions of statecraft and in doing so to elevate the status of its positive law.

St Augustine of Hippo (345 – 430)

St Augustine was an important figure in this development and one who played a significant role in the development of both medieval and, paradoxically, Reformation thought. Philosophically he stood at the sunset of classical antiquity and the pre-drawn of the Middle Ages. He combined both Christian and Hellenistic tradition in his thought which he was ideally suited to do as one who was a Christian Bishop but had formerly been a teacher of classical rhetoric.

Augustine was born in 354 in the region of Carthage of a pagan father and a Christian mother, St Monica. He himself did not become a Christian until well into adulthood. His interest in philosophy was sparked by reading a lost work of Cicero — the *Hortensius* — whilst a student of rhetoric (the then equivalent of 'greats') at Carthage. Initially he became a Manichean, that is, one believing that the universe is founded upon conflict between two equal and opposite forces of good (God) and evil (Satan). This system of thought founded by Mani (executed in 277) saw evil as a positive force which would be struck down only ultimately and not as a mere perversion or negation of Godliness. Man was seen by the Manicheans as a compound of these two inimical forces and pulled in opposite directions by them. Augustine became dissatisfied with this view and his studies of neoplatonism led him back to Christian orthodoxy. This occurred at Milan where he was appointed Professor of Rhetoric in 384 and came under the influence of the Bishop, St Ambrose. He was baptised in 386 and ultimately ordained a Priest. In 396 he became Bishop of Hippo where he died in 430 during a barbarian attack upon the city.

St Augustine was thus a Christian priest with a background in Hellenistic philosophy representing in his own person a fusion of the traditions. He wrote a number of highly influential works, of which, for the present purpose, two are of especial importance: *De Libero Arbitrio* (Upon Free Will), written in stages over a period from shortly after his conversion up to 395, and his greatest work *De Civitate Dei* (Of the City of God), completed in 397.

His writings reflected the effort of the Church to come to terms with the secular institutions of a formerly hostile, even persecuting, Empire of which it was now the representative of the official, though not universal, religion. Even at this stage, with the benefit of hindsight, some dim foreshadowing of the future struggles between the medieval Church and Holy Roman Empire may be discerned. St Ambrose, the mentor of St Augustine, had himself refused communion to the Emperor Theodosius until he repented for a massacre ordered by him upon political grounds. Herein may be seen an early assertion of that primacy of the spiritual over the temporal power, at least in certain matters, which was to form the meat of the conflict between Papacy and Empire and form the core of medieval naturalist thought.

For St Augustine, law was the 'poena et remedium peccati'.[6] Thus he taught that those under the coercive influence of positive law are still governed by a higher law (Eternal law) because all justice is derived from it, whereas those who seek concordance with Eternal law have no need of the curb of positive law.[7]

St Augustine was not dismissive, however, of the importance of positive law within the existing state of the world. In *De Civitate Dei* he presented human development as the product of conflict between two urges towards virtue and towards vice (or rather the love of God and the love of vicious pleasures). In general he assumed that the Church should be an instrument for the establishment of the City of God: however, he saw every reason to hope that a secular emperor should be in a state of grace and, of course, there is every reason to imagine that some churchmen were decidedly not so. One may readily imagine the category into which St Augustine would have put Pope Alexander VI (Borgia) or Pope Julius II.[8]

His view of relations between the spiritual and secular elements of society led Augustine to a close analysis of the respective roles of Divine and Positive law in which he admitted his debt to the Greeks. At one point he commented upon the closeness of some Judaeo/Christian and Platonic ideas, even to the extent of suggesting that Plato might have been acquainted with the Prophet Jeremiah,[9] although this is actually highly unlikely.

In the Augustinian scheme all things at all times were seen as governed by the Eternal law (*Lex Aeterna*), that is, the will of God. Thus he wrote: 'Lex aeterna est qua justum est ut omnia sint ordinatissima.'[10] That is to say that the Eternal law is that law by which it is just for everything else to be ordered.

The role of positive or 'temporal' law (*Lex Temporalis*) was seen as much more limited, in effect to the coercion of those wilfully inclined to err and stray in ways harmful to the rest of society. In fact Augustine saw positive law as maintaining order among the perversely inclined through fear.[11]

He outlined the relationship between Eternal and temporal law in a simple form by arguing that temporal law, like all things in the created universe, is subject to Eternal law representing the will of God. Thus he said that — '. . . in temporali lege nihil est justum ac legitimum, quod non ex lege aeterna homines sibi derivaverint.'[12] That is to say that nothing just and (truly) lawful is to be found in temporal law which has not been derived from Eternal law. St Augustine conceded that temporal law is necessarily mutable because it is required to face changing circumstances, but the fundamental principles of Eternal law from which any temporal law should be derived are immutable.[13]

This still leaves the question of the status of a purported exercise of temporal law-making power whose product in fact runs counter to Eternal law. The answer to this problem in the Augustinian scheme was what might be reasonably anticipated. In *De Libero Arbitrio* Augustine wrote: 'Lex esse non videbitur quae justa non fuerit',[14] which is to say that no (true) law could be unjust. This is not the prima-facie absurdity implied by the bald statement, lex iniusta non est lex. The notion that an unjust ordinance would automatically be devoid of practical effect would have seemed at least as absurd in the late Roman world as it would today. The correct implication is rather that the temporal law derives its moral claim to command compliance by virtue of concordance with Eternal law. A temporal positive law which conflicts with Eternal law might indeed have coercive force but, unlike 'good' laws, would make no claim upon the conscience of the subject.[15]

It should be stressed that St Augustine saw temporal law as essentially penal, a means of curbing vice and necessitated only by the existence of sin. The idea of civil litigation among the faithful would have been anathema to St Augustine as much as to St Paul.[16] Augustine did not actually argue even that the temporal law curbed, or sought to curb, all sin — he argued in fact that it curbed only that sin which reflected adversely upon public order.[17] In contrast, all sin runs contrary to Eternal law.

For St Augustine, then, positive law (that is, the Lex Temporalis) was an institution bound by sin and having relevance only in relation to it. In a perfected state the Eternal law as made manifest to man would secure full voluntary compliance without any need for coercive restraint from divergence through temporal law. Here the extent to which St Augustine was a Christian Platonist should be obvious.

Plato advanced an abstract Ideal perceptible through the insight of a perfect ruler (the 'philosopher-king') but in the absence of any such gifted person as demanded by *The Republic* allowed for the less flexible operation of a code of positive law outlined in the *Laws*. For Plato the moral worth of a positive legal provision would be adjudged according to its approximation to the Ideal. In an analogous manner St Augustine saw positive law as a debased and partial reflection of Eternal law rendered necessary only by sin. The great difference is that for St Augustine the higher prescription was not an abstract philosophical ideal but the concrete will of God which alone imparts moral authority to positive prescription or, in the alternative, withholds it. Augustine's scheme formed the basis for the elaboration of medieval naturalism leading to the work of St Thomas Aquinas. Unfortunately naturalism also proved capable of misapplication at times along the path of its development.

Natural law and the Papal/Imperial conflict

The Roman Empire in the west formally came to an end in 476 when the last shadowy Emperor, Romulus Augustulus, was deposed by the barbarian King Odoacer. The Empire in the east continued with varying fortunes until 1453 when Sultan Mehmet II 'Fatih' defeated the Emperor Constantine XI and captured Constantinople. The Empire of the west split into a number of barbarian kingdoms and principalities with occasional partial restorations of the imperium by the more forceful Byzantine rulers, including Justinian who ordered the compilation of the Corpus Iuris Civilis.

This left the Apostolic See as the remaining symbol of Imperial unity in the west until Christmas Day 800 when Pope Leo III (795 – 816) crowned the Frankish King Charlemagne Emperor of the Romans and acclaimed him Caesar and Augustus after Mass in St Peter's, allegedly much to his surprise. Thus was initiated the Holy Roman Empire in the west which continued rather tortuously for 1,000 years or so until its formal termination by Napoleon after the Battle of Austerlitz (actually it metamorphosed into the Austrian, later Austro-Hungarian, Empire).

The coronation of Charlemagne was a source of medieval controversy. The fact that the Pope crowned the Emperor, by invitation or otherwise, was advanced by some subsequent popes as evidence of the superiority of the spiritual over the temporal power — indeed of the proposition that the imperium lay in the gift of the Holy See. The Emperors were to make equally extreme counterclaims to a right of investiture of Bishops.

None of this was inherent in Augustinian doctrine, for St Augustine, while asserting the moral superiority of the spiritual power over the temporal power had never denied to secular institutions their proper sphere of action. The theoretical basis of relations between the two powers was actually laid down by the Doctrine of the 'two powers' affirmed by Pope Gelasius I (492 – 6) in which each power, church and state, was asserted to be supreme in its own sphere and bound not to trespass upon the proper preserves of the other. Of course the boundary between the two spheres was not, and is not, easy to define. There were soon examples of extreme claims trespassing on either side of the fence. The Papacy, on the basis of Imperial coronations and the (forged) Donation of Constantine which supposedly conferred temporal powers upon the Pope, demanded temporal as well as spiritual primacy. In return the Emperors shamelessly sought to make inroads upon the spiritual power. This was based upon a misunderstanding of the conception of the role of the Church — it had been seen as having power to criticise secular acts and indeed to withdraw moral authority from them but not one of supercession so as itself to become in effect the temporal power.

As the Middle Ages proceeded a more elaborate theory of natural law began to develop based in part upon the rediscovery of some of the formerly lost classical writings, notably those of

Aristotle which became the great inspiration of philosophy in the Middle Ages from a theoretical viewpoint. In order to achieve this the Church had first to find grounds for the 'rehabilitation' of the classical philosophers who had of course been pagans. St Augustine had seen some of them as unwitting Divine agents, even suggesting that Plato might have been familiar with the writings of Jeremiah through some Egyptian intermediary, but none the less classical writings remained suspect to the Church through the taint of paganism. The solution to this problem was simple as manifested in the *Decretum Gratianum* written in the mid twelfth century. The argument was as follows: classical naturalist theory was based upon observation interpreted through the medium of human reason. Both nature and human reason are fruits of the will of God and thus it is possible for man to gain some insight into the workings of the Divine will through rational observation of natural order.[18] Thus the insights of Plato and Aristotle were made acceptable to the medieval church as insights of human reason into a Divinely created order even though perceived by men who were pagans.

St Thomas Aquinas (1225 – 74)

The most significant contribution to the development of naturalist theory in the high Middle Ages was made by the Dominican theorist St Thomas Aquinas. Aquinas was the seventh son of Count Landulf of Acquino and his family originally hoped that he would become a Benedictine and possibly rise to be the Abbot of a great monastery. Instead, to their dismay, he chose to join the Dominican Order and became a writer and teacher. He studied under Albertus Magnus at Paris and Cologne and is mainly associated with the University of Paris at which he became a Professor of Theology in 1256 at the early age of 31. He worked at various times in a number of other institutions and produced a very considerable number of major works. For the present purpose the most important are the *Summa Theologica* and *De Regimine Principum*. His great work, the *Summa Theologica*, was designed as a general account of theology for students of the subject. It was left unfinished in 1273 after a mystical experience undergone by Aquinas during a celebration of the Mass convinced him of the futility of earthly endeavour. *De Regimine Principum* (Upon the rule of Princes) was originally intended as advice upon the practice of

government to the King of Cyprus.[19] Aquinas died in 1274 on his
way to attend the Council of Lyons at the summons of Pope
Gregory X (1271-6).[20] He was canonised in 1323 after some
initial doubts — at one point an Archbishop of Paris cast doubts
upon his orthodoxy — and has been influential in the Western,
especially but not only the Catholic, world ever since.

Aquinas produced a masterly synthesis of Aristotelian and
Christian thought, proceeding upon a basis closely related to the
views expressed in the *Decretum Gratianum* (see above). Aquinas
declined to make any such clear-cut distinction between the state of
nature and the state of grace as St Augustine had found it necessary to do.

For Aquinas, nature, including human nature, was a Divine
creation even if one corruptible by sin which was perfectible by the
action of Divine grace. This allowed Aquinas, like Aristotle, to
believe that as a consequence of man's reason and ability to make
choices it lies within his nature to live in political societies making
decisions upon the basis of rational considerations. Upon this view
human institutions, including the law and the state, could be perceived as 'natural' and (therefore) Divinely ordained, existing
irrespective of sin and having the capacity for perfection through
grace. This was a marked advance from the Augustinian view of
such institutions as, at best, temporary expedients necessitated by
the fact of sin.

Aquinas devoted Questions 90 to 97 in the first portion of the
second part (Prima Secundae) of the *Summa Theologica* to the issue
of law. He argues that God is the source of all authority and thus
that acts of human authority are Divinely ordained so long as they
are performed within their proper limits, citing St Paul in support
of this proposition.[21] The great issue is of course the nature of the
'proper' limits of human authority. Although Aquinas saw human
social institutions as the 'natural' outcome of the nature of man as
a social animal, he concurred with St Augustine in seeing human
law as dependent upon concordance with the will of God for its
claim to moral suasion. He saw both law and Divine grace playing
their own roles in the guidance of human action, saying,
'Principium utem exterius movens ad bonum est Deus, qui et nos
insturit per legum et juvat per gratiam'.[22] In light of the more
exalted role accorded to law by Aquinas he naturally treats it in
much greater detail than St Augustine had found necessary.

Aquinas defines 'law' in general as follows: '. . . nihil est aliud
quam quaedam rationis ordinatio ad bonum commune, ab eo qui

curam communitatis habet, promulgata',[23] which is to say that it is nothing but an ordinance of reason made and promulgated for the good of the community by the person to whom its care is entrusted. We have thus three basic elements in 'true' law-making set out in this definition: rational aim for the common good; enactment by authority; and promulgation. These elements are basic features of a wide spectrum of 'naturalist' opinion and do not in themselves have any necessary 'religious' connotation. It is notable, again in marked distinction from the Augustinian conception, that this definition contains no reference to coercion as an element of 'law', nor indeed any to sin. Aquinas did not deny, however, that in practice, in the present state of mankind, coercion will inevitably be an incident of law. He explains in *Summa Theologica* that those who by nature or the operation of Divine grace are inclined to virtue will need no more than fatherly guidance towards it whereas others who are headstrong and wayward must be coerced away from evildoing in order that they shall not disrupt the lives, and the inclination to virtue, of others. In time such coercion might even set the conditions in which the wayward might be led actively to seek a better way of life. Thus Aquinas remarks, 'Hujusmodi autem disciplina cogens metu poenae est disciplina legum'.[24] In other words, training in virtue through the fear of punishment is a discipline provided by the law. It is noteworthy that the coercive element of law is explained by Aquinas in the same way as it is by Augustine, as a product of the need to restrain the wilful from sin. Aquinas differs from Augustine in his wider conception of law as having a 'natural' role in human societies not dependent upon sin and coercion.

The Thomist conception of 'law' is in fact very wide indeed, certainly far transcending the limitations of human positive law. The idea of law as an ordinance of reason ('rationis ordinatio') includes all rules of reason up to and including the will of God. The Divine will is of course the highest reason playing the same functional role in Thomist theory that cosmic reason played in Stoic theory, albeit in a manner much more active and direct. The crucial point of the Thomist theory of law is that law is seen as a *rational* phenomenon, one which derives its moral stature from concordance with the highest reason, the will of God, which is also the highest 'law'. This leaves the important question of the means whereby the content of human law is to be related to the ultimate rational law for mankind, and the whole universe, which is to be found in the Divine will. That will is of course presupposed to be 'reasonable' since it is regarded as being in fact the source and basis of universal rationality. Aquinas gives an elegant answer to the question of the relationship between the laws of man and the law of God which admits the roles both of Divine revelation and of rational human perception. Aquinas argues that law can be seen in a number of different forms, at least as perceived by man. He then proceeded to formulate a scheme of relationships ultimately showing the connection between the will of God, the highest 'law', on the one hand and the law of man, that is to say positive law, on the other.

The highest law he termed ETERNAL LAW. This is the will of God governing the motions of the universe and is 'law' in its widest significance comprising 'natural laws' as understood by the scientist as well as the various usages of the term by philosophers and lawyers. As a medieval Christian theorist Aquinas had to consider the question of how it could be that the righteous living by Grace and therefore 'not under law' could none the less be governed by the Eternal will which he himself had defined as a form of 'law'. This issue is considered at length in *Summa Theologica*.[25]

The basic Thomist conclusion is that the virtuous act in accordance with Eternal law by natural inclination and the operation of Divine grace whereas the wicked lack the necessary insight and are subject to the consequences of sin decreed by the Eternal law. In short, the Eternal law is the perfect prescription but the wayward are necessarily coerced into compliance and are thus in a different way from the virtuous 'under' the law. Aquinas concludes: 'Et secundum hoc beati et damnati subsunt legi aeternae',[26] which is to say that both the blessed and the damned are the subjects of Eternal law.

The whole of Eternal law is not known (or even, presumably, knowable) to man: it is instead partially knowable to him through two sources which form the next level in the Thomist categories of laws, that is to say the Divine law and the natural law. Divine law is stated by Aquinas to be that portion of the Eternal law which is revealed to man in Holy Scripture, whereas natural law is seen as that portion of the Eternal law which is perceptible to man through the operation of human reason (and thus comprehensible to pagan thinkers such as Aristotle). Finally Aquinas placed Human law which St Augustine had called temporal law. This law is made by man for his benefit but it depends upon concordance with the known portions of Eternal law (through Divine law and natural law) for its moral claim to be obeyed.

This scheme of relationships may be set out diagrammatically as follows:

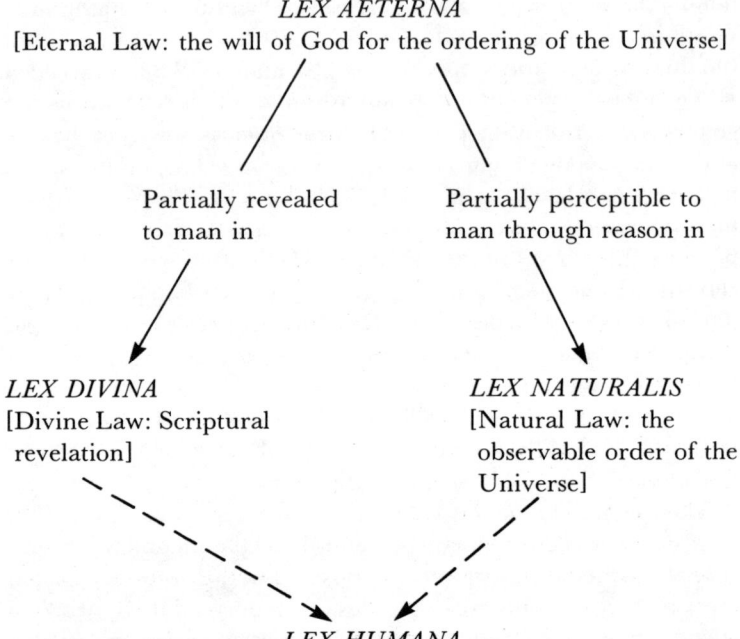

LEX AETERNA
[Eternal Law: the will of God for the ordering of the Universe]

Partially revealed
to man in

Partially perceptible to
man through reason in

LEX DIVINA
[Divine Law: Scriptural
revelation]

LEX NATURALIS
[Natural Law: the
observable order of the
Universe]

LEX HUMANA
[Human positive law, made by man but deriving its moral
authority from concordance with Eternal Law as from time
to time revealed or perceptible to mankind through Divine
or Natural Law]

In the Thomist system the Church was seen as the interpreter of God's will on Earth and thus able to condemn human laws which conflicted with Eternal law and to release their subjects from the moral obligation of obedience.

The higher law represented by Eternal law as manifested through the media of Divine and natural law is clearly the same ultimate prescriptive standard which St Augustine called the Lex Aeterna but the Lex Humana, which is more or less equivalent to the Lex Temporalis of Augustine, has been given a new respectability and status within the natural order by Aquinas.

The consideration of positive law in *Summa Theologica* opens with the fundamental question of the purpose and utility of the institution. It commences from the fairly obvious proposition that an enforced appearance of virtue is infinitely less valuable than the voluntary practice of actual virtue and thus that in terms of virtuous life, positive law must seem inutile.[27] For Aquinas as for many others, including Aristotle and Confucius for example, the refutation of such arguments lies in the educative function of law. On this basis the idea is advanced that although man has reason he also needs guidance through law in order to fulfil his potential as a creature and, because sin has rendered his reason corruptible, law at the present time must take a coercive form. Brute creation does not need such guidance, coercive or otherwise, because through the operation of instinct they cannot do other than live the life proper to them. Man in contrast through the faculty of reason has choice and is quite capable of leading forms of life grossly improper to his nature and indeed shows a marked propensity for doing so and hence stands in need of guidance. Thus Aquinas said in *Summa Theologica*: 'Dicendum quod, sicut ex supra dictis pater, homini naturaliter in est quaedam aptitudo ad virtutem; sed ipsa virtutis perfectio necesse est quod homini adveniat per aliquam disciplinam.'[28]

As we have seen, Aquinas saw laws in general as rational ordinances made and promulgated for the common good by a ruler. 'Laws' were seen by Aquinas as 'bad' or at least tainted, if made for some purpose other than the common good — for the personal advantage of the ruler, for example. Augustine had seen such 'laws' simply as abominations; Aquinas called them 'tyrannical' in the proper sense of that word as involving an exercise of power without validating authority. Aquinas did not claim that such ordinances were devoid of actual force, indeed in his day no less than in ours their force was all too obvious. Instead he called them perversions of true law without any moral claim to obedience in conscience. Thus he concluded: 'lex tyrannica, cum no sit secundum rationem, non est simpliciter lex, sed magis est quaedam perversitas legis'.[29] That is to say that a tyrannical law which is contrary to reason is not simply a 'law' but is rather a perversion of true law. It is therefore to be seen in more modern terms as an abuse of law-making power. So bad positive 'laws' emerge as corrupt simulations of law having the outward appearance but not the inner reality of a 'true' law concordant with Eternal laws. The distinction being drawn by Aquinas parallels that drawn by H. L. A. Hart between authority and power as between the demands of a government and a gunman.[30] The test of moral validity for human law is defined in a key passage in *Summa*

Theologica where Aquinas states that:

> In rebus autem humanis dicitur esse aliquid justum ex eo
> quod est rectum secundum regulum rationis. Rationis autem
> prima regula est lex naturae, ut ex supra dictis patet.
>
> Unde omnis lex humanitus posita intantum habet de
> ratione legis inquantum a lege naturae derivatur.[31]

That is to say that in the human perception 'justice' is derived
from reason and the natural law is the highest rule of reason. Thus
human law derives its claim to obedience from natural law. St
Thomas then immediately adds the significant statement that: 'Si
vero in aliquo a lege naturali discordet, jam non erit lex, sed legis
corruptio',[32] that is, if a human positive law should conflict with
natural law then it is not true law but a corruption of law. This is of
course essentially the same assertion made earlier in connection
with the idea of a 'tyrannical' law[33] ('lex tyrannica, cum non sit
secundum rationem, non est simpliciter lex, sed magis est
quaedam perversitas legis').

Aquinas did not mean by this that in order to have any moral
claim to obedience a positive enactment must copy natural law
slavishly (concordance with the Lex Divina was of course another
matter). He taught rather that human laws could properly relate to
the natural law in either of two ways, by direct extrapolation or as
specific formulations of more general natural norms. He states in
Summa Theologica: 'Sed sciendum est quod a lege naturali dupliciter
potest aliquid derivari: uno modo sicut conclusiones ex principiis
alio modo sicut determinationes quaedam aliquorum com-
munium!'[34] That is to say that ordinances may be derived from
natural law as if from a premiss or as specific applications of a
more general ordinance.

Ultimately Aquinas concluded that as all authority comes from
God, the proper use of it must accord with the Divine will and any
human ordinance in conflict with the higher law could not be binding in conscience. To put this in more modern terminology, law-
making power is held on trust from God and its exercise in breach
of that trust is not authoritative. Aquinas also stated that in
circumstances of unforeseen emergency it was proper for a subject
to follow a course of action for which the law did not provide since
that must have been the will of the rational legislator, had the
possibility of the relevant circumstances been drawn to his
attention.[35]

In *De Regimine Principum* Aquinas considered the exercise of the human authority whereby positive laws are enacted. He again asserted the 'naturalness' of human political society upon the basis that man as a reasoning creature, unlike the animals, needs direction to achieve his proper ends.[36]

St Thomas stressed that governments exist for the benefit of the governed rather than that of the governors. A ruler who rules for his own selfish ends is not one who rules by true authority but is a mere 'tyrant' imposing his will through the force at his disposal — rather as St Augustine compared unjust governors to bands of robbers. The purpose of governmental power in general (and of law-making power in particular) is presented as being the maintenance of the peace of the community, citing St Paul in support of this contention.[37] In general Aquinas thought this best achieved by a virtuous monarchy because the dissension inherent in other forms of government might itself be disruptive of peace. This seems more a reflection of the reality of medieval politics and the fact that St Thomas was writing to a king than an assertion derived from Christian doctrine. St Thomas admitted that the power of kingship may all too readily tempt its wielder into error and corruption. He therefore considered the question of how one should properly react to tyranny.[38] He concluded that some degree of oppression should be endured because of the greater perils of anarchy or of the replacement of tyranny with yet more severe despotism worse than the prevailing situation. Ultimately he rejected the morality of tyrannicide, as did Isidore of Seville, holding it to be contrary to Apostolic teaching. He claimed that the proper answer lay in appeal to some higher authority — then ultimate appeal would lie through the ·Church of God. In the original Thomist system it was the Church, and in particular the Papacy, which was seen as having the ultimate power to strike down 'bad' laws and to release their subjects from the obligation to obey. In the last resort this could be done through the excommunication of a king or government as, for example, in the case of King John.

It is an elementary point that legal provisions which are unexceptionable when created may, through changes of circumstances, become harsh, burdensome and wrongful.[39] The fact that pressure for change bears upon positive law led Aquinas to consider the mutability of laws, even when in origin they were 'good'.

The Lex Aeterna, as the will of God, was seen as necessarily immutable because of the perfection and inerrancy of the Almighty. On the other hand the Lex Humana was, and is, patently highly mutable. Aquinas found no conflict in the difference because man cannot wholly comprehend the mind of God or thus be fully cognisant of the Lex Aeterna. From time to time mankind's perception and knowledge of the Lex Aeterna may increase either through further revelation[40] or through rational enquiry into the nature of things.[41] In consequence of any such clarification of understanding the details of the prescription of Eternal law would, from the human viewpoint, seem to change even though there would be no actual alteration. There could, in short, be a change of perception but not of substance so far as Eternal law was concerned. Such increases in human knowledge would require changes to be made in positive law in order to maintain concordance with the higher law. Aquinas, while admitting the mutability of positive law, did not favour any undue variation in the Lex Humana. He argued that constant alterations of prescription weaken its effectiveness and thus changes should be made only when actually necessary. Thus he wrote:

> . . . ergo dicendum quod ea quae sunt artis habent efficaciam ex sola ratione; et ideo ubicumque melioratio occurit est mutandum quod prius tenebatur. Sed leges habent maximam virtutem ex consuetudine, ut Philosophus dicit . . . et ideo non sunt de facili mutandae.[42]

That is to say that what is made by human art may be changed in the interests of improvement, but, since law gains much of its effectiveness from the tradition of compliance, legal provisions should not be altered too frequently or readily — a contention supported by Aristotle.[43] These considerations apply of course only to 'good' laws; 'bad' laws contravening 'true' reason are *ex hypothesi* ripe for change and in any case only of defective 'legal' quality in the first place.

The theory of law set out by Aquinas is a more subtle analysis than that of St Augustine. The Lec Humana is admitted as a 'natural' aspect of the social life of mankind without necessary relation to sin. In the Thomist perspective it is the coercive incident of positive law rather than its existence as such which is related to sin. The perception of human law as a rational order related to the ultimate rationality of the Divine will and deriving its 'authority' from concordance with it leads in effect to the enunciation of what may be termed a 'proper purposes' doctrine of law-making. Aquinas would not have differed materially from Bentham in his view of law as the command of a sovereign backed by a sanction so far as 'bad' laws are concerned. They indeed depend upon coercion alone for their effectiveness, but have no claim upon conscience beyond that derived from the general interests of social stability; indeed such an abuse of law-making power produces only a corrupt appearance of 'law'. For Aquinas 'law' is essentially a moral phenomenon and the power to make it exists for purposes of a clearly defined nature, derogation from which vitiates the moral claim of the ordinance concerned. Coercion is thus admitted as an incident of positive law but not as a defining characteristic in the manner found in early positivist theory. This in no way conflicts with the positivist insight that upon a practical lawyers' perspective laws are made according to formal procedures which sufficiently identify legal rules for such immediate purposes. Aquinas's argument goes beyond this and identifies true law as an inherently moral phenomenon which suffers in its ultimate quality when morally defective. The line in short is drawn between an ordinance which 'obliges' through mere force and one which imposes an 'obligation' in conscience upon a level much more fundamental than that considered in the same terminology by the positivist analysis of H. L. A. Hart.

The work of Aquinas, the 'Common Doctor', was massively influential in the Middle Ages. It has remained so in the Catholic world and has attracted renewed interest beyond it as the moral claims of law have again become a focus of interest and concern. In the compelling logic of his analysis Aquinas has come to be seen as a paradigmatic classical naturalist. His work both of synthesis and development remains basic to any understanding of the mainstream development in naturalist legal theory.

Duns Scotus (1265 – 1308)

Aquinas was by no means the only medieval thinker whose work impinged upon legal theory. Notable among such other relevant thinkers was Duns Scotus. Otherwise known as John the Scot with the honorific title of the 'Subtle Doctor', Duns Scotus was a Franciscan who apparently taught at Oxford, Paris and Cologne. He is known to have sided with Pope Boniface VIII in his quarrel with King Phillip IV ('the fair') of France following the publication of the extreme papalist bull 'Unam Sanctam' in 1302. This bull asserted that as all power was vested in Christ, so on Earth it was in the Church, and in particular the pope as vicar of Christ, that power vests. On this basis kings were claimed to be beholden to the popes for their office. Such a doctrine would have given popes power over the entire exercise of secular power and not mere power to remonstrate with and condemn the sinful misuse of power. Duns Scotus emphasised the importance of will over the faculty of reason upon the basis that the former is free but the latter is not, being shackled by the consequences of observation and perception. He saw the universe as governed by the will of God and therefore by Divine love. Consequently, and in accordance with the teaching of the New Testament, he saw the pre-eminent norm as the love of God which is immutable and transcends human perception and reason. Duns Scotus admitted a perceptible 'natural law in that some forms of sin are inherently 'evil' in being inherently injurious to human nature and therefore not only forbidden by God but clearly wrongful to the rational perception of man. Any positive ordinance contrary to such perception would always seem 'wrong' and in fact contravene the basic norm of Divine love. One can imagine major problems in the application of such a principle. It is necessary to make a careful distinction between general disapproval and perception of Divine ordinance in considering human assessment of 'wrongfulness'.[44] Duns Scotus considered that some acts, however, are merely banned by God *pro tempore* in his absolute will and could, in changed circumstances, be commanded by Him instead without any contradiction in the immutable principle of Divine love.[45] In his view it follows from the nature of God that ideas of 'justice' and 'goodness' in law and elsewhere can only be measured against the standard of Divine love to which all things are relative. This is, of course, a very much less Aristotelian approach than that of Aquinas and one that, by its nature, has far less concern with the functioning of formal legal structures. Its precise effect upon human law is less easy to see than is the case with the Thomist model or indeed with the Augustinian.

William of Ockham (c. 1290 – 1349)

Another, and near contemporary, Franciscan thinker was William of Ockham, also British, but this time from Surrey. He lectured for a while at Oxford but his teaching career foundered upon inconclusive charges of doctrinal error. While endeavouring to answer these charges at Avignon[46] he became involved in a dispute between his order and the pope over the precise nature of the Franciscan vow of poverty in which he opposed the papal position. As a result he found it necessary to flee from Avignon. He took refuge with Ludwig of Bavaria whose side he took in the then raging dispute over the temporal power of the Papacy. These activities led to excommunication and it is not known whether subsequent attempts at reconciliation succeeded before his death.

For William of Ockham all the motions of the universe are the product of the will of God and consequently all proper norms of actions and restraint are derived from the Divine will. Prima facie this would suggest a purely revelatory concept of obligation. However, Ockham argued that although all these things are ordered by the illimitable will of God, that will had in fact been exercised in the imposition of a rational natural order. Consequently he asserted that the Divine will was therefore in some measure deducible through human reason. For Ockham, as for Duns Scotus, some things were 'good' or 'bad' for human nature and perceptible as such to human reason in the form of 'natural law' — this notwithstanding the fact that such tenets derive their moral authority from God and not the intermediate fact of nature.

William of Ockham deduced three types of ordinance bearing upon human conduct: (i) universal and evident manifestations of the Divine will which were *ex hypothesi* immutable; (ii) evident ordinances derived from natural law through rational human perception; and (iii) lesser ordinances dealing with immediate problems but without fundamental significance. This latter category would in the modern world include such rules of convenience as driving on the left-hand side of the road. The substantive content of such a rule is immaterial as long as all agree upon the same rule at the same time, that is, so long as there is *some* known rule.

Politically William of Ockham accepted temporal rulers, such as Ludwig of Bavaria, as having a 'natural' and proper role to play in social order and not as mere executive lieutenants of the Papacy. This would not preclude the Church, however, from remonstration and the application of spiritual sanctions where rulers used their power in a clearly 'immoral' way. In the last resort, in medieval political theory, the Church could call upon secular powers to remove an obdurate ruler, the highest secular authority being the Holy Roman Emperor.[47] This view has more of the practical flavour of Thomism although again less concerned with the detailed relationships of forms of law and law-making.

Dante Alighieri (1265–1321)

The poet Dante was an ardent if rather idealistic supporter of the Imperial cause in the conflict between the Guelphs and Ghibilenes. He adopted a similar view to the doctrine of the 'Two Powers' earlier sanctioned by Pope Gelasius I. Dante was of Thomist persuasion and greatly admired the pre-eminent 'Common Doctor' despite his being a churchman. Indeed in the *Divine Comedy* Dante placed Aquinas with the Doctors of the Church in the Heaven of the Sun wherein it is he who points out to Dante the other denizens of that region.[48] In *De Monarchia* (Of Monarchy) Dante argued that the authority of both pope and emperor in their respective spheres came directly from God without any need for intermediation. He asserted that this was a necessary condition for the maintenance of the unity of peace called for by the Apostle Paul. He asserted that the ills of his own time came from improper trespass by the spiritual powers in the duly appointed sphere of the temporal power. As always, however, Dante admitted the critical role of the Church in the denunciation of sin whether on the part of rulers or otherwise.

Of the medieval theorists it is St Thomas Aquinas, with St Augustine, who has had the greatest impact upon the development of naturalist legal theory. His continuing influence can be seen in the modern writings of the neo-Thomist school.[49] A particularly notable example of modern Thomism can be seen in the work of John C. H. Wu. In the course of his main work[50] Wu states the case for natural law in particular relation to the development of the Common law in England and the United States. His conclusions rely very much upon the work of Aquinas and indeed his approach is overtly Thomist.

Perhaps the lasting value of Thomist legal theory is its essentially realistic assessment of laws. Laws may be 'bad' and 'unjust' yet still be effective and good law on any positivist assessment. Aquinas does not deny that effectiveness but does deny the moral claim to obedience of such 'laws', at least beyond a certain point of necessary toleration in the interests of social stability. In the end result this is not to say that all ordinances must be moral but that those which are not are spoilt law which has in effect been made in breach of the moral conditions upon which law-making power is held. Although the organs of spiritual and temporal power are no longer as in his day and the relevant moral decisions are necessarily more individual, the questions he asked retain their importance today. Whether or not the Thomist answers seem obvious, they do provide a closely argued definition of the boundary to the propriety of temporal action beyond which lies tyranny both in the technical Thomist and in the more popular sense of that word.

Notes

1. See Ch. 2.
2. For an outline discussion of Judaic naturalism as such see Ch. 1.
3. 1 Cor. 15:56.
4. Mark 12:17.
5. Romans 7:7 and 12. In this context 'known' should of course be taken in the sense of ability to identify.
6. I.e. the penalty of and remedy for sin.
7. See St Augustine, *De Libero Arbitrio*, I.XV:107.
8. In this context the satirical work *Julius Exclusus* of Erasmus may be read with some amusement.
9. *De Civitate Dei*, VIII:II.
10. *De Libero Arbitrio*, I.VI:15.
11. Ibid., I.XV:32.
12. Ibid., I.VI:15.
13. Ibid., I.VI:14.
14. Ibid., I.V.
15. In *De Libero Arbitrio*, I.III, the obvious point is made that if all temporal 'laws' were *ex hypothesi* 'good' then the martyrs would have to be viewed as justly condemned. Such a conclusion would be utterly untenable within the Augustinian, or any other Christian, form of naturalism.
16. See 1 Cor. 6:1–8.
17. See *De Libero Arbitrio*, I.V:13.
18. An observation admitted by St. Augustine as the Lex Naturae perceptible through the medium of human reason.
19. This was probably Hugh III but might conceivably have been his predecessor, Hugh II.
20. There was a rumour that he was poisoned at the instance of Charles of Anjou. Dante repeats this in the *Divine Comedy* (Purgatorio, Canto XX:69) in the course of an onslaught upon the misdeeds of the House of Capet, but there seems to be no real evidence for the assertion.
21. *Summa Theologica*, 1a 2ae, 96:4 quoting St Paul at Romans 13:1. Latin quotations from the *Summa Theologica* are taken from the text used by the Dominican editors for the new translation issued in 1966.

22. *Summa Theologica*, 1a 2ae, de lege.
23. Ibid., 1a 2ae, 90:4.
24. Ibid., 1a 2ae, 95:1.
25. See ibid., 1a 2ae, 93:6.
26. Ibid., 1a 2ae, 93:6.
27. Ibid., 1a 2ae, 92:1.
28. Ibid., 1a 2ae, 95:1.
29. Ibid., 1a 2ae, 92:1.
30. H. L. A. Hart, *The Concept of Law*, Ch. 2.
31. *Summa Theologica*, 1a 2ae, 95:2.
32. Ibid., 1a 2ae, 95:2.
33. See (30) earlier.
34. *Summa Theologica*, 1a 2ae, 95:2.
35. See ibid., 1a 2ae, 96:6.
36. See *De Regimine Principum*, I:1 – 9.
37. In Ephesians 4:3.
38. See *De Regimine Principum*, Ch. VI.
39. To borrow a (now outdated) phrase from the realm of Company law.
40. That is, an increase in the Lex Divina.
41. That is, an increase in understanding of the Lex Naturae.
42. *Summa Theologica*, 1a 2ae, 97:2.
43. See Aristotle, *The Politics*, II, 5.
44. The problem is of the same order as that involved in using popular 'disapproval' as the test for the propriety of the use of law to enforce moral precepts, as suggested by Lord Devlin in *The Enforcement of Morals*.
45. See Duns Scotus, *Reportata Parisiensa*.
46. Then the seat of the Papal Court during the so-called 'Babylonian exile' from Rome.
47. In theory this was the form of the 'teeth' of most medieval naturalism, although the practical dentition of most Emperors was rather weak, even when they themselves were not in conflict with the Papacy.
48. *The Divine Comedy*, Paradiso, Canto X:94, *et seq*.
49. The modern neo-Thomist school of thought is especially strong in France and includes such figures as Jean Dabin.
50. Wu, *Fountain of Justice*.

4

Theories of the Ages of Reason and Enlightenment

The period of the seventeenth and eighteenth centuries represents, in jurisprudence as in many other areas, a watershed in the development of European thought and may in effect be regarded as the beginning of the modern period. In the preceding centuries the intellectual and political life of Europe had undergone two major upheavals, the intellectual ferment of the Renaissance and the religious and political revolution of the Reformation which permanently shattered the institutional framework within which, for example, Thomist thought had originally developed. These developments engendered an intellectual climate in which fundamental assumptions could be questioned and basic issues re-examined. Like all neat categorisations of historical eras, the terms 'age of reason' and 'age of enlightenment' must be treated with great caution as necessarily gross simplifications and potentially highly misleading. The categorisation in terms of rationality and enlightenment reflects in part a tendency to a rather self-conscious and often somewhat arid intellectualism but also reflects a genuine spirit of enquiry and a desire to find rational frameworks of analysis for the discussion of major issues. The seventeenth century in particular was a period of fierce, and often violent, controversy as what was in many ways a new international order appeared while the eighteenth century in large measure built up the systems of thought which in the last decade of the century and in the next were to bring about the fiery birth of the modern intellectual and political world.

In jurisprudence the era was one of experimentation. As with all experiments, the results of some were more quaint than valuable but, equally, theoretical perceptions of great and lasting importance were developed. In the present context two fruits of the era call for particular consideration; these are the group of theories known collectively as 'social contractarianism' and the work of Immanuel Kant.

The Social Contractarian method

'Social Contractarianism' is not a unified theory, it is instead a method of approach shared by a number of theories the essential concerns of which vary quite widely. The essence of the method is an enquiry into the rational social expectation as a means of determining the legitimate ambit of formal social prescription and in particular of positive law. This enquiry is conducted through the rhetorical device of an original 'social contract'. In effect the question is posed: 'If social order had been the product of agreement between free and rational individuals, upon what basis and to what end would they have set up their society?' The central concern is thus the proper extent of rational and formal restraint upon individuals in a society and the area properly reserved to the liberty of the individual. For the social contractarians the answer to this basic question lies in the analysis of the proper purposes of social organisation.

In one sense the use of the term 'social contractarianism' has proved rather unfortunate. There is a frequently encountered canard to the effect that as a matter of anthropological fact no primal assembly of 'free individuals' ever gathered together to 'agree' upon the basis of social life and therefore social contractarianism is misconceived and naïve. This argument is readily countered. Few, if any, social contractarians believed literally in a historical 'social contract' — the contract itself is merely a rhetorical device which is a convenient means of presenting basic questions and conclusions about the nature of society and social obligations. Social contractarianism is in fact a form of legal and social philosophical analysis, not a misconceived antique form of anthropology.

As an idea the notion of a 'contractual' basis for social obligation long predated the seventeenth century.[1] Elements of the idea may be discerned in the Old Testament[2] in which it is clearly indicated that the law of God was accepted by the ancient people of Israel rather than being merely imposed upon them. The notion is manifest in such Hellenistic thought and is certainly to be found in the writings of Plato in *The Last Days of Socrates*[3] in the idea of the duty to the law, even to a 'bad' law, based upon acceptance of the benefits of life in the community regulated by the law. Something of the same idea of mutuality can be seen in St Thomas Aquinas's discussion of the office of kingship. Aquinas argued that the authority of government is Divine in source but that the mode of exercise of it is a matter upon which the community may choose and may indeed change their mind should a given form of government become tyrannical. In *De Regimine Principum* he gives the example of the deposition of the last king of Rome, Tarquinius Superbus, and the establishment of the Roman Republic in support of this contention. He is careful, however, to stress that the deposition of tyrants is a matter for action by the public leaders of the community and not a justification for individual acts of tyrannicide.

The seventeenth-century thinkers thus had a historical tradition of 'contractarian' theory upon which to draw in the formulation of their theories. It is indeed a tradition which continues and in modern dress can be found in the use of the rhetorical device of the 'actors' in the 'original position' by John Rawls in the derivation of his theory of justice.[4]

The significance of the social contractarians of the seventeenth and eighteenth centuries was that they used the idea of the contract in the rational evaluation of law and society as a basis for the model of legitimate social structure in its own right, rather than merely as an explanation of the functioning and practical acceptance of prescription otherwise derived, as had earlier thinkers. In short, contractual bases of obligation were raised from an instrumental to a primary role in the explanation of law and the obligation imposed by it. The 'social contractarian' school covered a wide range of opinion but the work of three thinkers in particular, Thomas Hobbes, John Locke and Jean Jacques Rousseau, shows the pattern of developing social contractarian thought over the period in question.

Thomas Hobbes (1588 – 1697)

Thomas Hobbes lived through a tumultuous era of English history. He was born in the year of the Armada, reached manhood in the gathering constitutional storm clouds of the reigns of James VI and James I, lived through the reign of Charles I, the Civil

War, the Commonwealth and the Restoration, to die within ten years of the deposition of James II and the 'Glorious Revolution' and invitation to William III and Mary II in 1688/9. This background is important in the understanding of the political thought of Hobbes with its emphasis upon stability and order, qualities far from prominent in his own political experience. In his great work *Leviathan*, published in 1651, Hobbes sought to set out principles for the establishment of a stable social order which would secure its subjects from the primary perils of dislocation and anarchy and by virtue of doing so establish its claim to be obeyed. As a witness to civil war he considered that only such a secure order enabled mankind to maintain a level of existence above the merely brutish.

The starting point for Hobbes was the proposition that human beings on average are so naturally similar to one another in strength that a life of unregulated 'freedom' would soon degenerate into permanent conflict between the individuals which would prevent human life from ever rising above a brutish level. Even granted that the strong might from time to time establish local ascendancies these could never be more than temporary and precarious and the lot of the common man would in no way be thereby improved. Thus without some power exercisable over all and able to secure obedience human life would soon degenerate into a state of permanent conflict. Hobbes set out the consequences of this condition which has become famous:

> . . . where men live without other security, than what their own strength, and their own invention shall furnish them . . . there is . . . continual feare, and danger of violent death; and the life of man, solitary, poore, nasty, brutish, and short.[5]

This may almost be read as Hobbes's own impression of the English Civil law, which most certainly informed his rather gloomy opinion of human nature in general. He considered that men seek power over others as a means to the end of increased wealth, influence and other 'goods' and secondly that men will always seek to avoid 'evils' and in particular the evil of their own death. In short he argued that human beings are motivated by the desire for power and by a natural instinct of self-preservation. Granted the assumptions about human nature the appalling Hobbesian vision of the unregulated 'state of nature' follows inevitably. The underlying purpose of social order is then presented as the means whereby this state of things is avoided and civilised life is rendered possible. It is this purpose which is spelt out in Hobbes's conception of the 'social contract'. The contract for Hobbes was essentially a surrender of anarchic freedom in return for a guarantee of security which was the basis of the legitimacy of the state and its laws.

Hobbes rooted the social contract in two basic natural laws which are set out in detail in *Leviathan*.

The first is that '. . . every man, ought to endeavour Peace, as farre as he has hope of obtaining it; and when he cannot obtain it . . . he may . . . use, all . . . advantages of Warre'.[6]

The second rule is that '. . . a man be willing . . . to . . . be contented with so much liberty against other men, as he would allow other men against himselfe'.[7]

The first rule thus asserts an inclination to seek peace with a reservation of the right to self-defence; the second reflects a basic concept of 'fairness' in human relations which is a necessary aspect of any equitable social order. Both these principles are overtly concerned with the need to restrain the ambit of personal licence through the medium of collective restraint in the cause of social order. From the argument for social order Hobbes proceeds to advance the argument for government upon the following lines: (1) man is by nature competitive and unrestrained competition is incompatible with civilised life; (2) man desires the benefits of peace but in their absence reserves the right of self-defence — which in unrestrained exercise leads to the problem of (1) above; (3) the best means of avoiding this débâcle is for each individual to agree to the limitation of his personal powers in favour of a social order which is able to impose peace to the benefit of all; (4) a mere surrender of natural freedoms of competition and self-defence in favour of some concept of social order will not guarantee peace, however, because an abstention can always be reserved; (5) thus the natural capacities must not only be given up but actually and definitively be transferred to other hands, to be precise, into the hands of a political superior — the sovereign.

The Hobbesian social contract is thus a transfer of power to a political sovereign who in return guarantees the peace and social order which licentious freedom would destroy. This, according to Hobbes, is the basis of the individual's obligation of obedience to the state. He expresses the point thus: '. . . when a man hath . . . granted away his Right, then he is . . . OBLIGED or BOUND not to hinder those, to whom such Right is granted . . .'[8]

This, then, is the Hobbesian account of social obligation and of the duty to obey the positive laws made by the state. Individuals transfer their personal 'political' capacities to the state in order to gain the benefits of peace and security and having done so are then under an obligation to obey the authority which is thereby constituted.

The most obvious objection to Hobbes's scheme is that no evident means is advanced of calling the sovereign to account for his use of the authority conferred upon him, or even of determining what the proper limits of sovereign authority actually are. Hobbes did not actually ignore this issue but it was very much peripheral to his central concerns. His answer to the point was essentially that even 'bad' rule is preferable to no rule, a reflection of his primary concern with the need for order in the face of the perils of anarchy rather than with the substantive morality of government or law-making. Thus Hobbes comments that:

> . . . the estate of man can never be without some incommodity . . .; . . . the greatest . . . in any form of government . . . is scarce sensible in respect of the . . . horrible calamities that accompany . . . that dissolute condition of masterlesse men without subjection to Lawes and coercive Power . . .[9]

This is a gloomy conclusion, if not quite a counsel of despair, which was perhaps born of simple scepticism. Unprepared to take a Thomistic view of sovereignty as limited by any superior moral precept and thus unable to endow the 'lex tyrannica' with moral, as compared with formal or coercive force, to avoid the horrors of civil war or anarchy Hobbes was in the end driven to clutch at government, almost any government, as a source of security. Hobbes argues secondarily that rulers had no interest in oppressing their subjects since the vigour of the state depends upon the vigour of its people. This of course is not a satisfactory argument. The reasonable ruler would no doubt not be a tyrant, for moral as well as pragmatic reasons, but there is no reason to imagine that rulers will always be reasonable; indeed history strongly reinforces such sceptism. Hobbes in fact was not concerned with tyranny but with anarchy.

One is thus driven to enquire what is the *quid pro quo* which is demanded of the Hobbesian sovereign for the transfer of political power? The ruler receives power so that he can maintain the peace and order and obviate the perils of anarchy. What then if this rather basic consideration fails? In Chapter 21 of *Leviathan* Hobbes considers the circumstances in which the subjects' obligation to obey will be abrogated. He lists a number of such circumstances, being principally: (1) capture and release of an individual by a foreign state on terms of subjection by that state; (2) abdication of the ruler; (3) banishment, in which case the ruler could not logically demand a continuation of obedience; (4) transfer of obligation through international treaty — in short novation, cancellation, unilateral breach and transfer, to pursue 'contractural' analogies. One of these cases, however, deals with the problem of the 'bad' ruler or tyrant. The only case of failure on the part of the ruler which Hobbes does concede is that in which the sovereign fails to maintain the order which is his *raison d'être*. Hobbes's reasoning is that the obligation to the ruler is generated by the need for the maintenance of order and security and when that need goes unfulfilled the 'natural' right of personal self-defence, originally surrendered to effective sovereignty, resumes.[10] A sovereign who fails to supply or maintain that peace forfeits his claim to obedience because he has failed to perform the basic contract upon which the obligation rests.

There is thus a duty imposed upon the sovereign, the breach of which can abrogate the obligation of subjects. Continuing obligation depends upon the maintenance of peace and order. However, enquiry must surely be made into the quality of this peace and order — there are after all few things more peaceful and ordered than a graveyard. Hobbes was not entirely insensitive to this issue. In Chapter 30 of *Leviathan* Hobbes makes some consideration of the nature of the sovereign's duty as a ruler. The duty of the ruler to maintain the security of the people is said to embrace 'not . . . bare preservation, but also all other Contentments of life, which every man by lawfull Industry, without danger or hurt to the Commonwealth, shall acquire to himself'.[11] In short Hobbes, writing in the early years of the development of a capitalist economy, saw the role of government as the maintenance of stable social conditions in which individual initiative for self-betterment could flourish. None the less such matters of the quality of rule were left to the conscience of the ruler for which he would be answerable to God, and to God alone. It is only if the ruler fails to supply or maintain the essential social order that Hoddes concedes the termination of obligation through failure to perform the 'social contract'. Hobbes in fact makes the case for social stability in contrast to strife through the surrender of individual power to a political sovereign. With the quality of the sovereign's rule he is much less concerned, as the essential vacuity of his rather peripheral consideration of this issue in *Leviathan* demonstrates.

Hobbes's views were received as a shockingly amoral advocation of naked power politics in his own time and the idea of Hobbes as a grim apostle of totalitarianism lingers today. It is certainly true that Hobbes was centrally concerned with the power of government but this should not be misunderstood. Hobbes in some ways prefigured the positivist thought of the nineteenth and twentieth centuries in that, although his theory of government is certainly purposive albeit in a rather limited way, and in that sense quasi-naturalist, it is not concerned with any issues of substantive morality in government or law. This is not to say that Hobbes thought the morality of government to be unimportant — indeed *Leviathan* makes it clear that he did not, but, like Bentham, he in effect considered such issues to exist outside his innate frame of reference. In confronting the problems raised by civil strife and social dislocation it is not surprising that the main emphasis is placed upon stability, and is not unreasonable given the choice between civil disorder or order to choose the latter. Hobbes in fact was using the social contractarian method to argue the case for social order, and in the context of his times he may perhaps be forgiven if he placed an implicit trust in the willingness of sovereigns to behave in a morally appropriate way which in a less fearful age would be considered dangerous.

John Locke (1632–1704)

John Locke in the next generation turned the social contractarian method to other problems and became an advocate of constitutionalism. From 1666 onwards Locke was closely associated with Anthony Ashley Cooper, the Earl of Shaftesbury, a highly controversial figure in Restoration politics and a particular enemy of James, Duke of York, later King James II. This connection strongly coloured Locke's political views. He fled abroad after Shaftesbury's conspiracy to cause the Duke of Monmouth to usurp the throne, although there is no evidence that he was personally involved in the attempted coup. He eventually remained in refuge in Holland until James II was overthrown in the 'Glorious Revolution' of 1688/9 and replaced by William III and Mary II as joint sovereigns at the head of a government with which he was in very good standing. Locke's theories in fact formed the ideological basis of the 'Glorious Revolution' and the constitutional arrangements which followed it. He is thus a figure of outstanding importance in the history of English constitutional development as also in that of the USA, the Constitution of which owes much to Locke's ideas.

Like Hobbes, Locke used the social contractarian method in developing his ideas of government and state but the focus of his concern was quite different. His ideas upon government and the legitimate exercise of power are set out in his *Two Treatises of Government*. The first of these is an attack upon the idea of the divine right of kings; the second sets out Locke's perception of the basis of civil government. Like Hobbes, Locke commences from the position of a hypothetical 'state of nature',[12] the remedies to the defects of which are analysed through the medium of a 'social contract'. Locke's 'state of nature', however, differs markedly from the brutish anarchy envisaged by Hobbes. According to Locke the state of nature although without formal regulation was not wholly licentious, since there was from the beginning a 'law of nature'. This he saw as essentially a 'no harm' principle which obliged each person to avoid injury so far as possible to the lives, liberty and property of others upon the basis of mutual respect. This principle in a 'state of nature' grounds rights not only of personal self-defence but also of mutual defence against harm among individuals.[13] This led Locke to the conclusion that there is in nature a general and undifferentiated right to enforce a rational principle of mutual freedom from harmful incursion which is equally vested in all people in addition to the immediate and much narrower principle of personal defence. These for Locke are distinct bases of 'punishment', the general basis being for the restraint of delict in general, the personal basis being for the taking of reparation for some particular injury suffered.[14] These general and personal rights to enforce a rational principle against delict make Locke's 'state of nature' already in essence a 'social' order, albeit a very loose and open-textured one, in a way in which Hobbes's was certainly not.

Within this state of nature Locke also argues that there exist certain definite 'rights' which are not dependent upon any principle of civil government, these being encapsulated in the concept of 'property'. It is important to realise that 'property' in this context has a much wider meaning than its modern connotation of physical or pecuniary possessions. 'Property' in the sense used by Locke includes rights to personal freedom and economic entitlements as well as possessory rights over things. Indeed upon Locke's construction the latter are derived from the former two. The argument is this; every person has a 'property' in himself and in his own skills; thus whenever he fashions something through his own labour he adds something of himself to the thing over which he thereby acquires proprietory rights.[15] This concept, derived from Roman law, is almost a description of acquisition of title to a *res nullius*, a naturally occurring thing without former ownership, and, taken literally, is quite useless in the context of any economy ever so developed as that of seventeenth-century England. In the modern world it would, for example, hardly be said that a shipyard worker gains specific proprietory rights over that part of a ship such as the *Queen Elizabeth II* upon which he happened to work. Of course Locke's argument must not be taken so painfully literally. The proposition actually advanced is that human beings have a natural 'property' in themselves and in their labour. Thus no one may properly demand the labour of an individual by subjection. On the contrary, the individual has the right to the fruits of his or her labour which means, in effect, the right to proportionate reward for work done. This can be seen as an argument of economic individualism which reflects the developing capitalist economy of England in Locke's time. It is in fact a basic 'bourgeois' theory of economic relations.

All of these 'rights' and entitlements are regarded by Locke as having existence prior to the concepts of civil government and positive law. With so much treated as already inherent in the 'state of nature', what then is the purpose of civil society and the content of the 'social contract' at its root? The answer given by Locke, essentially, is security. Locke concedes in effect that the enforcement of natural rights through the random agency of individuals in a 'state of nature' could only be patchy, uneven and unsatisfactory. There is also the further problem that in the exercise of their personal rights men would of necessity be judges in their own cause with their judgement and impartiality at best questionable. In short, through insufficiency, through excess of zeal or through simple rage there would in a 'state of nature' be an inequity of maintenance of 'rights' which would be productive of insecurity of 'property' in the broad sense. The answer to this problem and the foundation of civil society given by Locke is the surrender of individual powers of protection and enforcement to a government in a political society which, having much greater force and being impartial as between persons can maintain natural rights with greater surety and efficacy. This is the substance of Locke's 'social contact'. It lies in the surrender of individual power and judgement to a governmental authority which then has power to maintain perceived natural rights in a political order. The state so created will then place obligation upon those subject to it, whose collective judgement it is taken to represent.

Order as such is not then the primary concern of Locke's social contract: the aim is rather order of a very specific sort designed to maintain a community life founded upon clearly enunciated and pre-existing social rights. This is all quite distinct for Hobbes's views and there is yet more significant distinction to be noted. The surrender of rights to the sovereign in Locke's conception is not absolute and does not therefore entrust an unlimited power to the sovereign. The purpose of government is presented as the achievement of specified ends which are taken to be the general aspirations and judgements of the community founded upon natural reason. The authority of government is not unlimited but dependent upon the continuing of the community wherein resides ultimate sovereignty.

Such a conception is of course relatively valueless, in the absence of means of implication, and this is the weakness of Hobbes's conception of the duties of the sovereign. Locke agrees that if a civil government behaves in a manner contrary to the implication of the delegation of power made it by the community then its law will to that extent become tyrannical and its authority may by the same token be vitiated. In such a case the members of the community are entitled to resume their natural power and select a different form of government which may better be trusted to secure their 'property', which was the original and proper end of government. Thus we return, by a different route through social contractarian methodology, to the basic naturalist conception of law-making as a power held on trust to be exercised for the 'proper' benefit of the community. In some ways this parallels the Thomist view. There is, however, one major difference: Aquinas distinguishes 'lex' from the 'lex tyrannica' saying that the one has authority and imposes obligation whereas the other has only coercive force. Locke equally sees the 'lex tyrannica' as a breach of the trust of government, but regards this as a ground for political revolution rather than a denial of the status as such. In this analysis power is given to the sovereign by the community as a transfer of natural individual rights, which rights may be resumed if the terms upon which the donation was made are breached. Until such a resumption takes place, the obligation owed to civil government remains. This of course follows the contractural logic of Locke's argument. Locke's approach was thus far more substantial in the duties which it imposed upon the state as the *quid pro quo* for its monopoly upon power. He did not, however, find it necessary in answering the problems raised by the constitutional clashes of the reign of James II to go so far in his theory as did the final social contractarian thinker calling for attention in this context, Rousseau.

Jean Jacques Rousseau (1712 – 1778)

Jean Jacques Rousseau was nothing if not a controversial figure. He attracted both admiration and opprobrium in his own time and continues to do so today. He was born in 1712 in Geneva, a city-state for whose system of government he later claimed to have some admiration although his writings were far from pleasing to the authorities there. It was in France, however, that Rousseau made his greatest mark as a thinker and also there that his work had its greatest practical impact. He wrote a number of political and philosophical works of which much the most famous is his great statement upon civil society and government, *Du contrat social*, published in 1782.

It is probable that Rousseau was familiar with the work of Hobbes and Locke but, in his assumptions and conclusions, he differed from both of them in significant respects. Hobbes was concerned with insurance against civil strife and Locke with the limitation of arbitrary government whereas Rousseau was concerned with the principles upon which a truly virtuous social order could be based. He believed the society which he saw around him to be a distorted and corrupted social order which tended to make men worse rather than better by inculcating in them false pride and other vices. Like other social contractarian theorists he commenced from a rational 'state of nature', but in this case one which was a state of unrealised potential from which man had gone into moral decline as a consequence of badly conceived social orders. His conception of the state of nature was neither so rapaciously brutal as that of Hobbes nor merely insecure and inconvenient like that of Locke: it was more an amoral state of independence in which mankind might be happy but could not develop his inherent moral potential for lack of motivation or the means of doing so. Rousseau argued that man, as a social animal, finds the means of his social development within a social medium, but may develop for good or ill having until then shown a marked propensity to do so for ill. This is the implication of the famous opening statement of *Du contrat social*, 'L'homme est ne libre, et partout il est dans les fers',[16] which is to say that man was born free yet he is everywhere in chains, the chains being not only those of servitude but also the intellectual shackles imposed by misconceived social structures.

There is some evidence that Rousseau originally conceived of the 'state of nature' as a condition of primal innocence, but it is clear that in *Du contrat social* he perceived it was a pre-moral condition in which mankind was independent but not 'free' because of the lack of any moral framework by reference to which 'freedom' could have any meaning. None the less Rousseau admits natural laws to exist as part of the character of man and he argues that these come to be reflected in an urge to form social groupings. Upon this analysis it is not fear or insecurity which impels mankind towards a 'social contract' but originally the collective advantage to be gained from group activity in, for example, hunting and agriculture. This is fuelled also by the urge of man towards association with his fellows. The social contract in fact arises, according to Rousseau, from the inability of mankind to develop morally or otherwise in isolation and the resultant need to develop a settled mode of community life.

Following this logic Rousseau saw the 'social contract' not as a surrender of individual power to a political sovereign but as a compact made among free individuals to enter into political society together. The contract then becomes the guiding spirit of the community, the *volonte generale* which is to say the 'general will'. Thus each individual is said to surrender his political will to the composite will of the community and to be thereafter governed by that general will which is also the proper expression of his own morality or potential for morality. In Rousseau's scheme the citizen is said to be 'free' in the sense of not being subjected to the will of any other individual (such as the Hobbesian sovereign) but is made subject to the will of the community as a whole which defines the parameters of right and duty. A man who thus obeys the rational extension of himself in the general will is not amorally 'independent' as in the state of nature but has the liberty of development which only a moral framework of reference can supply.

There are a number of possible objections to this scheme. As a sovereign power the general will must seem amorphous in the extreme and there is no evident reason why such a concept should at first sight be thought to differ from Locke's conception of the state of nature. Secondly, if the general will is merely the popular will Rousseau's 'liberty' begins to sound like subjection to majority opinion which may well be conceived to be a particularly odious form of tyranny. Rousseau makes careful efforts to avoid these pitfalls. He does not in fact envisage the general will as popular opinion but more as the opinion which would be held by an informed and moral population. This is what Rousseau had in mind in asserting that the general will is always morally sound and correct but that the opinion of the populace may be misled.[17] Rousseau also does not present the general will as a viable mode of *government* in anything but the smallest and most limited societies. Legislative validity in Rousseau's view can rest only in the general will but implementation and executive action in a community of any size is conceded to be vested in a government which should be one which understands and enforces the general will, *inter alia* through positive laws.[18] It is stated that the law-maker should be a person of superior perception acting upon the general will and, thus, clearly not a mere demagogue acting upon popular opinion. The actual form of government is left fairly open, Rousseau having conceded that different societies might well find different forms of government suitable to their needs. The important limitation is that, whatever its form, a government has a legitimate authority to make laws and to regulate only within the terms of the social contract which means in fulfilment of a general will. Thus for Rousseau a law which is authoritative as opposed to merely coercive is one which is a concrete and specific reflection of the general will. Other prescriptions are the acts of a despotism and a tyranny and, being a defiance of the general will, are without moral suasion or claim to obedience.

It is important to notice here that Rousseau conceives the rationality reflected by the general will to originate in what he terms the 'Divine Providence'.[19] His difference of opinion with much earlier thought lies in his wish to derive principles of human social organisation from the consideration of human rationality, not necessarily in the ultimate derivation of that rationality. The general will itself is the product of natural reason and therefore had certain definite limitations. Rousseau asserts expressly that the general will cannot will enslavement because that is contrary to natural reason which seeks moral 'liberty'. He further states that man is 'free' in relation to matters beyond the ambit of the social contract.

Rousseau has often been stigmatised as 'totalitarian'. There can be no doubt that his social conceptions were authoritarian and at first sight his general will bears an alarming resemblance to Nazi ideas of a debased form of *volksgeist* as 'the sound instincts of the people'. This latter doctrine of course became an instrument of arbitrary action on the part of the party which had no connection with any moral or even legal framework — it was in fact the foundation of the 'lawless' state of the Third Reich in Germany. This is a gross simplification, however, of Rousseau's argument. The general will is not popular opinion or prejudice; it is the expression of the rationally derived moral aspiration of the community and as such has limits and sets limits which would be intolerable to any modern totalitarian regime and indeed *was* inconceivable to despotisms of the eighteenth century. The interesting point about Rousseau's version of the social contract is that it vests sovereignty not in a government, an external 'sovereign', but in the community itself. A government serves the general will and if it defaults it may be replaced by something more appropriate without any such break and remaking of the contract as Hobbes or Locke would have required. Rousseau's social contract is a compact for a rational social order and not for any particular form of government.

The use of the social contractarian method by the theorists of the seventeenth and eighteenth centuries can be seen to have produced a wide variety of conclusion upon the proper form and scope of legitimate government. Some commentators have argued that this diversity of conclusion is evidence of fundamental unsoundness in the social contractarian approach as a whole. It certainly cannot be said that thinkers such as Hobbes, Locke and Rousseau produced identical opinions. Hobbes argues for 'strong government' for the avoidance of the horrors of civil strife. Locke advances a 'constitutional' case for limitation upon despotism upon the basis of a more 'substantive' social contract than that required for the Hobbesian analysis. Rousseau's argument in contrast goes not to the 'contractual' basis of any particular type of government but to the basis for entry into 'society' in the first place as a means for the rational pursuit of human moral development. These conclusions are not of course by any means identical, but there is on the other hand no particular reason why it should be anticipated that social contractarian thought should always tend to the same conclusion. Any such assumption rests upon characterisation of 'social contractarianism' as a theory of society and government in its own right, in the same sense that basic 'Marxism' might be so regarded. It has already been argued that such a characterisation would be false and that in fact 'social contractarianism' should be treated as a method of enquiry rather than as a 'theory' *per se.* Once this is understood the divergences of conclusion derived from the method become less startling because it becomes clear that basically different issues are being considered by the theorists concerned through a social contractarian method. Weak government as such would hardly be an aim if there is to be government at all, but at the same time the ambit of governmental power should surely be defined in a manner fit to obviate arbitrary and unaccountable rule. On a different level it seems not unreasonable to argue that social structures should be seen as based upon the moral aspirations of the community. All these issues can be discussed through the medium of the social contractarian method but remain none the less different questions open to different answers.

It may well be that in practice many social contractarian thinkers considered the issue which they immediately addressed to be the single most significant question to be asked and other issues to be merely peripheral, as appears from Hobbes's discussion of tyranny. However, this should not divert attention from the significance of the method with its emphasis upon the importance of human social aspirations in the assessment of law and government wherein lies the continuing value of the social contractarian analysis.

In striking contrast to the often very particular speculations of the social contractarians is the work in relation to jurisprudential matters of the vastly influential philosopher Immanuel Kant who, a near contemporary of Rousseau, contributed a profound insight into the general moral nature of law.

Immanuel Kant (1724 – 1804)

Immanuel Kant cannot strictly be termed a legal theorist but his work is none the less of immense importance in any consideration of the moral nature of law and legal obligation. He was born the son of a saddler in Königsberg in 1724. After attendance at the university there and a period as a private tutor he was in 1770 appointed to the chair of logic and metaphysics at Königsberg where he remained for the rest of his life.

It is ultimately of the essence in any naturalist legal theory that the 'authority' of law, its claim to impose obligation rather than merely to coerce, is to be found in its moral quality rather than in its formal identity. All such theories involve of necessity some criterion of basic morality by which to judge positive laws. It is contended that such tests in the field of law are purposive in nature whether that purpose be found in the will of God or by rational enquiry into the human condition or, indeed, by some combination of these methods. It is none the less a major difficulty in such moral enquiries to find precise underlying principles to which propositions or actions which are 'moral' must be directly referable. It is his contribution to this area of thought which renders Kant's work of great importance in the context of the immediate discussion.

That mankind considers himself to hold 'moral' opinions is beyond denial but what is problematic is whether or not such concepts are truly distinguishable from other sorts of understanding. Can 'moral' concepts be distinguished from, say, strongly held prejudices and, if so, upon what are they founded? In answer to this question Kant sought the basic moral principle, which is to say that underlying principle to which any action which is morally 'good' must be capable of reference. His ethical theory is to be found in the *Groundwork of the Metaphysic of Morals* published in 1785 and in the *Critique of Practical Reason* published three years later in 1788.

Kant commences his argument from the working hypothesis that moral judgements may be 'true', as opposed to mere conceit or opinion, and then proceeds to enquire into the bases upon which such truths could be maintained, arriving finally at the primary basis of moral judgement.[20] He then sought to prove the basic moral principle by analysing rational insight into the principles of actions, proceeding by this means back to the same original principle.[21] In the *Groundwork of the Metaphysic of Morals* Kant argues that the only phenomenon which can be considered to be purely 'good' is a good will. The same results might be produced, according to circumstances, by actions resulting from a 'bad' will but only a 'good' will is necessarily 'good' irrespective of circumstance or even degree of achievement. Such a will is, in short, 'good' *per se* and not merely 'good' in its practical product. How then is a 'good will' to be defined? To will is to decide upon a course of action and not merely to desire a result; a will is then seen by Kant as 'good' if it is a proper fruit of rationality. In the case of mankind a rational will is defined in terms of 'duty'. Thus for Kant the will, decision upon a course of action, is 'good' only if it is reached pursuant to duty. This aspect of Kantian thought has been much criticised as an apparent linking of aspiration to virtue with a grim sense of obedience. This, however, is not what is conveyed by the Kantian sense of 'duty'. There can be no objection to a person desiring to do or enjoying doing what is his or her 'duty'; 'duty' here affirms the inherent 'rightness' of an action which is done because it is 'right' — whether or not it also fulfils a desire or aspiration of the actor.

If a 'moral' action is one which is willed pursuant to duty in the sense of concordance with what is 'right', it must be determined how in fact 'right' for this purpose is to be defined. Kant's argument that the morality of an action is founded upon the maxim by which the actor proceeds in deciding upon its performance requires that such maxims be referable to some general moral law. The general moral law at this level must clearly be a principle of universal rationality and this leads Kant to the fundamental principle enshrined in the famous 'categorical imperative'. This is that a man should act only upon a maxim which he could also will to become a universal law. The essence of this basic concept is that any maxim founding a 'moral' action will be one which could be operated by all people for their general good and not merely by an individual for particular advantage in a given case. It is a principle of uniformity providing that all 'moral' actions are founded upon compatible maxims which concord with a general rationality rather than merely representing transient or particular desires. The concept can be expressed at its most crude in the idea that no person should act upon a maxim which he would not be willing to admit as a foundation for universal action, including in respect of himself.

Kant argues that the categorical imperative provides an absolute test for the morality of any given maxim. He demonstrates this through a number of examples of 'immoral' maxims for action. Thus if a man acts upon the maxim that he will borrow money at need, promising to repay although he knows that in fact he will not do so, that maxim could not be made universal because if it was the whole concept of 'lending' and 'borrowing' would be entirely subverted. Thus the maxim conflicts with the categorical imperative and may be judged an 'immoral' basis for action as leading to contradiction when made of universal application.

In his account of Kantian theory Körner suggests that, in a much more rigorously developed form, there may be a link between Rousseau's notion of a 'general will' which is necessarily morally correct and Kant's tests of conformability with universal moral law.[22] It is certainly the case that both conceptions link morality to the possibility of general as opposed to particular good but, as Körner points out, Rousseau affords us no real criteria by which to distinguish the moral from the immoral in practice. Kant's categorical imperative by contrast does not purport to offer any substantive guidance but rather a means whereby substantive maxims for action can be related to a basic test of universality. The criterion afforded by the categorical imperative is thus universal and non-substantive, but can it in fact determine the morality of all maxims? The principal problem case is an instance in which a choice of alternative but incompatible 'moral' maxims for action appears to exist. An obvious instance here is provided by the law of marriage.[23] There are three possible forms of matrimony: monogamy, polygamy and polyandry. The adherents of these various forms of marriage naturally assert the moral excellence of their own arrangements and, commonly, decry the 'immorality' of the alternatives. This implies that the underlying maxims are incompatible and that therefore at least two, if not all, of these possibilities are in fact 'immoral'. These maxims can readily be identified. In the case of Christian 'Western' marriage the relationship can be defined as '. . . the voluntary union for life of one man and one woman, to the exclusion of all others . . .'[24] If this becomes a universal maxim then polygamy, polyandry or 'arranged' marriages are of necessity 'immoral'. It is not obvious how the scheme of the categorical imperative can take account of such apparent moral alternatives. It may of course be argued that some aspects of these forms of matrimony are indeed 'immoral' but it must surely be conceded that to a considerable extent the range of difference results from simple cultural diversity, in short representing genuine 'moral' alternatives. The problem is of course resolvable if one questions the level at which the basic definition of Western Christian marriage in *Hyde* v *Hyde and Woodmansee* is set. It may be a particular cultural application of a more basic maxim to which the test of the categorical imperative can be applied satisfactorily across the range of cultures. It may be significant in this context that modern matrimonial practice does take account of different cultures not conforming to the *Hyde* v

Hyde concept without the subversion of the institution of marriage. If this is accepted then the problem of cultural diversity does not constitute an objection to the operation of the categorical imperative.

The categorical imperative sets a test for the informing principle, the maxim of an action. Actions, however, are generally undertaken with ends in view and these, as well as the informing maxims, fall within the purview of moral assessment. The moral nature of the relationship of means and ends was not ignored by Kant. The solution to the problem is found in the 'principle of right' which is the proposition that humanity, whether in the person of the actor or in any other person, should never be treated merely as a means to an end but always accorded respect as an end in itself. This is a basic principle enjoining respect for human individuality *per se*. The application of the principle may readily be demonstrated. Take, for example, the problem of pornography. This is often addressed as an issue between 'morality' in a rather constrained 'Victorian' sense and 'freedom'. Upon the application of the principle of right the matter at issue is actually somewhat different. The subject of pornographic material, usually a woman, is by definition being treated as an object — not in the celebration of her human individuality but as an impersonal almost mechanical means to the end of the sexual stimulation of the recipient of the material concerned. The humanity of the subject is thus degraded and the fundamental 'immorality' of pornography is thereby exposed. The commonly encountered arguments that the readers or viewers of pornography enjoy it or that the subject of pornography 'do it for the money' or even enjoy their part in it is not relevant upon this perspective. No one, whether recipient or subject, can be 'right' to participate in the degradation of the humanity of any individual person and it is this which would rest at the base of any Kantian objection to the preparation and dissemination of pornographic materials.

It should be added that although in the Kantian, as in any other, thesis morality appears as a constraint upon action, it is in fact founded upon reason and is ultimately a principle of freedom in the development of human potentialities. According to Kant knowledge of right and justice exist *a priori*, but, because human perception is clouded by emotion and irrational impulse, natural principle is necessary and appears as a constraint upon action even though it is in fact the expression of moral freedom.

On this understanding human positive law, a formal prescription designed for the general guidance of action, should concord with the categorical imperative and should tend to the furtherance of humanity in accordance with the principle of right. It should not, for example, tend to the exploitation of the many in the interests of the few, or even of the few in the interests of the majority. A law which does not meet these criteria is without rational justification and is morally insupportable. These are not of course criteria for the assessment of positive law alone but a concordance of human and universal reason applicable to all human actions including the making of positive laws. The value of Kant's moral theory from the viewpoint of the legal theorist lies in its generality as a means of relating maxims of law to universal reason. The tests are not substantive in nature but seek to assess the principles informing positive law in terms of compatibility with a universal rational scheme. Unlike social contractarianism this is not merely a method of enquiry into particular questions but a test in its own right of the rationality of law-making which must play a vital role in any 'naturalist' discussion of the proper purposes of law-making and the propriety of the content of given laws.

The rationalism of the seventeenth and eighteenth centuries contributed valuable new methods and insights to the study of legal theory, in some respects foreshadowing the innovations of the nineteenth century. There are, for example, strong hints of later positivism to be found in the work of Hobbes. It is misleading, however, to seek some great divide between a preceding 'age of faith' and the 'ages of reason and enlightenment'. The context undoubtedly differs but the basic issues do not: the focus remains the authority and proper scope of 'law'-making as compared to the imposition of arbitrary or 'tyrannical' demands. The concerns of the social contractarians can be seen as particular instances of these basic issues, the universal reason of Immanual Kant is in the end functionally convergent with, if different in form from, the Lex Divina of St Thomas Aquinas. In this perspective the development of 'naturalist' enquiry can be seen as continuous rather than disjunctive and so capable of rendering an analysis of 'law' which is in fact the fruit of a process of development rather than of random and incompatible speculation.

Notes

1. Elements of a notion of consensuality at the root of obligation can be

81

seen in both ancient Judaic and Hellenistic thought. See Chs 1 and 2 earlier.

2. See Ch. 1 earlier. In particular the mode of presentation of the Mosaic law to the people of Israel.

3. See Ch. 2 earlier.

4. J. Rawls, *A Theory of Justice.*

5. Hobbes, *Leviathan*, Pt. I, Ch. XIII, p. 62.

6. Ibid., Ch. XIV, p. 64.

7. Ibid.

8. Ibid., p. 65.

9. Ibid., Ch. XIX, p. 94.

10. See Hobbes, *Leviathan*, Pt. II, Ch. XXI, p. 114.

11. *Leviathan*, Ch. XXX, p. 175.

12. It appears from *Leviathan* that Hobbes may at least to some extent have believed in the reality of the 'state of nature'. Locke, however, clearly did not.

13. Locke, *Two Treatises of Government*, Bk. II, Ch. II, s. 6.

14. Ibid., Bk. II, Ch. II, ss. 6–8.

15. See Locke, *Two Treatises of Government*, Bk. II, Ch. V, especially at ss. 44.

16. Rousseau, *Du contrat social*, Bk. I, Ch. I, p. 1.

17. Ibid., Bk. II, Ch. 3.

18. Ibid., Bk. II, Ch. 6.

19. A point rendered less surprising than might be otherwise thought if it is recalled that Rousseau at various times wavered between adherence to Calvinism and Roman Catholicism.

20. See Kant, *Groundwork for the Metaphysics of Morals*, Chs I–II.

21. See ibid., Ch. IV.

22. S. Körner, *Kant*, pp. 139–40.

23. Körner makes reference to this particular issue, see *Kant*, pp. 140–1.

24. Per Lord PENZANCE in *Hyde* v *Hyde and Woodmansee* (1866) L.R. 1 P.&D., 130 at 133.

5

The Positivist Insight

It has become a convention of legal theory to treat naturalism and positivism as inherently opposed doctrines with an inevitably gladiatorial relationship. The positivist thinkers of the nineteenth century are thus considered to have mounted an attack upon naturalist concepts with a view to their supercession by a more rigorous and 'scientific' theory of law. It is undeniably the case that an attack was launched upon the debased quasi-naturalism current in English law schools in the late eighteenth and early nineteenth centuries but it does not follow from this that naturalism and positivism are necessarily mutually exclusive doctrines. The conventional treatment may in fact be argued to be misleading and productive of a sterile debate which reflects more the original form of expression of the positivist argument than any matters of substance. The origins of this perceived dichotomy are to be found in the nature of the era in which the theory of legal positivism was first propounded.

The nineteenth century was in many ways a dynamic era for both good and ill. Amongst its other attributes it was a time of scientific discovery and rapid technological advance in an intellectual climate which prompted the asking of fundamental questions in jurisprudence as in other fields as a result of which many comfortably established modes of thought were unseated and overthrown. The very optimistic spirit of this age was clearly expressed by Jeremy Bentham in writing that in the last quarter of the eighteenth century: 'The age we live in is a busy age; in which knowledge is rapidly advancing towards perfection. In the natural world, in particular, everything teems with discovery and with improvement.'[1]

At the beginning of the nineteenth century English jurisprudence was quasi-naturalist in form, but it was a naturalism
founded upon crude *a priori* assumptions of a type exemplified in
Blackstone's *Commentaries*. The essence of this view was that
positive law reflected 'natural rights' and was therefore *ex hypothesi*
moral. This crude caricature of naturalist theory made the extraordinary leap from the proposition that 'true law' will concord
with moral perception in consequence of its proper purpose to the
idea that all positive prescription can therefore be assumed to be
moral. It was this type of view which Jeremy Bentham in a celebrated comment described as 'nonsense upon stilts'.[2] This
approach was not one which any major naturalist thinker had
actually advanced, nor indeed an assertion which common sense
or empirical observation would permit, in the early nineteenth
century or at any other time. The fundamental weakness of any
such reasoning was exposed by David Hume who complained that
no separation was being made between 'is' and 'ought' propositions. The former are descriptive and the latter normative in
nature,[3] and to argue that laws 'ought' to concord with morality is
not thus at all the same thing as to assert that they in fact do so. To
confuse these two basic propositions was the basic error of
Blackstone and many of his contemporaries.

Legal positivism developed in England as an attempt to set jurisprudence upon a surer footing in the light of the 'scientific' spirit
of the era. The endeavour was to analyse law as it 'is', leaving the
question of what it ideally 'ought' to be as an entirely separate and
distinct issue. Jeremy Bentham expressed the distinction clearly as
that between Expository and Censorial jurisprudence. This he
explained in the following terms: 'To the province of the *Expositor*
it belongs to explain to us what, as he supposes, the Law *is*: to that
of the *Censor*, to observe to us what he thinks it *ought to be*.'[4]

The essence of a positivist theory of law is the adoption of a
purely formal criterion of identification of law which takes no
account of the moral quality of the prescription concerned. Thus
in the United Kingdon that which is enacted by the Crown in
Parliament is the law of the land and binding upon those subject to
it whether it be moral, amoral or even immoral. This amounts to
the proposition that legislation which is morally defective is not
thereby formally invalidated or unenforceable. This is self-
evidently correct, but it does not follow that morality is not
relevant to legal obligation nor does positivism actually argue this
to be the case any more than naturalism seeks to deny that

immoral prescription exists or may be imposed.

The founding father of English legal positivism was Jeremy Bentham (1748–1832). The full extent of his contribution to jurisprudence has only become known in the present century with the discovery of some formerly unpublished works and as a result the title 'Father of English Jurisprudence' has conventionally been awarded to Bentham's disciple, John Austin (1790–1859), although in fact he developed and elaborated Bentham's ideas without necessarily always improving upon them. Bentham's definition of law was straightforward and expressed in terms of the volition of a sovereign attached to a sanction. For him law was in essence the declaration of the will of a sovereign concerning the conduct of subjects, obedience to which is motivated by the anticipation of attached consequences, which is to say 'sanctions', relating to compliance or non-compliance as the case might be.[5] This is the basic positivist definition of 'law' which may be summarised as 'a command of a sovereign backed by a sanction'. This is a 'voluntaristic' theory in which law is seen as the expression of the *will* of the sovereign without any necessary subjection to moral limitations other than any which the sovereign himself might choose to observe. A legal command then breaks down into three basic elements: (i) a declaration of will, (ii) which is made by a sovereign and (iii) which secures obedience from its addressees through apprehension of an attached consequence, which is to say a 'sanction'. The most obvious question arising from this is what are the distinguishing marks of sovereignty. Bentham distinguishes a sovereign by a habit of obedience.[6]

Austin elaborated this conception somewhat by adding that this is a positive mark of sovereignty to which a negative mark must be added for completeness of definition. He expressed the point thus:

> In order that a given society may form a society political and independent, the superior habitually obeyed by the bulk or generality of its members must not be habitually obedient to a certain individual or body . . .[7]

Through the combination of Bentham and Austin we thus have a definition of sovereignty as a person or body who or which is habitually obeyed by the bulk of a given society but is not habitually obedient to any other person or body. It is worth noticing here that although the language of Bentham and Austin in respect of the sovereign is personal and therefore suggestive of autocratic monarchy, both in their writings expressly considered a collective or institutional sovereign. Austin was careful to add to his 'negative' mark that a sovereign may, and in fact must, take account of the demands of other governments and of the desires of his subjects without losing the negative mark of sovereignty. It is only the habitual acceptance of superior direction which is presented as a negation of sovereign status.[8]

The law is then seen as the expressed will of such a politically supreme individual or body. Within this scheme any idea of an 'obligation' to obey can be dismissed as analogous to the 'nonsense' of 'natural rights' since obedience in general is seen as a matter of political habit and in particular cases by fear of the application of the threatened sanction. The theory is thus voluntaristic (will-based) and coercive in its appreciation of law and is accurately described as a 'command theory'. Bentham's view was not actually the recipe for tyranny which the simplest statement of this view might seem to suggest. In the first place the habit of obedience required as a mark of sovereignty is generally unqualified in a legal and jurisprudential sense, but not in a political sense. Obviously the habit of obedience can be withdrawn or transferred — in which case a new sovereign will be set up in the place of the old. Indeed to Bentham, as a rational witness of the French Revolution, this must have seemed too obvious to require emphasis. There remain, however, some jurisprudential qualifications to be made in that sovereign bodies can and do accept legal or quasi-legal limitations upon their conduct without apparently ceasing to be sovereign. These may briefly be considered under the headings of Treaties and general Public International Law, written constitutions, confederal and federal arrangements.

Bentham saw treaties as matters of agreement in the exercise of sovereign power; a sovereign might be bound in honour by such agreements but could not in general be legally bound by them if he was to remain a sovereign. Modern commentators have asked how this relates to the modern effect of Public International Law and such local international regimes as the law of the European Economic Communities. Bentham would have denied the name 'law' to both these phenomena, unless perhaps he had seen the latter as a form of confederal arrangement. Austin in *The Province of Jurisprudence Determined* specifically excluded Public International Law from his category of law properly so called, relegating it instead to the sphere of 'positive morality'.[9] This removes the problem from a classical positivist viewpoint since any restraint upon a sovereign thus derived ceases to be 'legal' in nature. This view is not particularly objectionable. Although both Public International and EEC law are binding and obligatory within their own terms of reference, in general, opinion of English law is that such rules are brought into English law by an act of political will. In other words, a dualist rather than a monist view is on the whole adopted.[10] This may be rather questionable from a purist viewpoint but it does have a salutary element of realism. Even conceding the existence of 'directly applicable' EEC legislation, it may be conceded that the Austinian 'negative mark' is unaffected because the political sovereign may be said to have *chosen* the exterior prescription. There can be little reasonable doubt that in constitutional terms for a British government to resile from its international obligations would be viewed in municipal law as a political decision within the competence of the Crown, even though 'unlawful' in terms of the relevant international legality. The potential immorality of such a course of action is an issue of which positivist theory deliberately takes no account.

If international limitations upon sovereign power may be fitted into the Benthamite perception as being non-legal and, ultimately, non-binding, confederal and federal constitutions are potentially much more problematic. Such arrangements involve, with written constitutions generally, the enactment of some form of entrenched constitutional law which is more than a matter of constitutional morality and which purports to restrain the expression of the sovereign will in defined and material particulars. The basic question here is can the sovereign will effectively limit the future ambit of the expression of his will? Obviously he can. The underlying problem, however, is whether such a self-denying ordinance can be binding upon a sovereign as a matter of law rather than moral sentiment or political reality. Bentham concedes, rather awkwardly, that this may happen in two sort of circumstances. One state may agree to the sovereignty of another, or two or many states may agree together to a confederal or federal union and in such a case the agreement might impose limitations upon the joint authority.[11] Even this may be seen, however, as a sort of qualified 'habit of obedience' rather than as exterior obedience on the part of the sovereign. Written constitutions enforceable by judicial process as in the United States of America are more problematic. Bentham admits the possibility of judicial restraint upon the sovereign[12] although he viewed the idea with marked disfavour as an irresponsible dilution of sovereign power — as in effect making the judiciary part of the sovereign body. Thus he wrote:

> Applied to practice then, the effect . . . is, by an appeal made
> to the judges, to confer on those magistrates a controlling
> power over the acts of the legislature.[13]

Bentham went on to qualify this by stating that

> There is a wide difference between a *positive* and a *negative* part
> in legislation . . . *repealing* a law . . . is a great power: too
> great indeed for Judges: but still very distinguishable from,
> and much inferior to that of *making* one.[14]

The end result is that in such a constitutional structure Bentham
would, with marked distaste, admit of a sort of collective
sovereignty in which as in the United States there is a judicial
power of review of legislation.[15]

Austin's views upon sovereignty were more absolute than those
of Bentham and, whereas the latter was content to accept the conventional wisdom that the sovereign in the United Kingdom is the
Crown in Parliament, the former defined the sovereign as the
monarch, the House of Lords and the electorate of the House of
Commons because he feared that otherwise a hiatus in sovereignty
would occur during Parliamentary elections which would be a
breach of his conception of sovereignty as illimitable and
indivisible. Even granted that the electorate in Austin's day was a
very much smaller proportion of the population than is now the
case, this seems to lead him into the extraordinary position of
asserting a command theory of law in which the population is
partially in a habit of obedience to itself.

If 'law' is defined as the command of an ultimate political
superior backed by a sanction, what is the nature of the duty to
obey laws? Both Bentham and Austin essentially dismiss this as a
futile question. Law-making is seen by them as a political act
which is either successfully imposed or not; it is certainly not perceived as an inherently 'moral' act capable of generating abstract
'duties' or 'obligations'. Thus, while the habit of obedience
persists, enunciation of the will of the sovereign continues to be
'law' whether that will is morally good, bad or indifferent. To
speak of inherent moral or other limitations upon the will of the
sovereign is therefore according to Bentham a naïve misuse of
language.

If moral suasion is denied, why then is law obeyed? A mere

habit of obedience is not sufficient explanation. Why should such a habit commence, other perhaps than through acceptance of excellence, which has already effectively been ruled out? The answer lies of course in the third element of Bentham's definition of 'law', the sanction. This idea is conventionally presented as an unsubtle bludgeon, which is certainly one of its elements, but that is by no means the totality of the concept. Bentham considered that

> . . . there is nothing by which a man can ultimately be *made* to do it, but either pain or pleasure.[16]

The implications of this for jurisprudence are explained in detail in the succeeding paragraph, in which Bentham asserts that

> There are four distinguishable sources from which pleasure and pain are in use to flow . . . the *physical*, the *political*, the *moral*, and the *religious*: and inasmuch as the pleasures and pains belonging to each of them are capable of giving a binding force to any law or rule of conduct, they may all be termed *sanctions*.[17]

It is of course primarily the physical and political sanctions which Bentham has in mind in the context of law. Thus efficacy of law is conceived in terms of sanctions and their application. In Bentham's case this is almost, but not quite, entirely a coercive and punitive concept. He conceded that 'sanction' could include reward as well as punishment, pleasure as well as pain.[18] Austin was less flexible than Bentham in this regard and linked the idea of sanction to its signification of an unpleasant consequence. This led Austin to formulate the famous, or notorious, 'sanction of nullity'. This arises where a law does not prescribe or proscribe conduct in its own right but rather prescribes a means to an end. If the prescribed procedure is not followed the end will not be attained and this failure is described by Austin as a 'sanction of nullity'. The oddity of this conclusion may really be demonstrated. The Wills Act, 1837, with subsequent legislation, prescribes the requirements for the making of a valid will; if those requirements are not met the testament will fail and, according to Austinian analysis, it is fear of the 'penalty' of such failure which causes people to comply with the Act in drafting their wills. Now it cannot be doubted that a wrongly drafted will fails or that such a result is undesirable, but is fear of this 'penalty' really the motive for compliance? There are two principal objections to such a conclusion. Firstly, the incompetent testator, or even more the testator with an incompetent solicitor, presumably dies content in the comforting but false illusion that he has done the proper thing and his property will pass as he desires upon his death. It must then seem a dubious argument that the threatened sanction has acted upon his mind at all — and yet he has 'disobeyed' in the only way possible. Secondly, if the 'sanction' does operate, it does so after the death of the delinquent testator and the 'penalty' is then inflicted upon the wholly innocent intended devisees and legatees. It is surely a preferable view to regard the Wills Act as a set of instructions for the drafting of a valid will enacted with the intention of ascertaining with due certitude, post-motem, the deceased's intentions with regard to his or her property. The proper analogy is not so much with penal enactments as with instructions accompanying 'self-assembly' furniture. If the instructions are followed one may hope for a piece of furniture; if they are not the chair or whatever it might be may collapse — this is not a 'penalty' for breach of the instructions, it is simply the inevitable product of incompetence. So it is also in the instance of the Wills Act. The Benthamite 'reward' sanction resolves this difficulty quite easily but Austin, in the rigid pursuit of a doctrine of sanction, has precluded himself from seeking that resort.

Thus far we have the severely anti-naturalist argument of law as habituated force without moral dimension which is the conventional view of positivism. This view appears to be confirmed by Bentham himself, who wrote that:

> As to the *LAW of Nature*, if . . . it be nothing but a phrase . . . if there be no other medium for proving a law of the *state* to be contrary to it, than the *inexpediency* of such law, unless the bare unfounded disapprobation of anyone who thinks of it be called a proof; . . . I see no remedy but that the natural tendency of such doctrine is to impel a man, by the force of conscience, to rise up in arms against any law whatever that he happens not to like.[19]

This indicates clearly the naturalism/positivism dichotomy that has encumbered jurisprudence since Bentham's day. However, a point which seems to have been forgotten or at least under-emphasised is that *A Fragment on Government* was specifically written as a rebuttal of the arguments upon government advanced by Sir

William Blackstone in the Introduction to his *Commentaries*. Blackstone advanced that brand of naïve and debased pseudo-naturalism which has already been cited as the spur to Bentham's positivist re-evaluation. It pays to examine exactly what it was that Bentham sought to deny. He denied the existence of ascertainable formal rules of natural law in any positive form and also that any such proposition can render actual contravening positive enactments void.[20] The Benthamite and Austinian analysis may thus conveniently be reduced to the propositions that: (i) the capacity to enact effective positive prescription is a political fact dependent upon a habit of obedience with no necessary moral dimension; (ii) 'law' is distinguished from other norms by origin in the will of a 'sovereign', which is to say a determinate political superior with no habit of obedience to any other; (iii) obedience to law is secured through threat (and possibly promise) of sanction which will be operative until such time as the habit of obedience is broken; (iv) the sovereign will may by limited formally only by express agreement and even that is not desirable; (v) there are no inherent moral limitations upon the law-making function by which an apparent 'law' may become non-law.

There are some obvious difficulties with the simple 'command' model of law. If law is the will of the sovereign *simpliciter*, two immediate problems present themselves: in the first place, what is the status of supposed 'laws' which are patently enunciated by some person or body other than the sovereign? In the second place, how is it that the will of sovereigns long dead continues to operate even though the present sovereign may be assumed not to have a detailed knowledge of their prescription? The first problem, primarily that of case law in its function as precedent, is conventionally regarded as a form of delegation of authority. The second is usually avoided by the fiction that the sovereign never dies — the king is dead, long live the king! Bentham's concern to follow a severely expository jurisprudence led him to anathematise the use of fictions both in jurisprudential theory and in the doctrines of law *per se*. He thus rejected the idea of perpetual sovereign continuity as a foolish obfuscation and disparaged delegated 'law'-making as a dilution of true sovereignty, even indeed a usurpation. Yet judges do make law (even if they claim merely to interpret it) and William IV and his Lords and Commons are dead — but the Wills Act of 1837 is not. To this problem Bentham advanced the answer of the 'tacit command'. This was based upon the idea that what a sovereign 'permits' he also 'commands'. Thus a judge is permitted to make case decisions and those decisions and their continuing effects as precedents, if any, are consequently taken to be commanded by the sovereign who alone can constitute 'law'. Further, by not repealing earlier prescription a new sovereign tacitly 'commands' its continuation in application. Benthamite theory indeed goes further yet in asserting that any arrangement enforceable at law, such as a private contract, is also 'commanded' by the sovereign in that it can ultimately be implemented by permission of the sovereign power through the courts.

Tacit command has been treated as a major flaw in Bentham's description of law and it must be admitted that the language used gives a rather ridiculous impression. However, a word may be said in its defence. Quite clearly the Crown in Parliament can, and does, repeal earlier legislation; equally, judges are expressly delegates of the Crown in their judicial function. If these facts are to be accommodated in a fully imperative theory of law some form of implied imperation, which is essentially what the idea of tacit command is, is obviously necessary. The language is wrong: a permission cannot be a command — 'you may' is not 'you will'; but it is arguably true to say that by willingness to implement prior or delegated prescription, a political sovereign may be said to have 'commanded' its substance through a process of adoption. The need for the device may be criticised as symptomatic of over-literal application of the analogy between law and personal command, but, granted the assumptions of the simple imperative model, some such conception is inescapable.

The theory of law thus outlined is essentially a theory of power, in which law is seen as an imposed ordinance irrespective of its moral nature and which as an overtly coercive model deliberately rejects any concept of obligation as a quality of law. Is classical positivism therefore a theory of naked force espousing a heedlessly amoral 'philosophy of action'? In fact not. Bentham in *Principles of Morals and Legislation* was actually setting out the structure of principle for an 'ideal' criminal code, which may go far to explain the coercive nature of his general legal theory. His assertion was not that 'law' cannot or should not be made to serve moral ends, rather that it cannot rationally be assumed to do so as a necessary characteristic. Thus the existence of law is seen as an amoral fact, the ideal form of that fact being presented as a separate, if important, issue.

Bentham's conception of the ideal form of law was rooted in the

philosophy of utilitarianism. He stated the application of the idea
to law in the following terms:

> A measure of government . . . may be said to be conformable
> to . . . the principle of utility, when . . . [its] tendency . . . to
> augment the happiness of the community is greater than any
> which it has to diminish it.[21]

Thus the utilitarian idea of the desirable use of law is the facilitation of the attainment of the greatest happiness of the greatest
number, albeit at the potential expense of the greatest misery of
the few — as Bentham conceded. This clearly distinguishes 'good'
law-making from 'bad', although it does not derive from the distinction a qualification of 'law' quality as such. There is thus
admitted an idea of 'proper purpose' in law-making. This is
explicitly stated by Bentham in the remark that 'The business of
government is to promote the happiness of the society . . .'[22] But
this is clearly a matter which Bentham assigned to the sphere of
'censorial' rather than 'expository' jurisprudence. Although it is
difficult to quarrel with this assignment in terms of the separation
of 'is' and 'ought', it is important not to move from that separation to a denial of the importance of the moral quality of prescription in the understanding of law. In fact this becomes a matter of
choice of area of study as becomes clear from the jurisprudential
thought of Bentham's pupil, Austin.

In *The Province of Jurisprudence Determined*, Austin set out to define
the area of study which properly constitutes the ambit of 'jurisprudence' from a positivist viewpoint as compared to theology, moral
philosophy, political theory or any other circumambulent subject.
It is important to notice that he did not deny the importance of any
of these matters, merely that they could be relevant to the formal
determination of what is validly made positive law. He set out to
make a clear distinction between 'laws . . . properly so called' and
'laws . . . improperly so called'.[23] Austin set out his division in the
following terms:

> Of laws properly so called, some are set by God to his human
> creatures, others are set by men to men . . . laws improperly
> so called which are closely analogous to the proper, are merely
> opinions or sentiments held or felt by men in regard to human
> conduct.[24]

He then advanced three principal categories of 'law' and things analogous to law. These are (i) laws (properly so called) set by God to men, that is to say Divine law, (ii) laws (properly so called) set by man to man either as a political superior or as a private person by 'legal' right (for example, contract), that is to say positive law, (iii) (a) laws (properly so called) set by man to man other than as a political superior or by 'legal' right (for example, 'rules' of social conduct), and (b) laws (improperly so called) analogous to laws proper but being merely opinions or sentiments as to proper conduct, which Austin calls positive morality. Of these Austin considered positive law alone to be the proper sphere of jurisprudence, which he perceived as a 'science'. It is in the word 'science' with its full nineteenth-century connotation of verifiable certainty that the significance of this statement lies and his exclusion of moral considerations from the 'science' of jurisprudence is based precisely upon this point. Thus Austin wrote that

> . . . the goodness or badness of a human law is a phrase of relative and varying import. A law which is good to one man is bad to another, in case they tacitly refer it to different and adverse tests.[25]

In view of this moral confusion he denies that the morality of law can be an object of 'scientific' study. He does not deny, however, that judgements upon the moral quality of positive law can be made and even derived from a perception of a higher 'law'. This appears to be explicitly admitted in a statement in *The Province of Jurisprudence Determined* to the effect that

> . . . the expression '*positive law*' was manifestly made for the purpose of obviating confusion: confusion of human law . . . with . . . Divine law which is the measure or test of human.[26]

Austin's conception of the categories of law and things analogous to law may be set out diagrammatically as shown on page 95. Of these, positive law alone is seen as within the province of jurisprudence since it alone was seen as capable of precise and 'scientific' definition. Thus the theory defines law formally in terms of the application of known power and denies any definitive moral component. Upon this view the causes of obedience to law are attributed to the coercion imposed to the law-maker rather than to any moral suasion attached to the quality of the law concerned.

LAW PROPERLY SO CALLED	*LAW IMPROPERLY SO CALLED*
Divine Law	Laws of Science

Human Law

Positive Law	Positive Morality
Positive Morality	(Opinion or sentiment:
(Customary social 'rules')	Public International Law,
	Taste, etc.)

The analytical positivism of Bentham and Austin serves a valuable end in drawing the clear distinction between 'law' as formally enunciated rules and the moral questions which may be asked about those rules. The classical 'command' theory is susceptible to a number of criticisms, however. An immediate difficulty is the extent to which a straightforward analogy between personal command and rules of law can be pursued. In the end mere power and coercion afford too simple an explanation of the complex phenomenon of law and only by such awkward devices as the 'tacit command' can they be moulded into a complete account. No doubt obedience is in part explained by coercion and in part by mere habit, but without the element of perceived 'oughtness' which induces voluntary compliance it is difficult to see how any system of coercion could be sufficiently comprehensive or any habit strong enough actually to maintain a legal system in the long term. In short a simple command model of law may define *how* a law is formally enunciated but does not explain *why* it 'works' or is accepted.

It was in part the over-simplicity of the original 'command' model which led H. L. A. Hart into his major reworking of classical positivist theory. In *The Concept of Law* Hart set out to re-evaluate the basis of Austin's theory and to improve upon it in order to produce a more realistic picture of the working of a legal system. Hart started out from the deceptively 'obvious' appearance of laws as coercive commands and hence the attraction of the simple command model, as he expresses it: 'The most prominent general feature of law . . . is that its existence means that certain kinds of . . . conduct are no longer optional, but in *some* sense obligatory.'[27] However, he points out lurking complexities beneath the surface of this apparent simplicity. Two of these

95

difficulties are central to the issue of legal obligation. The first is essentially the problem posed by St Augustine of the distinction between laws made by the state and the impositions of a robber band, which is to say — the qualitative distinction between law and any other coercive demand. The second is the direct question of the linkage, if any, between legal and moral 'obligation'. Hart poses also a third issue which is the nature of legal rules — what makes a 'rule' and, once defined, are rules the whole content of law? These problems are termed by Hart 'recurrent issues' and summarised thus: '. . . How does law differ from . . . orders backed by threats? How does legal obligation differ from . . . moral obligation? What are rules and to what extent is law an affair of rules?'[28]

He considers first the coercive aspect of command. This is a problem anciently posed by St Augustine in the form of the assertion of the pirate to Alexander the Great that he had a small ship and was called pirate whereas Alexander had a great navy and was called Emperor.[29] Hart poses the same basic question in the updated context of a gunman robbing a bank.[30] The gunman may demand that a bank clerk hand over cash and will enforce that demand by the menace of a gun and may, indeed probably will, be obeyed. He will thus have issued a coercive demand which is in effect a command backed by a sanction. Equally, the state through the medium of the Inland Revenue may issue demands for the payment of taxes which are backed by a threat of sanction through legal process in event of default. This also is a command backed by a sanction. How, if at all, do these situations differ other than in terms of scale? There are in fact two essential distinctions here. Firstly, the demand of the gunman is addressed individually to the particular bank clerk and to no one else, whereas laws on the whole are addressed generally to all persons finding themselves in the circumstances contemplated by the prescription concerned. Secondly, the gunman's power over the bank clerk is exactly coterminous with the time that he has him in the range of his gun, whereas the prescription of law is a continuing phenomenon up to the time of repeal or other abrogation and is not dependent upon the immediacy of sanction. These considerations lead Hart to a concept of 'obligation'. The distinction drawn is that between *being obliged* to do something and being *under obligation* to do something. The one indicates immediate compulsion actually to perform some act or acts or refrain therefrom, the other indicates a continuing duty irrespective of compulsion or actual performance.[31] Upon this understanding the gunman 'obliges' the bank clerk by placing him *in terrorem* so long as he has him in his gun sight, the Income and Corporation Taxes Acts place the taxpayer under 'obligation' irrespective of threat or even of any actual payment. There is also the problem of the 'variety of laws', not all of which fit into a simple command model. Hart presents this issue as two specific objections to the idea of law as coercion: (i) *Content*, laws may confer powers or facilitate the free creation of legal rights as well as impose duties; (ii) *Range of Application*, penal statutes may not merely order others but impose duties also upon their makers. Thus MPs are as much bound by statutory provision as anyone else.

The simple coercive model will not then suffice. Hart seeks to maintain a more subtle definition of law based upon a distinction between two types of rule — those which impose duties and those which confer powers. He argues that almost any human society will have known rules which prescribe the conduct to be observed by its members in given situations and that such rules impose *duties* and may be called *primary rules*. In 'primitive' societies these will generally take the form of established tribal or other custom which is seen by Hart as 'pre-legal' rather than legal in nature. This is because as rules of usage they are *static*, in that they cannot readily be changed to meet new conditions and problems as they arise. They are also *uncertain*, in that no formally binding machinery of application and interpretation exists to settle 'problem cases'. Finally, they are *inefficient*, in that in the absence of formal means of implementation they can only be maintained by 'diffuse social pressure'.[32] With increasing social complexity a more sophisticated and dynamic system of regulation than static primary rules alone can afford is called for and thus the need arises for rules concerned with the identification, implementation and, where appropriate, amendment of the primary rules. These are the secondary or power-conferring rules. Hart initially categorised secondary rules as solutions to the three perceived defects of a 'primitive' system of primary rules. Thus uncertainty leads to *rules of recognition*, stasis to *rules of change* and inefficiency to *rules of adjudication*.[33] A 'legal' system properly so called then rests upon the union of primary and secondary rules which is able to administer and produce as well as merely to enunciate already established norms. Although not stated in such terms and overtly lacking its quasi-moral or purposive element, the method of this union of primary and secondary rules has certain evident affinities with Locke's conception of the social contract,[34] in that both presuppose the existence of ascertainable social norms but impose upon them a superstructure of implementation for reasons of convenience and safety from which the 'legal' structure is said to derive.

The most basic of the secondary rules is presented as the *rule of recognition* which Hart defines as one which specifies '. . . some feature or features possession of which by a suggested rule is taken as a conclusive affirmative indication that it is a rule of the group to be supported by the social pressure it exerts'.[35] In fact a rule of recognition serves to identify the primary rules to be applied and also the means whereby they are to be applied as well as generated in the first place. Hart thus remarks that 'Wherever such a rule of recognition is accepted, both private persons and officials are provided with authoritative criteria for identifying primary rules of obligation.'[36]

Where does this leave the unlimited sovereignty of the theories of Bentham and Austin? The rule of recognition, which defines who or what is the sovereign, differs fundamentally from the 'habit of obedience' to be found in classical positivism. The 'habit of obedience' is descriptive and certainly does not limit the sovereign power; the rule of recognition is not descriptive but definitive; it determines what the ambit of sovereignty actually is. This, it must be considered, is a more preferable account of the positive legal nature of sovereignty than any which can be afforded by the simple 'command' model.

The sovereign and the law are thus defined, but not yet clearly separated from Hart's gunman or St Augustine's pirate. Hart states the distinction in terms of *being obliged* and being *under an obligation* but does not relate these matters to moral sensibility or to feeling or opinion. Indeed while he admits that obligation and feelings of obligation are commonly coincident he feels it necessary to state that '. . . to *feel* obliged and to have an obligation are different though frequently concomitant things'.[37] This is of course true. To be placed under an obligation is not necessarily to 'feel' the fact; if this were otherwise, moral and legal norms would be much less susceptible to disobedience than they actually are. Hart in fact relates the distinction not to ascertainable moral norms or to sentiment of propriety but to the social context within which a formally enunciated norm of 'law' operates. Thus he states that '. . . the insistence on importance or *seriousness* of social pressure behind the rules is the primary factor determining whether they are thought of as giving rise to obligations'.[38] In fact this does involve, at least peripherally, the idea of attitude as is evidenced by the use of the formula 'thought of' in the above statement. The introduction of a moral element into the concept of law is avoided, however, by the idea of an *external* and an *internal* aspect of law. These are descriptions of forms of understanding of legal rules. The external aspect of a rule is the observable consequence of its existence and as such is merely predictive in operation. The internal aspect involves understanding of the normative nature of the rule; it is not merely a prediction of conduct but a *signal* for a particular pattern of conduct. Hart takes as an example a set of traffic lights. When the lights turn red traffic from the appropriate direction stops; this is a factual occurrence which could be predicted and acted upon by an outsider to the society without any knowledge of the reasons for the fact — perhaps the colour red has a doctrinal significance which would render proceeding in the face of it impious.[39] This is an external appreciation of the rule embodied in traffic lights. The internal appreciation in contrast involves understanding that the red light is a signal that traffic *ought* to stop in consequence of a rule to that effect. The violation of that rule is then not merely an aberration in prediction but actually *wrongdoing*, which is in itself a sufficient cause of hostility to the wrongdoer without further consideration of effect. It is this internal aspect which is said to distinguish obligation from being obliged. There is a clear implication that this distinction operates in fact upon the official mind but it nevertheless stands for the categorisation sought to be made. The outline structure of theory presented by Hart may now be summarised as follows. The overt duty-imposing role of law is performed by primary rules directed to the conduct of general classes of persons. Such rules, however, are not enough to constitute a 'legal' system. Law is generated by the addition to the primary rule structure of secondary rules or recognition, adjudication and change, which are power-conferring in nature. The union of primary and secondary rules produces a system in which the forms and use of law-making powers are formally defined and ascertainable. Legal obligation is the expression of the positive requirements of such a legal system as understood from the internal aspect.

Is this actually an explanation of legal obligation? Upon consideration this must seriously be doubted. Hart's theory is essentially an attempt to recast classical positivism in a more sophisticated mould and in this effort it largely succeeds. However, the expressed concept of 'obligation', while clearly different from being obliged, is not by any means the same thing as the idea of 'obligation' implied by naturalist theory. 'Obligation' in the Hartian sense is in essence the general perception of a duty imposed by a formally defined exercise of power, which is to say one within the ambit of the secondary rules of the system concerned. It is in short an aspect of a formal duty imposed within the recognised structure of a positive legal system. What then is ultimately different between the demands of a gunman or a pirate and those of the law as explained by Hart? The answer is in fact in terms of institutionalisation and scale of operation. The brigand extorts upon a local and personal basis; if very successful he may become a robber baron and even finally a tyrant king setting up a state complete with rules of recognition and all the other trappings of a visible legal system without actually changing the moral character of his rule. This is in fact virtually what Adolf Hitler did in Germany and Hart, in argument with Lon. L. Fuller, averred that upon his view Nazi positive law accorded with the then current German rule of recognition and was thus unqualifiedly 'law' presumably carrying 'obligation' as defined by the theory.[40] This should not be read as a criticism of Hart's theory of law. Positivist theory is expressly concerned with the formal criteria of identification of law and not with any moral dimension which there may be. Within that context it is indeed true that 'obligation' must appear as a formally instituted duty and should be understood in that limited positive legal sense. It is clearly and properly a theory concerned with the formal definition of power and not with 'authority' other than in the very attenuated sense implied by the rule of recognition. Against this background the choice of the word 'obligation' requires qualification. If A contracts with B to do something which is legal but immoral, then A will be under an enforceable legal obligation to perform that thing. Whether or not he is under a general or moral obligation to do the thing contracted for is an entirely different question which leads back to the issues explored by Plato in *The Last Days of Socrates*[41] and into the centre of naturalist argument. Hart is concerned with obligation in the former sense and does not address the issue of obligation in the latter sense. In effect we encounter here again the influence of Sir William Blackstone since it is, upon examination, the crude *a priori* assumptions of that debased form of naturalism which Hart decries when he comes to describe naturalism in general.

Hart concedes the existence of a form of naturalism which he terms the 'minimum content of natural law'. He rightly separates the categories of legal and moral obligation and then proceeds to analyse a form of teleological approach to naturalism. The essence of this is reduced from a perception of the 'good life' for mankind to a form of basic survivalism which leads Hart to the conclusion that basic generalisations about human nature indicate fundamental rules of conduct which any viable social structure must inevitably contain. These universal principles of human conduct rooted in basic human nature are said to constitute a 'minimum content' of natural law more viable than the more 'grandiose' forms of that concept. Hart advances a number of such basic factors which may inform such a minimum naturalism. These are (i) 'human vulnerability' which dictates limitations upon permissible inter-personal violence; (ii) 'approximate equality' among subjects of the law; (iii) 'limited altruism' meaning a system of 'mutual forbearances'; (iv) 'limited resources' leading to concepts of 'property'; and (v) 'limited understanding and strength of will'. This is a very reasonable account of a basic empirical naturalism which, again, has certain social contractarian undertones. This involves an implied purposive view of law and, despite its overt minimalism and the fact that it is in practice a morality of achievement rather than of aspiration, it is a tolerable working conception of naturalist principle. The arguable defect of this approach lies in its application which implies that default in the minimum 'natural' requirement will sap the vitality of law in the long term through failure to perform basic legal functions. This is really a pragmatic test of efficacy which, like R. W. M. Dias's idea of a 'temporal approach',[42] suggests that whereas formal positive criteria of identification operate in the present, the effect of natural defect operates in a continuum, the end of which is the revocation or other abrogation of the law concerned. As a political statement this may be adequately descriptive but it does not in fact amount to a concept of naturalist cause and effect. It amounts to saying that laws which do not serve the ends of social stability and cohesion are likely, ultimately, to be abandoned, and little more. This limitation is dictated by the original misreading of the actual nature of naturalist argument by positivist thinkers. Upon closer study it is being assumed that the naturalist view may be taken to be literally that 'lex iniusta non est lex', in the sense that an unjust law effectively does not exist. Thus Hart asks whether it is not better when faced with an objectionable and 'bad' law to argue that it *is* law but iniquitous[43] rather than to cast doubt upon its formal validity or quality as 'law'. The point is made clearly in the statement that

At least it can be claimed for the simple positivist doctrine that morally iniquitous rules may still be law, that this offers no disguise for the choice between evils which, in extreme circumstances, may have to be made.[44]

Here the rather sterile nature of the supposed naturalist/positivist debate becomes manifest. The 'choice between evils' which Hart presents cannot be avoided, not does naturalism in general seek to avoid it by such a simple sleight of hand as a denial that the 'unjust law' has objective existence or effect. The point is rather that whereas positivism identifies law formally as a duty-enunciated and therefore binding norm, defining obligation in terms of imposed duty, naturalism enquires into the moral claim of such norms to impose obligation beyond formally defined duty. To deny that rules exist or that compulsion to obey them may be applied would be futile but that is not the same issue as the question whether it is a moral duty to obey or, indeed, not to obey. The debates upon this question in, for example, *The Last Days of Socrates*[45] or the discussion of tyranny in the *Summa Theologica*[46] are not concerned with the formal existence of rules — which is not denied — but with the limitations upon the moral claim to obedience of those rules. At the end of the day positivism is concerned with the formal identification of law as a system of positive rules. Naturalism is concerned with the issue of the purpose of law-making and the moral claim of laws which relatively serve 'proper' or 'improper' purposes. The answers given differ widely because the questions asked are not the same, not because the one approach is any more 'right' than the other. The positivist insight is of immense value in its own right and in the context of naturalist thought properly determines the division between formalism and moral purpose in the study of law. Whether either forms the determinate 'province of jurisprudence' is a question to which the answer depends largely upon taste. The more useful approach is perhaps that both arguments contribute to the understanding of law which is surely the actual purpose of jurisprudential study.

Notes

1. Bentham, *A Fragment on Government*, Preface: 1.
2. Bentham, *Anarchic Fallacies*. He believed that the idea of 'natural rights' was an absurdity which obscured true understanding of the nature of law.

3. Hume, *A Treatise on Human Nature*.

4. Bentham, *A Fragment on Government*, Preface: 13.

5. See Bentham, *Of Laws in General*, (ed. Hart, 1970), p. 1.

6. Ibid., p. 18. Cf. the emphasis upon a habit of obedience by Aristotle, see Ch. II, earlier.

7. Austin, *The Province of Jurisprudence Determined*, Lecture VI, p. 212.

8. Ibid., pp. 214–15.

9. See this volume. This has been a sore point with public international lawyers ever since, probably needlessly. In Austin's day PIL was a matter of customary practice among 'developed' nations as they would not be called. Such a customary system obviously contained rules but could hardly be said to have the force or precision of municipal law. Today PIL is of course much more institutionalised and has a considerable element of quasi-legislation and case decision. None the less the analogy between PIL and 'primitive' municipal law remains useful. In denying the 'legal status of PIL Austin was saying that it was not a perfect analogue of developed national law, though this is not to say that it does not exist.

10. The applicability of EEC law in English law rests upon the provisions of the European Communities Act 1972. In respect of PIL the monist views expressed by Lord DENNING, M. R. in *Trendtex Trading Corporation* v *Central Bank of Nigeria* [1977] 2 WLR 356 should perhaps be seen in the special light of the rather peculiar development of the doctrine of sovereign immunity as a 'special case'.

11. See Bentham, *A Fragment on Government*, Ch. IV: 23. 34–5.

12. Ibid., 31–3.

13. Ibid., para. 31.

14. Ibid., para. 33.

15. These issues are discussed at length by Professor H. L. A. Hart in *Essays on Bentham*, IX, 'Sovereignty and Legally Limited Government'.

16. Bentham, *Principles of Morals and Legislation*, Ch. IV: 1.

17. Ibid., para. 2.

18. See Bentham, *Principles of Morals and Legislation*, Ch. VII: 1.

19. Bentham, *A Fragment on Government*, Ch. IV: 19.

20. Ibid., para. 26.

21. Bentham, *Principles of Morals and Legislation*, Ch. I: 7.

22. Ibid., Ch. VII: 1.

23. Austin, *The Province of Jurisprudence Determined*, Lecture V, p. 118.

24. Ibid., p. 122.

25. Ibid., pp. 128–9.

26. Ibid., p. 124.

27. Hart, *The Concept of Law*, p. 6.

28. Ibid., p. 13.

29. St Augustine, *De Civitate Dei*, Bk. IV, Ch. 4.

30. Hart, *The Concept of Law*, pp. 19–25.

31. Ibid., pp. 80–1.

32. See Hart, *The Concept of Law*, pp. 90–1. This is very much a practical Western lawyer's view of legal anthropology. There is in fact a considerable weight of evidence that, even in the absence of formally developed legislative and judicial machinery, 'primitive societies' are capable of fairly sophisticated techniques of dispute avoidance and/or

resolution. For a discussion of some of these issues see S. Roberts, *Order and Dispute* or, more compendiously, M. Gluckman, *Politics, Law and Ritual in Tribal Society* and also L. Mair, *Primitive Government.*

33. Hart, *The Concept of Law*, Ch. V.
34. See Ch. 4, earlier.
35. Hart, *The Concept of Law*, p. 92.
36. Ibid., p. 97.
37. Ibid., p. 86.
38. Ibid., p. 84.
39. During the 'cultural revolution' in China some red guards actually attempted to reverse the significance of traffic sign colours because they considered the colour red to symbolise progress. As implementation was patchy the experiment was not a success and in fact the general system was retained ultimately.
40. For a discussion of this issue see Ch. 8, this volume.
41. See Ch. 2, earlier.
42. See Dias, *Jurisprudence* (4th edn), Ch. 21, p. 695, *et seq.*
43. See Hart, *The Concept of Law*, p. 206.
44. Ibid.
45. See Ch. 2, earlier.
46. See Ch. 3, earlier.

6

Marxist Legal Theory

For the legal theorist Marxism presents a number of difficulties. In the first place it is not a legal theory, but a political and social-historical theory which necessarily has a legal dimension. Secondly, as Marxism has developed into Marxism-Leninism in the USSR and Marxism-Leninism-Maoism and beyond in the People's Republic of China, the perception of the nature and role of law has varied considerably. A third difficulty is an extreme problem of categorisation in the common terminology of Western jurisprudence. There are elements of both positivism and natural-ism in the Marxist perception of law, although the latter would in general be denied by orthodox Marxist thinkers in view of the claims to 'scientific' analysis made on behalf of Marxism.

Classical Marxism is a theory of society and history developed collaboratively by Karl Marx (1818–83) and Friedrich Engels (1820–95). Marx rejected what he saw as the irrational idealism which characterised much post-Kantian thought in Europe, and especially Germany, at the same time. He sought instead a theory of society based upon an objective and 'scientific' analysis of the processes and mechanisms of social development. In fact and inevitably, the selection of data and their interpretation involve a concealed value judgement which leads in the conclusion to the advancement of a political 'ideal' within the framework of an objective terminology. Certainly the process outlined is not only presented as descriptively accurate but also as leading to a con-clusion which is morally desirable.

The Marxist analysis of social development depends upon the concept of dialectical materialism. This is in effect a radical adaption of the earlier Hegelian dialectic. G. W. F. Hegel

(1770–1831) stood at the summit of post-Kantian German 'idealist' philosophy. Kant had demonstrated that every thesis has a contrary antithesis. Hegel proceeded further to argue that such apparent conflicts conceal a higher perception of reality termed a synthesis. The process of resolution of thesis and antithesis into synthesis was conceived as an indefinite process resolving contradictions into higher states of understanding, tending ultimately to the realisation of a philosophical absolute. The absolute is the only complete reality; all other concepts are merely moments in the achievement of the conception of the absolute. In historical and political terms the Hegelian dialectic teaches that history is a process of development which leads through stages of social thesis, antithesis and synthesis to the ultimate fulfilment of the human condition. Each successive era takes elements from the cumulative development of previous eras but destroys prior forms in favour of the new condition established by it. In this theory the process of development itself is seen as being of transcendent importance. Each era is significant only in so far as it contributes to the process of future development and each individual is important only in so far as he or she plays a role in the collective entity which is the state. The state is seen as the prime vehicle of social development and also as a phenomenon greater than the sum of its parts both in the present time and in the continuum, the development of which is in fact the principal end rather than merely the means of social existence. This emphasis upon the central importance of the state led Hegel to his paradoxical conception of 'freedom' as the performance by the individual of his role within the framework of the state as his social destiny. It also led Hegel ultimately into a rather uncritical worship of the Prussian state which took its place in a tradition which, perverted and vulgarised, was to lead to such dire consequences in the tendencies of German thought in the second quarter of the twentieth century.

Marx rejected the Hegelian dialectic as unrelated to real social conditions. However, Marx proceeded upon the basis of a dialectical analysis, albeit one founded upon quite different premises from that of Hegel. For Marx the mechanism of social development was not the state but economic class relationships within society and the nature of participation in the processes of production and exchange. According to classical Marxism, social beliefs, institutions and development are based entirely upon economic relationships which precede and determine their form. As the social fundamentals of production and exchange alter so, sooner or later, the social and political order which is derived from them must also change its form. Social form is always behind the development of economic reality and thus periodic synchronisation occurs through the medium of revolution. Thus Marxism is 'materialist' in the sense that it is grounded in the analysis of material economic relationships in the processes of production and exchange rather than in unverifiable and therefore 'unreal' ideal hypotheses. The idealised statism of Hegel is rejected but the dialectical element of his thought is retained. The nature of the dialectic is rooted in the Marxist theory of knowledge. Knowledge is essentially a form of perception and according to Marxist thought social knowledge takes the form of ideological perception in that it is based upon ways of thinking about the economic social base which can shift dramatically into new forms. As Hugh Collins has expressed it:

> Marxists . . . argue that . . . men must use ideological frame-works in order to interpret the material world. These ideologies act as grids for analysing experiences . . . these ideas are tested and examined, and this . . . lead to refinement and . . . to new social practices.
> The Marxist theory of ideology rests upon . . . the ideological nature of the acquisition of knowledge together with the way conscious ideas are formed by and help to shape the material world.[1]

Thus, on this view, perception of economic and social reality is moulded by the ideological nature of understanding. The ideological perception in any era will originally be that of the dominant class, but in time a subordinate class will develop a contrary ideology and this conflict between thesis and antithesis will eventually be resolved by revolutionary change in the forms of society. This is the Marxist dialectic and is essentially a form of social catastrophe theory in which form and perceived reality change at different rates as a result of which the form is periodically pushed abruptly into a new state reflecting a changed reality. Such change is brought about through the medium of class conflict. Classical Marxism supposes a clear-cut division of society into classes defined by common economic interests and roles in the processes of production and exchange and that the opposed interests of these classes produces conflict. Thus in the classical Marxist analysis social forms develop through a process of ideological appreciation of material economic relationships punctuated by revolutionary changes in social structure as formerly subordinate classes successively seize the dominant role.

Briefly the envisaged process of development commences in a state of primitive economic equality in which the means of production and exchange are held collectively by the whole community in a state of mutual interdependence. This primitive stage is succeeded, as the economic structure becomes more complex, by successive eras of class domination. This comes about through the diversification and separation of economic roles and the emergence of ownership and control of the means of production, which in turn confers economic and political domination upon the controllers and leaves others as subordinate class groups. Society passes through successive monarchic and feudal periods of control from which economic power passes to the bourgeois mercantile class in the 'bourgeois revolution' in the early industrial era. In the Marxist view this happened in England through the sixteenth and seventeenth centuries culminating in the period of the Civil War and finally the 'Glorious Revolution' in 1688/9 in which James II was overthrown to be replaced by William III and Mary II. At this stage the means of production and exchange are controlled by an owning and investing 'bourgeois' class whose interests diverge from those of the working proletariat and peasantry as subordinate classes. As the 'bourgeois' epoch proceeds so the ideological perceptions of the proletariat will diverge from the 'bourgeois' social order and in due course a 'proletarian revolution' will follow. This will bring to an end the process of class conflict because no further subordinate classes will remain. This was supposed by Marx to lead to a classless communist ordering of society in which there would be no domination of one group by any other and formal institutions of state would wither away in favour of a vaguely consensual ordering of things among the people collectively. Society is thus conceived as developing through the adjustment of forms to changing economic relationships by a process of class conflict and successive revolutions. This mechanism is perceived as fundamental, the institutions which reflect it, the state, the law and so on, are seen as 'superstructure' upon the economic base. These institutions do not determine the form of society, on the contrary, they are a mere reflection of ideology and economic power.

This Marxist interpretation of social development has, like any other theory, both its strengths and weaknesses. In the sense that social change clearly comes about through changes in expectation and perception which force alterations in form, it may reasonably be argued that history is essentially a dialectical process. It is also clearly the case that formal institutions are a reflection of social and historical development and not the reverse. The weakness in Marxist analysis lies in the selection of the data upon which the conclusions of dialectical materialism are based. The root difficulty here is the problem of 'class reductionism'. That economic relationships and class divisions have been and are very important factors in social development can hardly be denied: however, they are not isolated or singular factors, nor is the relationship between the two as simple as the Marxist analysis suggests. Social structures are surely the product of very complex interactions between people for which in fact 'society' is a collective noun, notwithstanding Hegel. Into these interactions go such matters as culture, ethical or other beliefs and inherited concepts of solidarity as well as purely economic factors. To concentrate solely upon economics as the base factor is severely to limit the analysis and to interpret all other factors in its light actually involves a distortion. The simple equation of power and economic benefit with perceived social class and the explanation of all conflict in terms of class antagonism also appears to be a dangerously over-simplified analysis. Ultimately it may be argued that ideology in the sense of conditioned perception is a vitally important shaper of social structures, but its development is a great deal more complex than simple Marxist analysis suggests.

From the Marxist perspective law is of course a part of the social superstructure which represents the interests of the dominant class and is in fact a prominent instrument of class repression. It was considered that law plays some role in all phases of class dominance but that it is an especially prominent feature of the 'bourgeois' phase of development. The superficial nature of law was stressed by Marx in statements in which the law is depicted as arising from concepts of private property which are themselves generative of class distinctions and antagonisms. It is certainly true that matters of property, not simply private property, play a considerable part in legal rules. However, the statement that 'real' law develops with the appearance of 'bourgeois' mercantilism is an arbitrary assumption about the nature of law which has little or no support in the evidence of social and legal anthropology. Law is a way of stating values, resolving disputes and generally setting out a known framework within which general day-to-day transactions can be conducted — often without any consciousness of the involvement of 'law' on the part of those involved. What Marx did was to take the coercive and economic aspects of law and define them as being the whole of the phenomenon. This is arbitrary, which is far from being a uniquely Marxist fault. It is significant, however, that the non-coercive communist 'ordering of things', predicted by Marx but nowhere yet fulfilled, would in fact perform many functions which on other appreciations would be termed 'law jobs'[2] but which are called non-legal by Marxists because non-coercive and not class-based. The definition is short, and like many other definitions, distinctly circular upon examination. This early Marxist idea of law was considerably developed when in due course the time came for its practical implementation.

The Russian revolution of 1917 was in many ways an anomaly in Marxist theory. Upon a Marxist analysis the Russian Empire at the turn of the century was only just showing signs of moving into a 'bourgeois' phase of development being at the time still semi-'feudal'[3] and certainly not a likely candidate for proletarian revolution in the short term. In the event the Imperial government collapsed in the face of the strains imposed by the First World War. Tsar Nicholas II abdicated on behalf of himself and his heir[4] and power was seized by the Mensheviks led by Kerensky who is taken to represent the 'bourgeois' era of domination in Russia. The Menshevik regime was overthrown by the Bolshevik party led by Lenin. Lenin himself originally trained as a lawyer, indeed he gained a 'First' in the state legal examinations in 1891 and practised law in the Westernised legal system adopted in Russia in 1864 as part of the reforms introduced under Alexander II (1856–81)[5] before devoting himself wholly to revolutionary activism. Lenin shared the Marxist view of law as an instrument of class conflict. However, as a former practising lawyer and as ruler of the Soviet Union from 1917 to 1923 he was unable to share the idealistic expectation of the withering away of the state and its institutions in favour of a co-operative order as a natural consequence of proletarian revolution. In practice Lenin revised Marxism into the form known as Marxism-Leninism which was to have, among myriad other effects, a major impact upon the development of Soviet jurisprudence.

Lenin considered that the proletariat, left to itself, is incapable of organisation beyond the level of trade unionism and that the proletarian revolution would thus degenerate into new class divisions and probably chaos. Thus he concluded that between the proletarian revolution and communism a more or less lengthy period of education and indoctrination would be necessary in order to eradicate remaining 'bourgeois' and 'counter-revolutionary' attitudes. The proletarian revolution was therefore to be followed by a further period of domination by a didactic communist party. This period is termed the 'dictatorship of the proletariat'; it is in fact the dictatorship of the party which is conceived as having the role of inculcating a communist ideology and extirpating all contrary ideologies. This is in essence what is meant by the 'leading role of the Communist Party', enshrined in the constitutions of communist states. Thus the apparatus of state was to be maintained in a transitional period until the aftermath of class conflict had been dissipated and the proletariat had been educated for communism. During this period law was to be retained, but not in deference to any Diceyan conception of 'rule of law' which the Bolsheviks derided as 'legal fetishism'. Law was to be used as a weapon in the eradication of 'bourgeois ideologies' and 'class enemies'. That done it would have no further use because as an ineradicably 'bourgeois' institution it could play no part in a genuinely 'socialist' or 'communist' society. Lenin's initial intention had been to maintain only the institutions of public law as a means of party control during the transitional period, regarding private law (equated with 'property') as part of the bourgeois trappings to be eliminated. This remained official policy from 1917 to 1921. At that stage, however, it was decided that a 'breathing space' was required in which Russian society could be led to full socialism as the prelude to communism more gradually. The practical expression of this idea was the 'New Economic Policy' which was applied during the last years of Lenin's rule from 1921 to 1923 and thereafter until 1928. The NEP involved a partial reversion to a mixed economy and this in its turn involved a readoption of some rules of private law, in a suitably controlled ideological mould.

The NEP was abandoned in 1928 in favour of a much more direct approach through the first two 'five-year plans' up to 1937, by which time a single economy and a classless society was expected to have been achieved, this being in many ways similar to pre-1921 policy. Throughout the period 1917 to 1937, however, Soviet law was officially considered to be a temporary party weapon wrested from the hands of the bourgeoisie to be abandoned as soon as the party's coercive and didactic task was done. This was the view held in 1927 by P. I. Stuchka, the first

President of the Supreme Court of the USSR and was the basis of the first development of Soviet jurisprudence which was very anti-legalist.

The principal legal specialist in the USSR during this period was Evgeny Bronislavovich Pashukanis (1891–1937). E. B. Pashukanis became a Bolshevik activist at the age of 21 and after the 1917 revolution he became the leading Soviet jurisprudential specialist and ultimately a Vice-Commissar for Justice. His views were very much those of the period of 'war communism' and the NEP, but he failed sufficiently to keep step with the major shift in policy under Stalin and fell victim to an attack orchestrated by Stalin's Procurator-General, A. I. Vyshinski. Pashukanis was 'liquidated' in 1937, one of the many victims of the Stalinist purges. His image has been considerably rehabilitated in the USSR in the period from the mid-1950s, although his jurisprudence has not been substantially re-adopted. His views, however, played a large role in modern Marxist debate upon law outside the USSR.

Pashukanis's most important published work was *The General Theory of Law and Marxism*.[6] In this book he explained the rules of law in terms of commodity exchange as an image of a monetary market economy. Pashukanis criticised those legal theorists who, like Petrazycki and Kelsen,[7] propounded ideas of law which emphasised legal norms as being of the essence of the nature of law. He contended instead that the standards and principles advanced by law do not actually regulate personal relationships and transactions but merely reflect the forces of production and exchange and the ideology of the class which controls them. The purpose of legal rules upon this perspective is to enable individuals to be treated as economic units whose relations can then be treated as formal transactions within a known framework. In short, and this is a basic point of Marxist jurisprudence, law is not an autonomous system of rules but a reflection of economic relations in the absence of which it is wholly without life or point. Thus, far from moulding commercial and economic relations into the form apparently demanded by legal norms, legal rules are merely the devised formal means by which 'real' economic relationships are expressed. Pashukanis extended this commodity-exchange view of law far beyond the overtly 'commercial' areas of law like contract. Family law is explained as a formulation of personal relations in terms of rules which are quasi-contractual and reflect a 'bourgeois' market economy. The analogy of bargain is extended also into the realms of public law. Thus constitutional law was argued by Pashukanis to be presented as a supposedly arm's-length bargain between state and people, an idea enshrined in the conceptions of 'social contractarianism'.[8] Pashukanis sought to demonstrate that this 'bourgeois' bargaining model of law as a structure of impersonal norms reached at arm's length is a distortion of reality concealing the subjection to the will of the dominant class. In his view bourgeois dominance took a legal form in particular because the bourgeois epoch is primarily identified with a capitalist trading economy of which law is a simile. This approach enabled Pashukanis to support the classical Marxist idea of law as an ineradicably bourgeois phenomenon which could never become inherently socialist or communist together with Marxist-Leninist gloss of the retention of law as a party instrument during the 'dictatorship of the proletariat'. Thus during the period of transition to communism law would remain because relics of bourgeois ideology would remain. Once the economic base of a market society had been eliminated the superstructural phenomenon of law would wither away in favour of the communist 'ordering of things'.

A number of points may be made about this form of legal theory. The economic centrality of the theory is of course the common feature of all Marxist thought, but the elaboration of the market idea of law is an important contribution to Marxist legal theory. It is clear that Pashukanis, like Lenin, was loosely positivistic in his concept of law in so far as he regarded it as the expression of rules by a ruling group without any necessary or inherent moral dimension. On the other hand the simple command or imperative model of law was rejected as an instance of 'legal fetishism' which ignored the economic base and ideological nature of law. Equally, Pashukanis, like all Marxists, would have denounced a naturalist approach as unscientific and unreal, being in effect moral fetishism. Yet, upon reflection, a curious paradox at the heart of Marxist jurisprudence becomes apparent. The progression through eras of class dominance to the proletarian revolution and ultimately to a communist ordering of society is presented as a 'scientific' and objective description of an inevitable process which is at the same time urged as morally desirable. Thus an argument based upon a selection of data proceeds to a conclusion which has been rendered inevitable by the adopted criteria of identification and which is in fact basically a value-judgement. This view may be supported by the conception of the Marxist-

Leninist 'dictatorship of the Proletariat'; coercive education would surely be unnecessary for the completion of a progression which was straightforwardly 'inevitable'. The presence of this value-judgement is significant in terms of jurisprudential categorisation. Law is being presented as a means of social control used in the course of class domination but which can also transitionally be used as a means of coercive didaction in the preparation of the 'desirable' conclusion of a communist society in which there would be no law but a consensual 'ordering of things'. The use of law in the supression of contrary ideologies and the maintenance of Marxism in the face of 'reactionary' opposition identifies law as a mechanism associated with 'erroneous ideology' and having meaning only in association with it. In a commuinist society, and in any event for the ideologically educated, law would have no relevance. There can in this be seen at least a mechanical, although not a functional, parallel with the approach of St Augustine.[9]

If 'bourgeois ideology' is substituted for sin, there seems no reason in essence why Pashukanis should have dissented from the Augustinian proposition that law is the 'poena et remedium peccati'— the penalty and remedy for sin. It is also significant that, like St Augustine, Pashukanis focused upon the narrowly coercive role of law in society and founded his views upon that perception. The subsequent 'ordering of things' is blandly categorised as non-law in an argument of inescapable circularity.[10] This is of course an argument comparing form and not substance. St Augustine had very different criteria and ends in view from those of Pashukanis or any other Marxist theorist. Augustine argued from external standards whereby the conduct of the state could be judged and by which its actions should be guided if it is to have any moral claim to obedience. Marxist theory proceeds upon the basis of a state ideology in which the state as a party entity has no need of 'authority' external to itself.

Be that as it may, the jurisprudence advanced by Pashukanis did not survive the 1930s in the USSR. As the period of the first two 'five-year plans' proceeded Pashukanis and other Soviet jurists undoubtedly expected that the time for the withering away of the state and law was imminent. Pashukanis's writing at this time became more and more anti-legalist and some commentators have claimed that Soviet judges in this period began to work towards the closure of their courts. It is difficult to say exactly what the real trend of the time was. However, it is certainly the case that the final result was the reverse of that anticipated by Pashukanis and the Soviet jurists of the 1920s and early 1930s.

The official policy of the years following the revolution had been formulated in the anticipation of world revolution in which the USSR would become the leader of the movement to world communism. The most prominent enthusiast for this approach in the 1920s and 1930s was Leon Trotsky. Lenin's successor in supreme power was Joseph Vissarionovich Dzhugashvili, who took the revolutionary name of Stalin. Stalin favoured a very different view which rested upon the idea of 'capitalist encirclement'. The argument went that a stateless communist society could not survive while there remained the political and military threat of non-socialist states, consequently the Soviet state could not be permitted to wither away. The new doctrine was 'socialism in one country' under which the Soviet Union was to develop a socialist society behind the protective walls of the party and the state. Although the ideology was different this was not entirely a new phenomenon in Russian policy. The very reactionary Tsar Nicholas I (1825–56) had similarly attempted to isolate Russia from foreign influence in an effort to prevent the import of 'revolutionary' contagion during the 1840s. In some respects Stalin's rigid control of outside contacts had a similar motivation from the other side of the ideological divide. It must also be said, and this was by no means a coincidence, that the new doctrine was highly conducive to the personal dictatorship of Stalin himself. The jurisprudence of Pashukanis did not fit easily with the new policy and his attempts to modify his position were not a sufficient accommodation. Pashukanis was liquidated in 1937 upon absurd charges of subversion and treason and replaced as the leading Soviet jurist by the architect of his destruction, A. I. Vyshinsky. The means of Vyshinsky's rise to prominence and his leading role as Procurator-General in the Stalinist purges have left him with a deservedly sinister reputation. Vyshinsky replaced the idea of law as a 'bourgeois' relic of temporary utility during the transitional era with the concept of 'social legality'. In fact Vyshinsky's exposition of legal theory in *The Law of the Soviet Union*, which he partly wrote and partly edited, was very much more crude than that of Pashukanis, having in common with it only the absolutely dismissive tone adopted towards all other views than those being expressed. The abusive tone, typical of Soviet writing of the time, did conceal an important change of jurisprudential view, however.

The new element of Vyshinsky's legal theory was the idea that law could in fact be made inherently 'socialist' in nature. In short that just as 'bourgeois' embodies in its norms the interests and ideologies of a bourgeois economic base, so in a socialist society the legal norms can be made to reflect a socialist ideology. What then becomes of the perception of law as an inherently non-socialist weapon of class domination? Vyshinsky's argument was that socialist law is proletarian law which 'dominates' anti-proletarian factions but is also in itself the perfect expression in rules of socialist ideology for the whole mass of the community. The development of this theory was politically necessary in order to support the acceptance of the permanence of the Soviet state and its laws. With the completion of this historical shift of emphasis the nature of obligation in the development of Soviet jurisprudence may be considered in context.

For the classical Marxist the idea of an 'obligation' to obey the law is either superstitious or an ideological distortion. On this view law is neither more nor less than an exercise of coercive power in its own interest by a dominant class. The development in the USSR of Marxism-Leninism and the jurisprudence of Pashukanis complicated this picture. Law was still seen as a simple coercive instrument, a juristic bludgeon, but now one which operated during the dictatorship of the proletariat to secure the ends of socialism and communism about which Marxist and Marxist-Leninist thought makes an evaluative as well as a predictive judgement. In the sense that one who disobeys legal norms, and thus incurs their coercive force, is acting in a way contrary to the perceived 'good' of socialist ideology there is here an implicit nascent concept of an 'obligation' to act in concordance with law as an aspect of good citizenship. This nascent concept of obligation in the limited legal theory of Pashukanis is only indirectly referable, however, to any strict form of naturalism and is subject to a number of important qualifications. The implicit quasi-obligation involved is based upon the presupposition of the rectitude of any law enunciated by the communist party in the exercise of its 'leading role' in the state. There is in fact no admission of a distinction between the power of party and state and the 'authority' of their actions. In the end the legal concepts of Pashukanis must be taken to represent a 'power' theory of law which through the medium of an implicit value-judgement takes on some of the form but not the substance of naturalism because the central value-judgement is defined and maintained by the positive law-makers themselves.

The 'socialist legalism' of Vyshinsky raises slightly different issues. The law in this view has become not a mere bludgeon which may be used temporarily in the advancement of socialist ideology but a social phenomenon which is itself inherently socialist in nature. A thing which is considered not merely usable in the advancement of rectitude but to be right in itself seems on first impression to impose obligation in a stronger form than the more distanced approach of Pashukanis. In a sense this is indeed the case. However, the only reference beyond the rules themselves is still to the party as the guardian of ideology so that at the end of the day the structure of obligation is entirely enclosed and does not make the distinction between 'power' and authority, as those concepts are properly understood. This must be understood against the background of the intended operation of Soviet law as a regulatory agency. It has been remarked that Western ideas of the 'rule of law' are alien to Marxist-Leninist jurisprudence. Law, whether or not inherently 'socialist', is in the Soviet system necessarily subject to the ideological override which follows from the very idea of 'socialist legality'. In practice this means that Soviet courts were and are enjoyed to enforce rules of law not as neutral directions in the Western manner, although Soviet jurists of course regard Western legal rules as being far from neutral, but in the light of ideology and overtly for the achievement of ideological ends. The purpose of presenting an ideological example is seen as of at least as much importance as the settlement of an immediate dispute. It must again be remarked, however, that this emphasis upon the ideological 'spirit' of 'socialist legality' is not a reference external to the law but to the nature of the Soviet state of which the Soviet legal system is a part.

The jurisprudential era inaugurated by Vyshinsky was referred to as one of 'stability of laws'. In fact the personal rule of Stalin had little connection with legality, 'socialist' or otherwise, and it is with the political terrorism of those years that Vyshinsky is especially associated.

Eventually after the death of Stalin he and his supporters were denounced as having derogated from the standards of socialist legality. The post-Stalinist and modern era in the USSR has seen important further developments in Soviet legal theory. In 1961 at the XXII Communist Party Congress the USSR was declared to have become a state of all the people, terminating the formal condition of 'dictatorship of the proletariat'. This was taken as a sort of interim achievement of communism and discussion of the withering away of law and other coercive institutions in favour of consensuality and social pressure revived. Comrades' courts as a less formal medium of problem-solving and a rediscussion of customary law as a people's law all manifested themselves as symptoms of this movement of ideas, subject always to the preservation of the leading role of the party in Soviet society. This was the main thrust of jurisprudential ideas in the Khrushchev era. Since the fall of Khrushchev there has been some further reorientation in Soviet jurisprudential thought. The emphasis of the Brezhnev, Andropov and Chernienko years in legal matters, which seems to be continuing into the Gorbachov leadership, changed from the dismantling of legal structures to an idea of bringing them closer to the public through popular participation. The Comrades' courts seem not to have been selected as a principal means of achieving this aim, mainly it would appear because the procedural norms of a more formal system are considered more efficient and to have the merit of uniformity in the administration of justice. This is sometimes taken as evidence of the 'Westernisation' of the Soviet legal system implying a move to conceptions of the autonomy of law and perhaps towards an Anglo-American positivist jurisprudence. It certainly seems to be the case that the institutionalisation of Soviet law has been accepted. However, this should be misunderstood or interpreted in too simplistic a manner. The 'separateness' of law in the USSR from other forms of social control is very much less than is the case in a Western system, official mobilisation of social pressure upon 'deviants' being especially emphasised. Perhaps more fundamentally the Soviet idea of law remains based upon 'socialist legality' in which the 'neutral' norms of formal law are always subject to the advancement of ideological interest. This concept of law of course lends itself readily to a crude state interventionism, but it is also further evidence of the rather ambiguous nature of Marxist-Leninist jurisprudence. On a more formal level the law is inevitably, and properly, regarded as a positivist phenomenon, but through the doctrines of socialist legality and such techniques as the 'shaming' of deviants through social pressure an element of somewhat crude proto-naturalism becomes discernible. How this may develop is not easy to predict but an evolution into a naturalist form is entirely possible.

The naturalism which may be nascent in Soviet jurisprudence is very incomplete, as indeed the system itself is not yet even a century old, but with the present institutionalisation of Soviet law the crudely coercive model of law has of necessity been laid aside. Such a development tends towards an idea of obligation in law and the non-autonomous nature of law in the Soviet conception leads towards more than an idea of a merely formal 'obligation', such as that essentially advanced by H. L. A. Hart.[11] The implication of this line of reasoning is in fact a developing conception of legal obligation in the full sense of one derived from evaluation by reference to exterior standards, here based upon a particular theory of social purpose. Whether or not this element of Soviet legal theory continues and matures remains to be seen. It is to be hoped that its observation and study will be reasonably free of the hysterical adulation which led the political left to regard even the Stalinist show trials with an unseemly approbation from the comfort of Bloomsbury, as also the unreasoning phobia which leads the political right to view anything suggestive of collectivism as equivalent to original sin.

The USSR is not of course by any means the sole example of a state with a Marxist-derived official ideology and it should not be taken as the only model for the development of jurisprudence upon a Marxist base. A rather different pattern of development can be found in the People's Republic of China. Modern China rejects the Confucian tradition; some of the traditional attitudes to law have survived into the modern era and transpire to blend with a neo-Marxist ideology rather more easily than might be anticipated.

The nineteenth century was a period of catastrophe in China. Major incursions into the country by Western powers found the Manchu Empire neither technologically nor politically well equipped to resist. The inherent conservatism of Confucian thought had by this time produced an ossification of official thought which at once induced a contempt for all foreigners, collectively viewed as 'barbarians', and vitiated any possibility of developing the technological means of resistance to foreign aggression and interference which in earlier times would not have been tolerated. The process was drawn out and is symbolised in the 'unequal' treaties of the era in which leases and extra-territorial rights were extorted from the Imperial government by Western powers. The Opium War of 1839 to 1842, in which Britain successfully fought China to maintain its 'right' to engage in drug trafficking in China at a time when the Chinese government and especially Commissioner Lin Tse-hsu in Canton were endeavouring to stamp out the importation of opium, led to the cession of Hong Kong. In 1895 the Sino-Japanese war led to the cession of Formosa (Taiwan) to Japan. The turn of the century saw a scramble for Chinese territorial concessions; France obtained Kwangchow Bay and rights in the Tonkin area, Britain obtained the Kowloon lease, Russia gained Port Arthur and Dairen together with an extension of the trans-Siberian railway through Harbin to Port Arthur, and Japan took rights in Fukien province. All this was a major cause of the so-called Boxer rebellion in 1900 which was actually a pro-dynastic anti-foreign movement. The siege of the Peking legations led to foreign intervention and relief of the Peking legations by a joint expeditionary force mounted by Britain, Germany, France, Russia, Austria, Italy, the USA and Japan. Not surprisingly conflicts also broke out among the external powers, notably in the Russo-Japanese war of 1904/5 upon the issue of the control of Korea which was resolved in favour of Japan by the Treaty of Portsmouth (New Hampshire). Most of these disasters occurred during the period of rule of the Empress-dowager Tzu-hsi through the medium of a series of ephemeral puppet Emperors. A cynical and corrupt ruler whose attitudes, conditioned by life in the harem, almost uniquely unfitted her to guide China through these stormy years, the Empress-dowager presided over the dissolution of Imperial China in a miasma of corruption and incompetence. She died in 1908 and revolution came in 1911 led by progressive nationalists among whom the most notable was Dr Sun Yat-sen. The Manchus were displaced and the last juvenile Emperor, Pu Yi, fled. He was later to add footnotes to history as a puppet of the Japanese in Manchukuo and later still as an example of communist 'rehabilitation' as a member of the People's Congress.

In 1912 the Republic of China was founded with Sun Yat-sen as first President. He, however, resigned in favour of the War Lord Yuan Skih-kai who had manifest ambitions to found a new dynasty with himself as Emperor but who eventually remained President from 1912 until his death in 1916. A confused period followed the First World War, including a civil war in 1922/3. In 1924 power was in the hands of the Kuomintong Nationalist Party under Sun Yat-sen. At this time communists were admitted to the Kuomintong and Mao Tse-tung became its Chief of Propaganda. After the demise of Sun Yat-sen in 1925 the leadership passed to Generalissimo Chiang Kai-shek who in 1927 expelled all communists from the Kuomintong. Internal conflicts in the 1930s paled into insignificance in the face of Japanese invasion through Manchuria upon various pretexts. This Sino-Japanese war eventually merged into the wider world conflict. After the Second World War in 1945 the USSR recognised the Nationalist Kuomintong as the government of China but civil conflict continued and in November 1948 the Communist forces took Peking and the Nationalist forces fled to Taiwan (Formosa) of which alone they retain control. The People's Republic of China was officially founded on 1 October 1949.

Through the turbulent half-century up to 1949 the Chinese legal perspective had been through a number of shifts of emphasis. By 1900 the traditional Imperial legal system had all but collapsed. The Imperial Civil Service examinations were abolished in 1902 and the system itself was on the verge of total collapse. As reformers came increasingly to the fore in the years before the fall of the dynasty in 1911, a number of important 'modernisations' were attempted and some of these indicated a developing revision of Chinese legal theory. The Ch'ing code, the Ta Ch'ing Lu Li, underwent its final major revision in this period being completed in 1910, the year before the revolution. The Nationalist authorities after 1912 tended at first to a simple rejection of the entire Imperial tradition including its anti-legalism. Initially some attempt was made to import Western codes of law despite their very non-Chinese assumptions and general nature. Many of the new Nationalist jurists had been trained in Japan and in consequence relied heavily upon Japanese models which were themselves closely derived from German originals. The inappropriateness of this soon became evident — indeed it requires little specialist knowledge to imagine that laws framed in Wilhelmine Germany and transposed to China through a Japanese filter would, at best, sit oddly. Once this was realised, Nationalist jurisprudence moved into a phase which has been well described as one of 'enlightened eclecticism'.[12] The ideal of this approach was to take useful elements from the laws of a range of countries and to graft them into the native Chinese legal tradition. In practice this meant that for many years the Ta Ch'ing Lu Li, as modernised in 1910, remained the core of Chinese criminal law. The almost complete lack of civil provision in Imperial Chinese law meant that the Nationalist Republic was obliged to import much overseas law in this area. Rules of civil law were developed fairly swiftly with inevitable reference to the German/Japanese model. The legal theory of this era was more or less 'Westernised' in nature. Law was officially seen as a normal and 'respectable' part of the social fabric in a marked departure from the Confucian canons.

However, the extent to which this re-evaluation of the role of law was accepted in popular attitudes is open to some doubt. It appears to be the case that many at least of the older generation in modern Taiwan, where the Nationalist system of law operates, retain in effect a traditional Confucian stigmatisation of the litigation process and those involved in it.

After the communist takeover in 1949 the legal theory of the People's Republic of China initially followed a severe Marxist-Leninist, soon to become Marxist-Leninist-Maoist, line. The standard Marxist-Leninist view of law as an instrument of class repression was adopted, including its extension as a coercive instrument of state for the imposition of socialist ideology upon the recalcitrant during the period of proletarian dictatorship. This again is the simple class conflict model of law, derived directly from Soviet jurisprudence. However, modern Chinese legal theory is not a mere mirror image of that to be found in the USSR. This is partly the result of different historical legal traditions and partly the product of the adaption of Marxism-Leninism to Chinese social conditions. The Russian legal tradition was very weak and if Marxist-Leninist disdain for legal institutions was not exactly inscribed upon a *tabula rasa*, it was certainly adopted in a society with comparatively little legal consciousness. From this developed the ideological concept of obligation already outlined. In China there was a very strong, but narrowly focused, legal tradition which emphasised the coercive and penal role of law in maintaining the perceived form of philosophical and social rectitude in the case of the wayward. The readiness with which this sort of idea can be transmuted into the concepts of law in the proletarian dictatorship is clear enough. Unlike Imperial China, or the USSR in its early years, Communist China also accepted the role of civil law, which had been engrafted onto the Chinese legal tradition in the years between 1911 and 1949. The original official idea of civil law is reflected in the statement that 'The civil law of the People's Republic of China is socialist civil law . . . Under the leadership of the Communist Party . . . it has . . . developed through . . . evaluation of our activity in revolution and construction.'[13] This is patently a post-Pashukanist view which in effect recognises the possibility, of a 'socialist legality'. The pattern of subsequent development, however, did not follow the Soviet lead to a concept of socialist obligation directly from this concept. Chinese tradition in any event associated obligation with Li rather than Fa and to this was added the Maoist element of Marxism-

Leninism-Maoism. Mao Tse-tung contributed the idea of progress through continuous revolution. Mao argued that if society was permitted to stabilise a bourgeois reaction would set in and the impetus of revolutionary progress would be lost, as had happened, according to Mao, in the USSR. From these ideas sprang the chaotic era of the 'Cultural Revolution'. During this period all formal institutions including law were disparaged as potentially if not actually 'bourgeois' or 'revisionist'. The main thrust of the cultural revolution was provided by Red Guards, young extremist activists who were, so to speak, a law unto themselves, led by the political grouping around Madame Chiang Ching[14] now known as the 'Gang of Four'. During this period formal law was all but abandoned in favour of 'popular tribunals' which were supposed to express popular ideological understanding in the correction of deviance or counter-revolutionary tendencies. In practice and inevitably such 'popular' justice was often mere persecution of unpopular characters and a means of settling old scores which in the end was little if at all distinguishable from simple gangsterism.

In the long run the practices of the cultural revolution proved insupportable and after the death of Mao the 'Gang of Four' fell from power in 1976. Chiang Ching and her associates were purged, but not in the manner of the cultural revolution, rather through the medium of a highly significant legal trial.[15] The form of the trial was interesting. In itself it represented a return to the concept of 'socialist legality' as distinct from the chaos of the cultural revolution. The following passage from the official account of the trial makes the point clearly:

> The years of lawlessness ended with the arrest of the Gang of Four in 1976 . . . It was recognised that socialist legality must prevail.[16]

The same passage continues, however, to stress the ideological nature of the trial and its outcome by stating that

> . . . the Lin Biao and Jiang Qing cliques were . . . charged . . . according to . . . law, although everyone . . . knew that they were guilty of . . . heinous crimes . . . it was . . . stressed that facts were the basis and the law was the sole criterion . . . the trial provided the people of the country with a lesson . . . on the rule of law.[17]

Thus the trial was conceived as an act of state representing at once the norms of socialist legality including its procedural guarantees and the ideologically didactic conception of law in mainstream modern Marxist-Leninist thought. The conclusions of the court were also significant in terms of the state of Chinese legal theory. The ten principal defendants were inevitably found guilty by the 37 judges of the special court, indeed the prospects for acquittal must be seen as having been negligible. However, the automatic capital sentences of Soviet 'show trials' under Stalin did not follow. Chiang Ching herself and Chang Chun-Chiao were sentenced to 'death with a two-year reprieve and permanent deprivation of political rights'.[18] The remaining defendants received sentences of varying periods of imprisonment and deprivation of political rights, the longest period of incarceration being 20 years and the shortest 16 years. The suspended death sentences upon Chiang Ching and Chang Chun-Chiao are especially interesting in so far as the clear aim of the court was a period of probationary ideological 're-education' which to some extent again combines Marxist-derived jurisprudence with the traditional Chinese idea of law as the maintainer of the social proprieties of Li. The same can be seen in the evident significance attached by the court to the penitent and constructive, or otherwise, attitude of the defendants. Here too can be seen the concept of socialist legality with its mixture of procedural norms and overt ideological commitment transcending the apparent neutrality of normative statement. The present situation in China seems to tend towards stated norms of law which faithfully follow socialist ideology from which in course of time a concept of legal obligation may be derived in association with ideas of ideological rectitude. The Constitution adopted on 5 March 1978 provided for the participation of 'representatives of the masses' as assessors in people's courts[19] and for the supervisory role of the Supreme People's Court over lower courts and its accountability to the National People's Congress in parallel to that of lower courts to local people's congresses.[20]

The idea behind these provisions is conveyed by the report of Chiang Hua, the President of the Supreme People's Court, to the Fifth National Congess in 1980 in which he said that

. . . we must ensure that people's courts are independent . . . subject only to the law. This is an important principle of a socialist legal system . . . efforts should be made to foster people's judges who are fair-minded . . . and dauntless . . .

> Supervision of judicial work by the people's congresses . . .
> people's courts at and by the masses is very important.[21]

Thus the law in modern China seems to be conceived as a formal structure of norms embodying procedural guarantees which serves the ideological purposes of Chinese socialism. It seems not to be considered a permanent, or at least long-term, social phenomenon and this tends towards the same form of argument of obligation as those already advanced in the context of discussion of modern Soviet legal theory.

Marxist thought in the West has not always followed either the Soviet or Chinese model, or indeed any of the other variants adopted by communist states. The modern revival of interest in the work of Pashukanis has been mentioned. Another theorist in whom interest has revived is Karl Renner who wrote of law from a Marxist viewpoint at the turn of the century.

Karl Renner was the first Marxist thinker to make a special consideration of law. He followed Marx in emphasising the paramount importance of the economic base in social development. Renner was interested by the apparent stability of legal concepts despite changing economic circumstances. This he analysed as a contrast between stability of *form* and mutation of *function*. His principal published work was *Institutions of Private Law and Their Social Functions*,[22] in which he sought to demonstrate that understanding of a legal concept involves an examination of its changing economic function rather than merely its superficial form. The most important concept for Renner is that of 'property'. He argued that concepts of property originated as an accurate expression of economic activity. Ownership, he claimed, originally involved typically the control of land whereby the owners fed and maintained themselves so that legal concept and economic activity corresponded each to the other in a direct and simple relationship. However, increasing complexity of economic activity subverted this simple correspondence of form and function and as the capitalist owner comes, through financial holding, to control the economic activities of others whom he employs, the concept of ownership changes from a measure of economic independence into a quasi-public power exercised over others. Thus although the *language* of ownership remains more or less the same, the use of the concept has changed from a simple economic statement into a complex system of relationships ultimately symbolising the exercise of economic power by the few over the many. From this evolved use of the concept of ownership flow many other legal concepts such as contract and, in particular, contracts of employment. This is not a free bargain as the language suggests[23] but the means whereby the capitalist 'owner' exercises what is in reality a quasi-public power over his workforce.

Like most early Marxist thought, Renner's theory is entirely destructive of any idea of obligation since law is here treated as developing from a statement of economic relations into a means whereby economic power is exercised, ultimately through various forms of coercion. Renner has by some commentators been denied the appellation 'Marxist' because his admission of the stability of legal forms seems to run counter to the Marxist conception of law as superstructural and therefore mutating. This view may be argued, however, to be very superficial. Marx did not speak of legal forms; he considered only the function of law as an incidence of social economic development, and the mutation of legal function is at the heart of Renner's analysis which would thus seem to involve no conflict with Marx himself. Be that as it may, the work of Renner contributes to a stream of Marxist thought which must be set against the observable quasi-naturalist tendencies in modern development.

What conclusions may then be reached upon the concept of legal obligation in the context of Marxism. It is a trite assertion that Marxism has much of the appearance of a secular 'religion', certainly it has many sects by no means in harmony with each other. The religious analogy should not be pursued too closely and the direct comparison between classical Marxism and the thought of St Augustine, later development and Thomism, in the area of legal theory sometimes made is a massive over-simplification ultimately unjust to all the thinkers concerned. There is, however, a certain parallel which may usefully be observed. It will be recalled[24] that St Augustine considered human law to be a corrective measure which was meaningful only in the context of sin, whereas St Thomas Aquinas argued that sin imposed a coercive form upon law but that law itself is an expression of the nature of man as a social creature having no necessary connection with sin. In Marxist legal theory on the other hand, classical Marxists and Marxist-Leninists, including Pashukanis, saw law as a coercive instrument of class repression. The later concept of 'socialist legality' treats law as capable of being an inherent part of a socialist and classless society embodying its norms and not necessarily either coercive or repressive. In both cases, although from vastly different perspectives and with very different intentions, the change is less one of basic social perception than of selection of legal definition. The respective earlier phases involve an emphasis upon coercion as a definitive factor in the identification of law so that non-coercive norms are treated as *ex-hypothesi* non-legal. Such a view precludes any argument of obligation in the immediate context of law, although not necessarily in the context of the principles from which legal norms may have been derived. The later phase widens the perception of law so that the coercive repression of deviance becomes an incident of law but not its totality. In this state a legal theory must take account of obligation since obedience is claimed even in the absence of coercion because of the nature of the rules or the system concerned. In the Marxist analysis the communistic 'ordering of things' is patently normative but popular rather than institutionally coercive. If law is not defined in coercive terms then the supposedly 'a-legal' ordering of things may be argued to become an 'ideal'[25] conception of law as a non-coercive structure of social norms in the absence of dissension and deviance. The 'obligation' to obey is then derived from the perceived rectitude of the informing ideology. It is arguably implicit in this position that a norm contrary to ideological requirements would be necessarily repressive not of deviants but of the masses and would therefore perforce rely upon coercion alone for its effect. If this argument is accepted the quasi-naturalism of the Marxist theory of law becomes evident. How this line of development will continue remains to be seen but it is noteworthy that in theory at least something not far removed from this view appears in the claimed aims of law of this type. The achievement of non-coercive and non-repressive law in the Marxist context as elsewhere is far distant and the reality of the intention is questionable but it none the less appears to be the case that in some aspects of Marxist-derived thought a marked 'naturalist' tendency and a nascent concept of 'obligation' is to be found.

Notes

1. Hugh Collins, *Marxism and Law*, p. 38.
2. In Karl N. Llewellyn's sense of the phrase.
3. In the proper use of the term the Russian Empire was not and never had been 'feudal' in nature.
4. As a historical technicality it is arguable that Nicholas II was not the last Russian Tsar since the throne technically passed to his brother the

Grand Duke Mikhail who very sensibly, however, turned down the opportunity with haste.

5. The legal system in Russia at the beginning of the nineteenth century was a chaotic, and corrupt, mixture of traditional jurisdictions and arbitrary administrative practices. A major scheme of reform was proposed by M. Speransky under Alexander I (1801 – 25) but this ultimately came to nothing. Even the reactionary Nicholas I (1825 – 56) conceded the problem and authorised the inevitable and utterly inconclusive committee but again nothing was done. Eventually under Alexander II very radical change was made introducing a completely new system based upon an intensive comparative study of European legal systems. The reformed system was introduced in stages region by region and was never wholly completed, partly because of lack of resources and partly because of reactionary opposition, especially during the reign of the obscurantist Alexander III (1881 – 94).

6. Now available in a useful translation by Barbara Einhorn as *Law and Marxism, A General Theory* edited by Chris Arthur and published by Ink Links Ltd.

7. The examples selected by Pashukanis, *The General Theory of Law and Marxism*, Ch. 3. Petrazycki, now an undeservedly neglected theorist, was a pre-revolutionary Russian jurist who after 1917 fled to Poland and became Professor at Warsaw. He advanced a psychologically based theory of law in many ways similar to the ideas of the Scandinavian Realists. He was in fact a near contemporary of Axel Hägerström, the founder of that school of thought, but each appears to have been unaware of the work of the other. Kelsen was of course the propounder of the 'Pure Theory' of law and therefore an obvious target for Pashukanis and Marxists in general.

8. This is a painfully literal interpretation of social contractarian ideas; see Ch. 4, earlier.

9. See Ch. 3, earlier.

10. There is of course no reason why Pashukanis should not have chosen any definition of 'law' which he found satisfactory, so long as it is remembered that that is what has been done.

11. See Ch. 6, earlier.

12. Bhatia and Chung, *Legal and Political System in China*, Vol. I, p. 32.

13. *Basic Problems in the Civil Law of the People's Republic of China*, trans. US Joint Publication Research Service, No. 4879, p. 8. Cited by P. M. Chen, *Law and Justice. The Legal System in China 2400 BC – 1960 AD*, p. 85. (and note 85, Ch. 4).

14. Wife of Mao Tse-tung. Her name is rendered in a more modern transliteration as Jiang Qing.

15. The official account of this trial has been published as *A Great Trial in Chinese History* by the New World Press of Beijing (Peking).

16. Ibid., Preface by Professor Fei Hsiao Tung, Director of the Institute of Sociology of the Chinese Academy of Social Sciences and a member of the panel of judges at the trial, p. 9.

17. Ibid.

18. *A Great Trial in Chinese History*, p. 233.

19. Article 41.

20. Article 42.

21. See, *Main Documents of the Third Session of the Fifth National People's Congress of the People's Republic of China*, p. 128.

22. Published in English translation in 1949.

23. This is not of course necessarily a Marxist point. The dichotomy of language and function in law is a commonplace — for example, the language of contracts for transport by railway or bus implies a bargain whereas in fact there is no such thing. If one wishes to proceed from A to B by such a method one must take the terms imposed — no choice is offered.

24. See Ch. 3, earlier.

25. This is one of the more startling aspects of Marxist conclusions in view of the avowed anti-idealism of Marx himself.

7

Naturalism and Post-war Problem Cases

The problem of the iniquitous positive law is fundamental to legal theory. The problem lies both in identifying iniquity and in deciding what is an appropriate response to it. Reactions have varied from that of St Augustine, who saw iniquity as subversive of legal status, to that of the analytical positivists who dismissed the problem to a realm other than that of jurisprudence. Useful discussion of these issues calls for some practical example of iniquity as a basis for theorising. Selection of an example involves the making of a necessary preliminary value judgement, but one which unfortunately causes little difficulty in the making.

The horrors of the Nazi regime in Germany are well enough known to require no detailed description here but they afford an example of which may widely be agreed to have involved a great measure of evil. This is not, unfortunately, because the Third Reich was uniquely evil but because the comprehensiveness of its military defeat made the detail of its iniquity in letter and in operation readily available for our study. The collapse of Hitler's Germany left a major problem for the Allied powers, and for the Germans themselves, in seeking to unravel the after-effects of the regime. In particular how to nullify the bad effects of Nazi government without destabilising the entire social order, much of which was morally neutral or even 'good'.

In order to seek a definition of what was actually 'bad' about Nazi government and law, subjective abhorrence not being enough, one must first examine its theory and practice. Nazism was a specific development of Fascism in Germany and its legal theory, like much of its thought, was closely derived from that of Fascism and especially from Fascist Italy. However, Fascism had older roots within Germany itself.

G. W. F. Hegel (1770 – 1831)

Hegel was one of the most influential of post-Kantian philosophers in Germany. His thought contained the seeds of many subsequent theories, including, paradoxically, both Fascism and Marxism. Hegel saw history as a process in which each development is derived directly from its predecessor but differs radically from it. He produced a complex theory of thesis and antithesis leading to the Hegelian dialectic under which all apparent contradictions are resolved in the understanding of the total nature of things. The foregoing is a crude (even wrong) statement but the general implication of Hegelianism is that any given person or thing is no more than a 'moment' in the Absolute. Historical tradition becomes a summation of what went before but is productive of something utterly different from what preceded it or what will follow it. The practical product of this highly abstract system of thought was an exaltation of the state and its processes. Just as the historical moment was seen as a minor element in a larger process so the human being was seen as a subordinate unit of a larger totality, the state. Hegel, somewhat eccentrically, saw this as 'freedom'. He did this by proceeding from the idea that the individual is the product of the culture in which he is reared to the notion that self-knowledge, and therefore 'freedom' can only be realised by recognition of membership of a larger and evolving community having a being greater than that of the individual. Thus for Hegel, a free person is one who identifies himself with the duties and responsibilities with which he is invested by the highest social institution of all — the state. Hence Hegelian 'freedom' has much in common with the conventional perception of subservience. Hegel found his ideal in the Prussian concept of the state which he saw as a totality greater than the mere sum of its parts.

The implications for legal theory of such a philosophy are clear enough. The state as the expression of the historic consciousness of the nation is enabled to mould the law to its own end without any restriction in terms of the personal interests of the subordinated individual subjects.

Friedrich Nietzsche (1844 – 1900)

The tendencies of this type of thought were taken to their logical conclusion by Nietzsche, the adopted philosopher of Fascism and Nazism, although the adoption was not necessarily one which he himself would have sought. In fact Nietzsche's views do not of necessity lead to Fascism although they are undeniably anti-pathetic to any libertarian tradition. Nietzsche, like Hegel, was a historicist who saw social development as a continuous process of development. However, unlike Hegel, and unlike Marx, he did not believe that historical forces led to any inevitable improve-ment, nor did he especially admire the institutional state as such.

Like John Stuart Mill, Nietzsche had a horror of the mass or 'popular' mentality, but his views drove him in an opposite direc-tion from that of Mill. Mill's elitism was humane and tolerant, believing that others should be allowed to do as they wish without harm to others, so long as Mill was left equally undisturbed. Nietzsche, on the other hand, was highly intolerant and produced the doctrine of the 'Strong Man', the *Übermensch*.[1] This view led Nietzsche to a violent rejection of Christianity, which he claimed 'chained' the strong with its doctrines of humility and fore-bearance. For Nietzsche the lion should have used his strength to consume the lamb and the little child and thus perpetuated his mastery.

Nietzsche believed that there can be no ultimate compromise between the interests of the 'strong' and those of the 'herd', and that the former must properly prevail. He did predict, however, that the 'herd' mentality could lead to cynical social manipulation through deliberately created myths, which is of course precisely what happened under Nazism. Notwithstanding this, Nietzsche's theories, themselves often polemical exaggerations of Hegel-ianism, lent themselves all too easily to the vulgar pseudo-philoso-phical perversions which lay at the roots of Fascism and Nazism.

'Fascism' has unfortunately become a term of political abuse meaning nothing more than someone politically to the right of the speaker whom he does not like. The term did, and does, however, have quite a precise political meaning. Fascism was claimed to be a 'philosophy of action' which found solutions and fitted them into a theoretical context later on, if indeed at all. Fascist social concep-tions revolved around the corporate state which was a hierarchy of political and economic corporations which organised the detailed life of the people. The supreme expression of the social order was the nation-state itself with the Fascist Party at its head and ultimately personified in the chief ruler, be he Duce,[2] Führer or Caudillo. Here then we have a combination of Hegel and Nietzsche; the state as the most significant social unit symbolised in the person of a 'strongman' whose action, unlike that of an autocratic monarch, is subject to none of the restraints of a received morality or of religious belief or doctrine.

The expression in legal theory of this philosophy of state was, as might be anticipated, the very antithesis of any Diceyan notions of 'rule of law'. Society was to be governed by (strong) men and not by laws.

Basic Fascist attitudes led to a ready acceptance of certain ideas in legal theory associated in particular with the work of the French theorist Duguit. The basis of this teaching was that modern society depends upon efficient economic production which itself depends upon proper performance of economic and social duty by individuals. On this view law becomes no more than an instrument for securing the performance of those duties. Duguit taught that naturalist conceptions of 'validity' and 'justice' have no meaning and that the only test of law is whether or not it 'works' in promoting social and economic efficiency.

The appeal of this type of doctrine to the Fascist state is obvious. Under it, the law becomes purely the servant of the ends of the corporate state and not in any sense the definer of the parameters of its action.[3] As the Fascist writer, Alfredo Rocco, wrote in his exposition of Fascist doctrine: 'Superiority of ends, supremacy of force, these terms sum up the idea of the Fascist state.'[4]

In Italy the law was always subordinate to the decrees of the Duce, who, as Hitler was later to say of himself in Germany, indeed WAS the law. Truly a Fascist leader could be said to be 'nec sub deo, nec sub lege, sed sub homine' and would have gloried in the fact.

In Germany itself the advent of the Nazis produced the demise of any 'rule of law', as Wilhelm Shirer commented in his account of the Third Reich.[5] German jurists proclaimed that Hitler's will was law and this message was specifically enunciated by Goering in a speech to Prussian prosecutors on 12 July 1934. After the Reichstag fire incident Hitler proclaimed that he himself was the 'supreme judge' of the German people with power to order the death of anyone whom he wished.

There was no procedural or substantive certainty about Nazi law: if the state wanted to eliminate a person it could and would do so with or without the backing of any formal rule. However, despite the abandonment of the substance of legality, the Nazi regime did not actually abandon the outward forms of legal procedure. To make this point a formal (that is, positivistic) distinction between law and non-law must be drawn. In German jurisprudential terms the distinction is between *Recht* ('law' in a formal sense) and *Geist* (in effect, spirit; in the Third Reich, the ideology of National Socialism). Law as Recht depends upon a demonstrable pedigree, that is, law-making by some formal process, however minimal, leading to a knowable result which is traceable to some constitutional process. Geist, of course, knows no such procedural limitation.

What then was the 'pedigree' of Nazi law? Curiously, in view of his contempt for the Weimar Republic, Hitler never formally abrogated the preceding Weimar Constitution although he early and thoroughly subverted it. His decrees were based originally upon an Emergency Presidential Decree for public protection signed on 28 February 1933 by the aged President von Hindenburg under Article 48 of the constitution as a result of Hitler's persuasion as Reichskanzler. In addition there was an enabling power in a Reichstag Act of 24 March 1933 which gave Hitler powers of decree renewable at four-year intervals. There was of course no question that the Nazi Reichstag would dutifully renew such powers as and when required. The personal government of the Führer was thus, on paper, just about within the terms of the Weimar Constitution in positivist terms. The normal legal and judicial institutions continued in being. German courts had in any event no great record of independence and it was made very clear that there was to be none under the Nazis. The ordinary courts were subjected to much political pressure in their decision-making and indeed to arbitrary interventions and reversals when their actions displeased the Party or the Führer. The forces of the state, and especially the secret police — the Gestapo, were effectively above the law, and the latter was in fact formally stated to be so by the Gestapo Law of 10 February 1936. If doubt is felt as to this one may turn to a statement of Dr Werner Best, a deputy of the Reichsführer SS, Heinrich Himmler, to the effect that, 'As long as the police is carrying out the will of the leadership, it is acting legally.'[6]

If a dissident, such as for example, Pastor Niemöller, was lucky enough to be acquitted or leniently treated by a court, he could and probably would find himself arbitrarily seized and remitted to a concentration camp by the Gestapo without any possibility of appeal or redress and most certainly no question of habeas corpus.

The ordinary courts themselves were generally subservient, though not universally so, but even this did not satisfy Hitler. Special political courts were set up to deal in cases in which the party was especially concerned not to let the victim escape. These Special Courts (*Sondergericht*), created in 1933, dealt with 'political' crimes. The bare outward forms of procedure were maintained but represented a hollow sham. Defence lawyers required party licences and were of course careful not to defend too vigorously. (Some who were careless ended up in concentration camps until they amended their pleadings.) Before these courts, acquittal was a near impossibility. In 1935 a new political Supreme Court (the *Volksgerichtshof*) was set up, mainly to deal with treason cases. This court, which met in closed session, consisted of two 'legal' judges 'assisted' by five more drawn from the army, the SS and the Nazi party. Its decision was final. It rarely if ever acquitted and its normal sentence was death. It was this body which under its dreaded President, Roland Friesler, ratified the obscene execution of Count von Stauffenberg and his co-conspirators which was recorded on film and played for the entertainment of the ruler of Germany and his dinner guests.

Finally to ensure that no political deviation in legal administration was possible, the Führer himself took powers to quash or order criminal proceedings as he might consider appropriate and frequently exercised them.

The picture that emerges is of a state in which the bare shell of legality was maintained while the reality involved naked political intervention at every level and even beyond that various political institutions which acted quite outside the framework of any institution except the party and the immediate whims of its leadership. The shell of law itself retained the forms of Recht, perhaps barely sufficient to satisfy a positivist test. The arbitrary interventions in legal process and decision-making could only be Geist, and thus non-law.

After the collapse of the Third Reich some basis had to be found for an attempt to undo of the injustices perpetrated under the regime, at least in those cases which remained amenable to human intervention. This, so far as legal matters were concerned, inevitably involved a retrospective reconsideration of judicial or quasi-judicial action. There was also the wider issue of the criminality of the Nazi state as such to be considered. It is simpler, however, to commence with the narrower issues of specific cases of injustice.

The simplest response would be to take an extreme naturalist position and argue that the actions of the Nazi state were so fundamentally iniquitous as to render all its laws and administrative action void. This will not do, however. A simple denunciation of all Nazi law as void would wreak almost as much injustice as the original laws. Many civil marriages were celebrated in the Third Reich under Nazi administration. Nazi marriage law contained a number of racial provisions forbidding the marriage of 'Aryans' to non-'Aryans' and must thus have produced many injustices. None the less it is hardly a proper response to declare all German marriages between 1933 and 1945 void and thus many modern German citizens illegitimate. Many other such examples could be devised. It is, in short, necessary to consider each instance of claimed injustice upon its own merit and this involves the formation of a theoretical basis of assessment.

Such a theory could take one of two basic forms: (i) a moderate naturalist approach might follow a type of practical line, derived from general naturalism, that law-making power is held for certain types of purpose. Laws outside such purposes would be an abuse of the power and avoidable; (ii) a posivitist approach which would accept the shell of Nazi legality as valid but would seek deviations and abuses from and of the formally stated process which would then subsequently be impeachable as improper in terms of the purported Nazi system itself. Variations of both types of approach have been used at various times in both German courts and courts of the Allied powers.

The neo-naturalist approach

In *Oppenheimer* v *Cattermole* (conjoined with *Nothman* v *Cooper*)[7] the House of Lords was called upon to consider the validity of Nazi nationality law.

The appellant, Meier Oppenheimer, was born in Germany in 1896 and was thus by birth a German citizen. He was a Jew and was employed as a teacher in a Jewish orphanage in Bavaria. When the Nazis took power in Germany he was for a while imprisoned in a concentration camp but in 1939 he was allowed to flee to the United Kingdom leaving his property behind in Germany. A decree of 25 November 1941 provided, *inter alia*, that a German Jew who was usually resident abroad was automatically stripped of citizenship of the Reich and provided also for the confiscation of any of their property remaining in Germany, for the furtherance of Hitler's 'final solution'. The Second World War ended with the unconditional surrender of Germany on 5 May 1945 and the Third Reich ended formally with the dissolution of the rump 'government' of Grand Admiral Dönitz at Flensburg on 23 May 1945. Oppenheimer became a British subject by naturalisation on 24 May 1948. In 1953 the Federal Republic of West Germany awarded Oppenheimer a reparationary pension as a former employee of a Jewish religious institution who had suffered under Nazi persecution. He was awarded an additional pension upon reaching the age of 65 in 1961. Both pensions were paid out of German public funds.

Under double taxation conventions between the United Kingdom and West Germany made in 1954 and 1964[8] such pensions were exempt from United Kingdom taxation if the recipient was a national of both the United Kingdom and Germany at the time of receipt, but not if he was a national of the United Kingdom only. The central issue of the case was therefore the application of German nationality law to the appellant.

Three provisions were relevant: (i) the German Nationality Law of 1913; (ii) the 1941 Nazi decree; and (iii) the 1949 Basic Law of the Federal Republic of West Germany. The law of 1913 provided that a German who habitually resided abroad and had no abode in Germany lost his German nationality if he acquired any foreign citizenship without the written permission of the competent German authorities. The content of the 1941 decree has already been indicated. Thus on the face of the 1913 Act, Oppenheimer lost his German citizenship by his British naturalisation on 24 May 1948. If the 1941 decree was good law he lost his nationality on the date of its coming into force on 25 November 1941. In either case he would not have come within the exemptions of the Anglo-German double taxation conventions. However, Oppenheimer's departure from Germany in 1939 was not voluntary and while such forced departure was clearly within the contemplation of the 1941 decree it was not of primary contemplation in the 1913 Act.

Article 116(2) of the 1949 Basic Law of the Federal Republic of West Germany[9] provides that

> Former German citizens who, between 30th January 1933 and 8th May 1945, were deprived of their citizenship on political, racial or religious grounds and their descendants

137

shall be regranted German citizenship on application. They shall be considered as not having been deprived of their German citizenship if they have established their domicile in Germany after 8th May 1945 and have not expressed a contrary intention.

In 1968 the West German Federal Constitutional Court held that article 116(2) had been formulated upon the basis that the 1941 decree was void *ab initio* but that persecutees abroad who had acquired a foreign nationality would either have to return into residence or reapply for citizenship in order to reactivate their former German nationality. The effect of Article 116(2) on the 1941 decree was not actually, therefore, one of complete avoidance so much as one of retrospective repeal. It was left open to those affected whether they wished to take advantage of the repeal or not — that is in effect to say that West German citizenship would not be forced upon those who might well not want it.

Oppenheimer had neither returned to live in Germany nor reapplied for citizenship. He contended in the action (i) that the 1941 decree must be regarded as having been void *ab initio* and without effect in English Law, (ii) that the 1913 Nationality Law did not operate to deprive him of German citizenship in the actual circumstances of the case, and (iii) that he therefore remained a German citizen even though article 116(2) of the Basic Law would not operate to reactivate his citizenship had he lost it because of his non-residence and non-application therefore.

The House of Lords held that even if Oppenheimer's second contention was correct, he lost his German citizenship in 1949 by not applying for citizenship in the light of his UK naturalisation. The undoubted fact that he had a right to West German citizenship did not actually make him a German citizen — the implication being that he had repudiated German nationality by not applying for its restoration to him under article 116(2) between 1949 and the date of the action.

In the course of the judgement various matters such as the status of enemy legislation during the continuance of hostilities were discussed. However, the most important aspect of the case in the present context was the conclusion of Lords Hodson, Cross of Chelsea and Salmon (Lords Hailsham of St Marylebone and Pearson dissenting) that foreign legislation confiscating assets and cancelling citizenship on racial grounds is contrary to International Law and so grave an infringement of human rights as not to be recognisable as 'law' at all by an English court.

Lord Cross outlined this view, and its practical difficulty saying

> A judge should, of course, be very slow to refuse to give effect
> to the legislation of a foreign state in any sphere in which,
> according to accepted principles of International Law, the
> foreign state has jurisdiction.

He continued

> But what we are concerned with here is legislation which takes
> away without compensation from a section of the citizen
> body, singled out on racial grounds, all their property . . .
> and . . . deprives them of their citizenship. To my mind a law
> of this sort constitutes so grave an infringement of human
> rights that the courts of this country ought to refuse to
> recognise it as law at all.[10]

Lord Hodson concurred and remarked also that

> The courts of this country are not in my opinion obliged to
> shut their eyes to the shocking nature of such legislation as the
> 1941 decree if and when it fails for consideration.[11]

Lord Salmon also concurred and added that

> The comity of nations usually requires our courts to recognise
> the judisdiction of a foreign state over all its own nationals
> . . . to refuse to recognise legislation by a sovereign state . . .
> on the ground that [it] . . . was utterly immoral and . . .
> could obviously embarrass the Crown . . .
>
> England was at war with Germany in 1941 — a war which
> . . . was presented in its later stages as a crusade against bar-
> barities of the Nazi regime . . .
>
> I do not understand how . . . it could be regarded as . . .
> contrary to international comity . . . for our courts to decide
> that the 1941 decree was so great an offence against human
> rights that they would have nothing to do with it.[12]

Thus a majority of the House of Lords came as close as any
English court has to proclaiming, 'lex iniusta non est lex', at least
in relation to enemy alien legislation.

Objection was raised in argument that many inherently repugnant foreign laws have in the past been accepted as 'law' and that
the accepted rules of comity between states generally provide that
this should be so. The case of *Aksionairnoye Obschestuo A. M. Luther* v
James Sagor & Co.[13] was cited as an example. In that case a Soviet
decree expropriating a private timber yard, before the recognition
of the USSR by the United Kingdom, was recognised as valid
once recognition was accorded to the Soviet Union. Lord Salmon
said of the argument that 'The alleged immorality of the Soviet
Republic's decree of 1918 was different in kind from the Nazi
decree of 1941'.[14] He pointed out also that the fact that the Second
World War was raging in 1941 was a significant distinction
between *Luther* v *Sagor* and the instant case.

The decision in *Oppenheimer* v *Cattermole* and *Nothman* v *Cooper*
was actually made on different grounds and there was a distinct
suggestion that a deciding factor against the validity of the 1941
decree was that it contravened received Public International Law.
However, a majority of the court were prepared to condemn the
decree as valid on basic moral (strictly 'human rights') grounds.
This is essentially a naturalist approach to an example of repugnant Nazi legislation. Certainly the idea that 'this law is too
immoral ever to have been law' is substantially different from the
view apparently taken in 1968 by the Federal Constitutional Court
that effectively 'this law was immoral and it has therefore been
retroactively repealed'.

A quasi-naturalist view of such matters may also be found in
United States' jurisdictions. In *Leidmann* v *Reisenthal*[15] a Jewish
family resident in Vichy France agreed to give very valuable consideration in the form of jewellery to a person who undertook to
assist them in escaping from the Vichy regime and the danger of
Nazi persecution. Their apparent benefactor then defaulted
deliberately and decamped with the assets received in consideration. The family in fact succeeded in escaping from France by
other means. Later the victims found their plunderer in New York
and sued him for the return of the consideration. It was argued
that the action sought to enforce a contract which was illegal under
the relevant law of its formation, that is, that of Vichy France.
Hooley, J. held on this point that in the actual circumstances of the
case the victims were terrorised into acting as they did and that in
consequence the remedy of recovery would not be barred by the
prima-facie illegality of the original contract in the foreign jurisdiction. Here Nazi iniquity acted in effect to override a normal

procedural obstacle in an action for recovery of money had and received, that is, an unjust foreign law is no legal obstacle in domestic law. Again the objection to the Vichy law is clearly quasi-naturalist in form.

The quasi-naturalist approach of *Oppenheimer* v *Cattermole* and *Leidmann* v *Reisenthal* was of course adopted outside Germany by courts of the Allied powers. A somewhat different approach was taken in post-war Germany itself when the issue of Nazi abuse of law came to be faced.

The quasi-positivist approach

One of the first German cases to consider this problem unfortunately became the basis of rather misinformed jurisprudential controversy. The case itself occurred in 1950.[16] In 1944 the defendant, who wished to be rid of her husband, reported to the Nazi authorities certain derogatory remarks which he had made about Hitler when home on leave from the German army. On the basis of her evidence the husband was condemned to death by a military tribunal under statutes forbidding the making or repeating of statements inimical to the Third Reich[17] or the impairment by any means of the military defence of Germany.[18] However, after a period of confinement the man was in fact sent back to the front. He survived the war and in due course the wife and the judge who had tried the case were themselves brought to trial. The indictments were found under paragraph 239 of the German Criminal Code of 1871 for unlawful deprivation of liberty.[19] The Provincial Appeal Court found the judges to be not guilty because they had acted within the parameters of an existing law, albeit a highly iniquitous and cruel law. It seems, however, that the Provincial Court expressly remarked that the laws concerned were *not* a violation of natural law. The wife was guilty, however, because she had not been under a duty to inform and had in fact done so for personal and malicious purposes knowing that such action in such circumstances was 'contrary to the sound conscience and sense of justice of all decent human beings'. Such informing had apparently been regarded as 'immoral' by most Germans at the relevant time.

The brevity of the Harvard report unfortunately renders it somewhat misleading.[20] The case was used as the basis of a discussion between Hart and Fuller, apparently based upon the belief that the Provincial Court had declared the statute invalid, which in fact it had not. The case seems to have been based upon acceptance of the positive law as 'law', albeit a highly iniquitous one. Thus the judge who applied the law was not guilty. The wife who chose to abuse the law for an improper purpose was guilty of an offence. This approach is in essence positivist but the case cannot be regarded as very satisfactory. If a law is valid it is difficult to see how action within its terms can be illegal, however immoral the action may have been. If there has been an abuse of process then of course an offence might have been committed. On the facts of the given case this would seem to have necessarily involved the judge as well as the wife.

This approach was indeed adopted in another and more satisfactory case of almost parallel facts.[21] In this instance again the husband was a German soldier. At various times the husband made remarks critical of the Nazi leadership to his wife and after the attempt of 20 July 1944 to assassinate Hitler[22] he wrote in a letter to his wife that had Hitler been killed the whole 'dirty mess'[23] would be over. The wife handed this and other dangerous letters over to local party leaders. Eventually in 1945 the husband found that his wife was extensively unfaithful to him and after an altercation she again denounced him to the Nazi authorities. The man was arrested and brought before a court martial. The presiding judge, rather remarkably and much to his credit, informed the wife at the outset that the accused faced the likelihood of capital punishment and that she was not obliged to give the evidence under oath without which the legal case would necessarily collapse.[24] The wife, however, insisted upon giving her evidence and the accused was in due course condemned to death. He was not in fact executed but after a period of confinement, presumably because of the catastrophic military situation of the Reich, he was sent back to the front in April 1945. After the war the wife was charged with unlawful deprivation of liberty and attempted homicide. In 1951 she was acquitted by a court at Wurzburg on the basis that the court martial had been duly constituted and had acted within the parameters of the existing law, and that the wife had been entitled to believe in the lawfulness of her behaviour since she knew the man's conduct to have violated a then existing decree. The court apparently felt that a more 'highly educated' person would have been guilty for so acting in the same circumstances. It is difficult to see, however, why any advanced degree of formal education is called for in the appreciation of such a situation.

The case then proceeded to the West German Federal Supreme

Court in 1952. The Supreme Court quashed the acquittal and referred the case back to the Provincial Court. The reasons given for the Supreme Court decision are interesting. The Court opined that the question of the legality of the court-martial proceedings must be decided uniformally. Thus, if the proceedings were improper so far as the wife was concerned, they must also have been so in so far as judges, court officials and others were concerned. If they were lawful then the informer, unless guilty of perjury, could be no more guilty than anyone else in 'due' proceedings under a law, even though that law was iniquitous. However, the Court was of the opinion that it was not necessary to consider the validity or otherwise of the Nazi decree because the sentence was determined by an improper construction of the decree itself, deviating from the normal principles of German criminal law.

In the first place the decree was concerned with subversive remarks made 'in public'. This phrase was given a wide interpretation by Nazi courts coming to embrace at least any statement made with a view to its reaching the public, however intimate the original circumstances of pronouncement. The Supreme Court held that if the requirement of publicity meant anything at all, as it must be assumed to have done, it must have involved a *mens rea* of expectation of breach of confidence on the part of the husband. In the absence of such *mens rea* communication between spouses must surely have been 'private', if any cummunication could have been. As there was no evidence of any such *mens rea* in the case the Supreme Court concluded that the court martial must have erred in its finding of guilt and indeed proceeded upon an unlawful application of the decree. In addition there was a massive range of penalties under the decree ranging from one day's imprisonment to death. A range of penalties implies a graduation of seriousness of offence. Since communication between spouses must, at most, have been a very minor offence, application of the maximum penalty must appear to have been a grave abuse, or rather non-use, of judicial discretion. The sentence therefore was also non-lawful.

As the court martial had acted unlawfully, so, concluded the Supreme Court, had the wife in her procurement of the action. She was therefore guilty as an accessory before the fact to unlawful deprivation of liberty up to the pronouncement of sentence and of attempted homicide thereafter. The reasoning behind this conclusion appears to have been that the wife had intended to use what was widely known as an arbitrary procedure designed for ends of political terror as a means of eliminating her husband. In effect, therefore, she had the *mens rea* of a crime and the actual unlawfulness of the court-martial proceedings supplied the *actus reus* of the crime itself. A mistaken belief in the lawfulness of the proceedings was held to avail only a person who could not be expected to have an ordinary awareness of the arbitrary nature and likely outcome of the relevant proceedings. The point was also made that the court martial itself had urged the wife to withhold her evidence and she had insisted upon proceeding.

This is a positivist solution to the problem. The status of the Nazi law as 'law' is not discussed; instead procedural defects and abuses are relied upon to hold the proceedings unlawful upon a proper interpretation of their own terms. The malicious initiation of such unlawful proceedings is then itself readily found to be culpable. The solution is neat and admittedly avoids many difficulties. It must also be admitted that such abuses of process are not difficult to find in the records of Nazi courts. However, the argument implies that had the court martial proceeded within the clear parameters of a stated procedure and discretion, then the wife would not have been culpable. Were the case to arise, this could not seem any more satisfactory than would a blanket condemnation of all Nazi law to be invalid *per se*.

There is here a jurisprudential Scylla and Charybdis. In seeking to avoid the amoral or even immoral pitfalls of such slogans as '*gesetz als gesetz*'[25] one may fall foul of the important principle '*nulla poena sine lege*'.[26] If one is to avoid the trap of unfairly retroactive impeachment of conduct which, far from being an offence, was officially encouraged at the date of commission, while at the same time refusing to accept that any evil may be legitimated by mere formal enactment, some clear and knowable criterion of judgement is needed. This was the problem faced by the Nuremberg Tribunal itself in dealing with the surviving Nazi leaders and with the criminal actions of the German state itself.

The jurisprudence of Nuremberg

In considering the criminal actions of the Third Reich and its leaders and officials, the Nuremberg Tribunal was faced with a number of problems. So far as the state itself was concerned a superior system of positive law was readily available in the form of the rules of the Public International Law. These rules do of course contain a large measure of moral aspiration and this is especially so in regard to denunciations of aggressive warfare, such as that contained in the inter-war Kellogg-Briand Pact.[27] None the less the guilt of the German state could be judged according to a readily available standard. The guilt of individuals presented greater difficulties. The two basic questions calling for resolution on this level are:

(i) When does any prescription superior to national positive law require an act or omission of an individual which may very well be culpable under prevailing national prescription? In short, when does a law become so iniquitous that there is a retrospectively enforceable duty to disobey? This question must be given a clear answer if any subsequent preceedings are to avoid stricture under the *nulla poena sine lege* principle.

(ii) In circumstances such as those facing the Tribunal at Nuremberg (and also the Tokyo Tribunal), can the natural desire for vengeance on the part of a victor adequately be separated from considerations of justice?

The second question may be answered briefly. It is true that certain criminal acts of the Axis powers were paralleled by certain acts of powers on the Allied side and that these latter have gone uncondemned, other than in the record of history. However, the iniquitous conduct of the Nazis was on a remarkably vast scale and, amittedly by the virtue of military defeat, was unusually open to inspection. The presiding judge at Nuremberg, Lord Lawrence, was at pains to stress the judicial nature of the proceedings of the tribunal and the need to proceed slowly and carefully, keeping in mind the precedent for the future which was being set. Similar opinions can be found expressed by other judges of the court (Biddle (USA), Donnedieu de Vabres (France), and Nikitchenko (USSR)) and by, for example, Rudenko, the Chief Soviet Prosecutor. The answer to the second question so far as Nuremberg was concerned may on balance be taken to have been in the affirmative, though such a conclusion would have been far less tenable had the post-First World War 'hang the Kaiser' movement taken shape and borne fruit.

The first question presents much greater difficulties. It resolves itself into two major sub-issues: (a) the division of national responsibility and individual culpability; and (b) the application of the *nulla poena sine lege* principle (the breach of which was one of the major complaints against the legal administration of the

Nazis themselves).

So far as the first point is concerned, the defendants at Nuremberg were clearly a 'sample' of the suspected major war criminals. Many other cases were dealt with by other tribunals (for example, the Belson Tribunal) and later by German 'de-Nazification' courts, some defendants acquitted at Nuremberg being punished subsequently by such courts. The Defence relied in essence upon a denial of individual responsibility based upon a claim that culpable acts were 'acts of state' for which the state alone was responsible. A variant of this was the 'superior orders' defence in which ultimately total responsibility was thrust back to Hitler, who was of course by then conveniently dead. Such arguments could hardly, and indeed did not, stand in the case of principal actors such as Hermann Goering. However, they also failed in jurisprudentially more interesting cases such as that of Field Marshal Keitel. Keitel claimed to be a 'simple soldier' who had done no more than obey the orders of his Commander-in-Chief. The evidence showed, however, that while other high ranking officers had resisted Hitler, for example by non-implementation of orders and some had openly defied him,[28] Keitel displayed a complete subservience to the Führer which had kept him in place as Chief of Staff. The conclusion of Nuremberg was that an unlawful superior order has no power to bind the addressee (that is, lex iniusta non est lex) and one who implements such an order will be culpable for the results thereof as well as he who issued it. This version is now written into military manuals although its application on the battlefield seems potentially somewhat problematic. This sort of doctrine is clearly workable where there is in fact an exterior point of reference[29] which can determine the point at which unlawfulness is reached and, as in with many Nazi defendants, where a major voluntary element can be shown. Thus Keitel did not have to submit so totally to Hitler; he chose to do so and received the rewards and later the penalty of that choice. Similarly in the case, for example, of Sergeant Möll who volunteered for the duty of operating the gas chamber at Auschwitz. It is clearly impossible for an unlawful order to serve as a subsequent defence for a volunteer, but the position of one who is coerced into obedience raises a more complex issue which must be reserved for the moment.

Upon the second point, the issue of *nulla poena sine lege* raises immediately the question which 'lex' we are talking about. Public International Law is not a complete answer because international prescription *per se* has little to say of the treatment by states of their own citizens and many victims of the Third Reich were in fact German citizens. If the law concerned is simply formal positive law then, on the basis of *gesetz als gesetz*, no action under Nazi legislation could be impeached so long as it was duly carried on within its own terms of reference. If, on the other hand, the reference is to some system of supra-positive prescription then definition is required if anything more than a subjective retrospective denunciation is to be achieved. Any such definition must obviously include some minimum expectation of the nature and functioning of law.

Conclusion

The disentangling of Nazi law led to fierce jurisprudential debate. Within Germany, Gustav Radbruch made a notable contribution. Before the war he had held the positivist opinion that law was 'law' no matter how morally defective, and that disobedience on moral grounds was a matter of personal conscience not concerned with legal validity. After the war he somewhat changed his view and argued instead that a certain level of morality and compatibility with human rights were inherent in 'Recht' and that beyond a certain point of deviance from such standards the positive law would yield to the demands of justice and morality.

In his discussion (*inter alia*) of the early Nazi 'grudge-informer' case,[30] Hart argued that a court of law has no choice in the application of duly made positive law, however morally defective that law may be. Like Radbruch before his change of mind, Hart therefore saw the choice of disobedience upon moral grounds as a matter of individual conscience (and risk) not having any effect upon the formal status of law as Recht. Fuller took a different view[31] similar to the later Radbruch, arguing that the incorporation of iniquitous aims in formal law deprives it of the ability to command obedience as compared to its ability to force compliance. In this dichotomy is stated both the difficulty and a possible solution to the practical problem of the iniquitous law.

Where a system of positive law and/or its administration is iniquitous according to a generally received morality it is quite right and proper for courts of other systems to refuse to be swayed by its prima-facie influence upon subsequent causes arising before them. This was what was done in *Oppenheimer* v *Cattermole* and

Leidmann v *Reisenthal* and amounts to nothing more exceptional than a refusal to allow the 'comity of nations' doctrine to be used as a cloak for barbarism.

In dealing subsequently with the after-effects of an iniquitous system within the relevant jurisdiction a number of distinctions seem possible and necessary. These may for sake of convenience be enumerated as follows:

(i) Formal law as 'Recht' should not perhaps be retrospectively questioned for to do so is to engender an element of uncertainty potentially as inequitable as the evil itself. To this extent one may agree with Hart or even with pre-war Radbruch.

(ii) Where law as 'Recht' is subject to arbitrary interference on the basis of an iniquitous Geist, as in the Third Reich, then cases involving a departure from the formal letter of the law as Recht may subsequently be impeached in purely positivist terms without need for reference to naturalist principle. An example may be seen in the decision of the Federal Supreme Court of the Bundesrepublic discussed above.

(iii) Only where the law as stated, as opposed to merely as applied, was iniquitous or where an immoral act (for example, of a 'grudge-informer') was carried out according to the letter of a formal positive law does the crunch case for the application of naturalist doctrine arise. Assuming that the rule may properly be seen as immoral, one is faced, as Fuller perceived, with a choice of evils. One may either ignore manifest past iniquity or one may retrospectively impeach conduct which was formally legal at the time of its commission. This is a decision which can only be made in terms of the moral standards perceived to operate, but the decision need not by any means be presumed to be properly made against retrospective action.

(iv) The less controversial role of naturalism is perhaps forward looking in the alteration of bad laws for their future improvement and the remission of their effects for those originally penalised by them. To this role surely not even the most adamant positivist could object.

The final question, that of progress in the search for a definitive naturalist standard, will be further considered at length in the next two chapters.

Notes

1. The *Übermensch* in Nietzsche's conception was not the racist Nazi stormtrooper into whom the vision was perverted but rather a man mighty in mind and spirit such as he portrayed in his own poem, *Also sprach Zarathustra*.

2. Mussolini was never the Italian head of state since Italy remained a monarchy throughout the Fascist era.

3. There are here some analogies, which should not be overstressed, with Hobbes's *Leviathan* — once chosen, once supreme and all but irresponsible. Interestingly both Hobbesian social contractarianism and Italian Fascism were products of, and reactions to, social dislocation; for the former the horrors of civil war, for the latter the post-World War One economic collapse in Italy (and elsewhere).

4. Rocco, *La Transformazione della stato*.

5. W. Shirer, *The Rise and Fall of the Third Reich*, p. 333.

6. Ibid., p. 337.

7. (1975) 1 All E.R. 538.

8. See the Double Taxation Relief (Taxes on Income) (Federal Republic of Germany) Order 1955, S.I. 1955, No. 1203, Sch. Art. IX(1) and the Double Taxation Relief (Taxes on Income) (Federal Republic of Germany) Order 1967, S.I. 1967, No. 25, Sch. Art. IX(2).

9. Effectively the West German Constitution.

10. (1975) 1 All E.R. 567.

11. (1975) 1 All E.R. 557.

12. (1975) 1 All E.R. 571 to 572.

13. (1921) 3 K.B. 532.

14. (1975) 1 All E.R. 572.

15. 57 N.Y. St R (2d) 875.

16. The case is reported and commented upon in 64 H.L.R. (1950–1) 1005.

17. Law of 20 December 1934.

18. Law of 17 August 1938.

19. 'Rechtswidrige Freiheitsberaubung'.

20. The fuller account of the case is given by H. O. Pappe in an article entitled 'On the Validity of Judicial Decisions in the Nazi Era', 23 M.L.R. 260.

21. An account is given of this case by H. O. Pappe, 23 M.L.R., p. 264, *et seq.*

22. This was the plot led by Count von Stauffenberg.

23. Trans. H. O. Pappe.

24. As we have seen this would not necessarily have saved the accused from the arbitrary intervention of the Gestapo.

25. The law is the law, that is, no matter how evil it might be.

26. No penalty without law.

27. This was a pact to abandon war as an instrument of policy. It is now reflected in Article 1 and Chapters VI and VII (Arts. 33 to 51) of the Charter of the United Nations.

28. For example, Von Blomberg, who was dismissed, and Rommel who was compelled to commit suicide.

29. Here Public International Law.

30. H. L. A. Hart, 'Positivism and the Separation of Law and Morals', 71 H.L.R. (1958), 593–629.

31. Lon L. Fuller, 'Positivism and Fidelity to Law', 71 H.L.R. (1958), 630–73. For a more detailed consideration of the Hart/Fuller debate see Ch. 10, this volume.

8

The 'Rights Thesis' of
R. M. Dworkin

An interesting and important contribution to the modern development of legal theory has been made by R. M. Dworkin, the successor to H. L. A. Hart as Professor of Jurisprudence at Oxford. His theory of law, the main elements of which are contained in the essays published as *Taking Rights Seriously*, is an attack upon the classical positivists' analysis of law as a structure of rules. In that the theory introduces a form of value judgement into the concept of law, most particularly into the analysis of the process of adjudication, it may be said to have a quasi-naturalist tendency although this is a statement requiring heavy qualification.

Dworkin attacks the positivist analysis of judicial decision-making as an exercise in the identification and application of relevant rules in relation to the facts of a given case as an inadequate and incomplete description of the way in which law actually functions. He does not deny that in clear cases decisions will in fact be determined by the straightforward application of rules. He argues, however, that 'hard cases' — those upon the outcome of which informed opinion may reasonably differ — cannot be resolved by rules alone but are rather decided by reference to non-rule desiderata of which the positivist model takes no account but which are not a cover for 'judicial legislation'. In practical terms the nature of the claim is easily demonstrated. In cases of breaches of planning control an enforcement notice served upon a person allegedly committing a breach is required to give certain information specified in s.87(6) of the Town and Country Planning Act 1971, a purported notice which fails upon its face to give this information is a nullity. Such an issue is clearly determined by the application of a simple statutory rule. However, 'hard cases' upon Dworkin's analysis cannot be solved by rules alone since in such cases the application of rules is *ex hypothesi* in doubt and judges must necessarily make decisions by reference to non-rule desiderata of which the positivist rules model takes no account. The criticism which Dworkin makes of the positivist analysis leads him to two further basic questions; the distinction between legal and moral propositions and the issue of judicial 'legislation' in hard cases. Almost any 'hard case' will demonstrate the nature of the issues but the famous decision in *Donoghue* v *Stevenson*[1] will serve as well as any other. It was in this case that the modern doctrine of negligence initially took shape. The issue immediately in point was the liability of manufacturers to ultimate consumers in respect of defective products where, as here, the defect of the product could not have been known to the immediate supplier. The law as it stood before 1932 did not provide for such a liability. However, the House of Lords in *Donoghue* v *Stevenson* found for Mrs Donoghue who had suffered injury from the consumption of contaminated ginger beer, from an opaque bottle in which the immediate seller could not reasonably have been expected to detect the defect, against the manufacturer of the ginger beer. The basis of the House of Lords' judgements, and especially the 'good neighbour' speech of Lord Atkin, laid the foundation for the development of the modern, much more general doctrine of negligence. How did the House of Lords achieve this doctrinal development? A doctrinal common lawyer might try to argue that a doctrine of negligence was already implicit in the body of the law requiring only the appropriate circumstances for its elucidation from pre-existing authorities. This is an attempt to treat the common law as judaic-theory treats the Torah, as a body complete in itself requiring only understanding by later ages. This is historically as well as jurisprudentially ridiculous. The Torah is ascribed to the necessarily all-knowing will of God, the common law development through the accretion of pragmatic solutions to individual problems as they arose against the background of constantly developing doctrines. *Donoghue* v *Stevenson* was a step forward in this process and was certainly 'new' in that sense. The realistic positivist, committed to a rules model of law, would therefore be driven to argue that such cases do in fact represent a process of invention by judges, being in effect judicial legislation based upon reference to some extra legal set of norms or values. Positivists like Bentham have in fact concluded that judges, however much they deny it, do legislate although they argue that this is highly undesirable and should so far as possible be obviated, for example, by efficient codification. Is it necessary, however, to take either of these views? Dworkin argues that it is not and asserts that these forms of analysis are the product of an undue obsession with rules at the heart of the positivist case. If law did indeed consist only of rules then the fact of judicial 'legislation' in hard cases would be inescapable, but Dworkin argues that law in fact consists of more than rules and that the non-rule desiderata supply the solution in hard cases. This is the starting point for a difference theory of law based upon a model which is not bound to the concept of rules.

To remedy the incompleteness of the positivist rules model of law Dworkin advances a 'rights thesis' which takes account of factors beyond rules which judges necessarily consider in the adjudication of 'hard cases'. In his analysis he advances three broad propositions: firstly, that law consists of more than rules; secondly, that there is not an absolute division between propositions of morality; and thirdly, that in the process of adjudication, even in 'hard cases', judges do not legislate — the conclusion being that law does not consist simply of rules, as the positivists claim, but neither does it afford scope for the exercise of arbitrary judicial whim, as some of the realists[2] claim. Instead law involves the application of rules in a political and moral framework, the desiderata of which must be included in any complete account of the operation of law. Any such analysis inevitably reintroduces into the concept of law some of the moral elements which the classical positivists have been so anxious to exclude and carries important implications for the discussion of the development of naturalist theories of law.

To express Dworkin's basic proposition in another way, a theory of law which takes account only of rules and the means of their identification is an incomplete theory because legal decision-making actually involves a range of factors which cannot be categorised as 'rules'. These non-rule factors in adjudication are described by Dworkin as 'standards'[3] and are divided into two broad categories as 'policies' and 'principles'. He distinguishes between the two categories by reference to objective. A 'policy' is, '. . . that kind of standard that sets out a goal to be reached, generally an improvement in some economic, political or social feature of the community . . .'[4] whereas a 'principle' is '. . . a standard to be observed . . . because it is a requirement of justice or fairness or some other dimension of morality'.[5]

By way of example, that standards of road use should be improved is a 'policy' but the idea that 'no man shall profit by his own wrong' is a 'principle'. The distinction is important because the former relate really to the practice of legislation and are properly used by judges only in the interpretation of the legislative decisions embodied in statute whereas the latter are essentially part of an adjudicatory tradition upon which judges can draw in the determination of hard cases. Dworkin emphasises this point in his discussion of the important issue of judicial 'legislation'. Obviously, if Dworkin's thesis is to be maintained, 'standards' must be clearly and objectively distinguished from rules as phenomena.

The issue is not merely semantic and to maintain the distinction Dworkin advances two principal arguments, one relating to the mode of application of standards as compared to law and the other to the means of incorporation of standards into law.

As to the first point, the substantive content of rules and standards does not necessarily differ materially in type; there is no particular reason why the proposition that 'no man may profit from his own wrong' should not be made into a general statutory provision and it has of course come to be incorporated in various case precedents. The difference lies rather in the nature of the impact upon decision-making in adjudication. Dworkin argues that decisions upon the application of rules are essentially absolute in nature whereas decisions upon the use of standards in adjudication are relative in nature. Once a judge has decided that a claimed rule is relevant to the circumstances of a given case, the issue of its validity is an all-or-nothing question. An apparent rule is either valid as a matter of positive law or not:[6] there is no possibility of any indeterminate 'grey area' between the two conditions. This is the conclusion of the basic positivist analysis in which some formal criterion of identification, such as H. L. A. Hart's 'rule of recognition', will determine absolutely the 'legal' status of any given proposition. A 'standard', in contrast, cannot be assessed by reference to any such absolute criterion. The application of standards in adjudication is not determined by the absolute criteria of validity but by the relative criteria of 'weight'. By this is meant that the impact of a standard upon a case decision will be determined by comparison of the significance of that standard with other standards which may be relevant in the immediate context. Thus in contrast with the assessment of rules a judge may consider a standard to be relevant to a case before him without its having a

154

determinant effect upon the outcome because some other relevant standard may carry greater 'weight' in the particular circumstances. However, the fact that a standard is so outweighed in a case does not reduce or vitiate its force in future cases because of the relativity of the concept of 'weight' as compared with that of 'validity'. Upon this basis standards are argued to be a separate phenomenon of the adjudicatory process and one objectively distinct from rules.

The second important distinction made between rules and standards lies in the different form of their incorporation into, and displacement from, the body of the law. In the case of rules the genesis and extinction of provisions are fairly clearly marked. The time of the coming into force of a statutory provision is precisely indicated either in the text of the statute itself or by the provision of an appropriate commencement order and the moment of repeal or amendment is similarly evident, usually through the operation of subsequent statutory provision. The situation may seem less clear in respect of rules derived from case law in that such rules are not usually suddenly enunciated or abandoned but are shaped by lines of case decisions through the operation of the doctrine of precedent.[7] They may, of course, be sharply abrogated by decisions of the superior courts, in particular the House of Lords. None the less such rules are necessarily traceable to 'authorities' even if it may be necessary to study a line of several cases in order to elucidate a developed rule. Standards, in contrast, are not incorporated into the law through enactment or precedent, although they will almost certainly be reflected in both processes, nor are they overtly repealed or overruled. Instead they are developed, and possibly subsequently diminished, through what may best be termed a sense of adjudicatory propriety engraved in the professional traditions of the judges. Dworkin says of this that 'The origin of . . . legal principles lies . . . in a sense of appropriateness developed in the profession and the public over time. Their continued power depends upon this sense of appropriateness being maintained.'[8] In short, standards develop from a continuing sense of what 'ought to be' in the process of adjudication. No one originally created a rule to the effect that 'no man shall profit from his own wrong'; the proposition instead developed into a principle from a widely-held notion of what, in this instance, ought not to be, which has become embedded in the interstices of the structure of legal norms. As a standard waxes, so too may it wane if in changing social circumstances it seems to become less appropriate.

As decreasing reference is made to such a standard it may, unlike a rule, eventually become vitiated through desuetude.

How conveniently is the case made out for an objective distinction between rules and standards? From a classical positivist standpoint it might be argued that what Dworkin describes as 'standards' are actually no more than general principles which are to be found enshrined in a variety of specific rules. If this is the case then the process of adjudication in hard cases can be analysed as a process of selection among rule provisions rather than one of reference to jurisprudentially distinct 'standards', thus preserving the basic positivist rules model of legal processes. In fact the rules model of positive law need not be by any means so rigid as Dworkin tends to imply. The concept of 'validity' is of course absolute in the sense that there is no 'grey area' between the states of valid and not valid but the question of application is by no means so simple. In a common law jurisdiction the doctrine of precedent operating through the processes of application, distinguishing and overruling in case decisions, allows the subtle development of case rules on a pragmatic basis from instance to instance. The labyrinthine development of the doctrine of negligence following the decision in *Donoghue* v *Stevenson* is a good example of the subtlety and complexity of this process. It is clear, however, that the answers to all legal issues cannot be found in existing rules and here, in hard cases, the process of adjudication does seem to resort to desiderata beyond legal rules which are none the less a part of the legal framework. The conceptual separation made by Dworkin between rules and standards can be said at least to provide a less strained analysis of the realities of adjudication than a scheme requiring the imposition of a rules model upon the whole process.

Once the idea of standards as a distinct aspect of adjudicatory reasoning is admitted, undermining the model of law as a system simply of rules, the relationship of 'standards' to moral and ethical considerations requires discussion. This leads to Dworkin's second major proposition, that there is not in fact any absolute line of demarcation between legal and moral propositions — in further marked distinction from the classical positivist analysis of law. The introduction of the idea of 'standards' into the analysis of adjudication has the effect of introducing a form of value judgement into the concept of law, thus, in effect, bringing moral issues into the very area from which the positivists seek to exclude them. It is in this fundamental sense that Dworkin describes his theory as anti-positivist. Before it can be said, however, that his theory is therefore in any sense quasi-naturalist the nature of the 'moral' perceptions being introduced into the concept of law requires examination.

Through the introduction of the idea of 'standards' into the analysis of adjudication in 'hard cases', Dworkin asserts that the judicial determination of what the law 'is' in hard cases rests upon the perception of a form of communal morality and that consequently no absolute distinction can be drawn between what the law 'is' and what it 'ought' to be. It is here that Dworkin draws his crucial operative distinction between the two types of standard, 'policies' and 'principles'. The formal difference between the two has already been set out[9] but there is also a major distinction in operation. Policies are set out as community goals and as such represents a form of reasoning which is more legislative than judicial; resort to them in adjudication in 'hard cases' tends towards the idea of judicial legislation which Dworkin is at pains to deny. The argument is, therefore, that judicial decision-making in hard cases is guided not by the external 'policy' goals which are discernible in the legislative process but by perceptions of the implication of an ascertainable framework of 'principles'.

There remains the important issue of the derivation of the substantive content of Dworkin's principles. It is clear that they represent in effect a form of communal moral, or rather quasi-moral, perception as apprehended through the formal medium of legal practice. Such a formulation, however, leaves the door open to a species of naked populism in pursuit of which 'principle' can be equated with majority opinion in the sort of 'decibel morality' into which Lord Devlin's assessment of the relationship between law and morality tends to fall.[10] Dworkin argues that legal 'principles' are in fact quite distinct from the fluctuations of popular opinion and prejudice and represent a genuine framework of moral reference, the conclusions of which may not infrequently actually be unpopular in the sense of flying in the face of popular prejudice. In brief, it is argued that 'principles' are derived from that abstract moral framework which is institutionalised in the community's general political structures, most notably of course in its constitutional bases. As an example of what is meant, there may be a constitutional acceptance of the idea of freedom of association. As a principle such an idea will operate to protect groups who may be very unpopular and deserving of suppression in popular opinion. The proper limitation upon the operation of the principle is not the unpopularity of the group concerned but the actually damaging nature of its activities, because the community has in principle committed itself to the idea of a right to freedom of association. Dworkin himself expresses the point thus:

> The community's true morality is not to be discovered by taking opinion polls about particular moral issues. It is to be discovered by asking what answer to a particular issue would fit consistently with abstract rights to which the community has already committed itself in its constitution and institutional practices — such as rights to liberty, dignity, equality and respect.[11]

The 'rights' to which the community is thus said to have committed itself are the basis of Dworkin's 'rights thesis'. In essence the operation of principle in adjudication is said to depend upon recognition of community 'rights' which carry 'weighting' against the achievement of more specific political and social goals of the moment and which are evenly distributed among the members of the community.

The tenability of the 'rights thesis' as compared with the general implementation of 'policy' in adjudication is important if the imputations of uncertainty and judicial legislation are to be avoided. It might be argued that there is in practice a large overlap between arguments of policy and principle which tends to undermine a 'rights thesis' of adjudication. One may consider, for example, that appeals to 'policy' have been made in the development of substantial parts of the law of tort — this is the case with both the law of negligence and of private nuisance. Dworkin, however, argues that such examples do not destroy the 'rights thesis' in adjudication because in such circumstances references to 'policy' can be construed as arguments about the rights of all members of the community which can 'outweigh' other particular rights. He asserts that

> . . . appeals to . . . scarcity of some vital resource . . . as a ground for limiting some abstract right . . . might be understood as . . . [appeals] . . . to the complexity rights of those whose . . . just share of that resource will be threatened if the abstract right is made concrete.[12]

Again this may seem to be an argument which is more semantic than substantive but in fact it is not. The idea of a framework of competing rights to be 'weighed' one against another provides a tenable description of a process of adjudication based upon ascertainable jurisprudential criteria as compared to one in which *ad hoc* solutions are found upon a basis of fluctuating policy considerations.

Dworkin's 'rights thesis' leads to a general argument upon the nature of adjudication which properly involves the balancing of competing claims upon what is in essence a principle of 'fairness', the derivation of which requires a general philosophy of law and society. To demonstrate the nature of the ideal judicial philosophy Dworkin poses the perfect judge — Hercules. This possesses in the highest degree the intellectual skills of both lawyer and political philosopher and is thus perfectly fitted to adjudicate. Faced with a case in which a range of conclusions is possible Hercules actually has a variety of available options in his decision-making, indeed this is the case *ex hypothesi*. In making his determination Hercules is not guided, however, by subjective inclination or by considerations of 'policy' exterior to the law concerned.[13] He will instead make his decision by balancing the available conclusions against each other in the context of the philosophy of law which underlies the institutional structures of his society, adopting that result which is most readily explicable in terms of that philosophy. Dworkin compares the situation of a judge in a 'hard case' to that of a referee in a game who is called upon to resolve some issue not catered for by the published rules of the game.[14] The referee in such a situation can only make his determination by asking himself whether the situation is one which can be permitted as being compatible with the continuing viability of the concept of the game itself. Similarly the judge deciding a 'hard case' must find an answer which most closely concords with the legal and institutional philosophy of his society.

Dworkin argues also that even in the adjudication of 'hard cases' judges do not 'legislate'. This has been, and continues to be, a bone of contention in the theory of adjudication which raises major problems both in relation to the nature of the judicial function *per se* and in the wider context of the relation of the judicial task to the democratic process. It has already been remarked[15] that on the one hand the common law may be treated as a repository of legal wisdom, elucidated originally by the judges from the custom of the realm, in which modern judges can 'discover' solutions without need for judicial 'legislation', or, on the other, it might be accepted that judges do in fact 'legislate' in producing solutions to new problems. This latter has been the positivist position since Bentham's day and indeed seems 'obvious' in light of the artificiality of the argument for the inherent completeness of the common law. Whilst admitting the 'fact' of judicial 'legislation' positivists generally, and most certainly Bentham, have tended to deplore it as a usurpation of the legislative function by persons not elected or called to that role. Bentham hoped that the perfection of codification, the apotheosis of the rules model, would pursue the legal process of this undesirable phenomenon. This view depends upon an identification of law with rules so that law can only develop through the devising of new rules. Dworkin's denial of the rules model through the analysis of law as comprising absolute standards enables him to deny that judges 'legislate' without having to resort to ideas of the seamless web of the common law.

The argument in essence concerns the nature of judicial discretion. The case for the existence of judicial legislation depends upon the acceptance of a judicial discretion to select among available solutions the problems in a more or less arbitrary manner. Dworkin argues that judges are not vested with such a discretion because there is a 'right answer' to all cases, even 'hard cases'. Judges do of course make judgements in their determination of issues but this is termed by Dworkin a 'weak' discretion, different in type from the 'strong' discretion of personal selections among alternatives. An analogy is drawn with moral judgements, a reasoned effort has to be made to find a right answer but this does not imply an arbitrary choice of options. By reasoning from the whole framework of law judges are argued to find 'right answers' to issues in litigation without having to resort either to undemocratic judicial 'legislation' or to claims for the inherent comprehensiveness of the common law.

Dworkin thus makes a strong case for a model of law which is not defined solely in terms of rules, which embraces a form of community morality and which permits the resolution of new problems by judges without recourse to undemocratic judicial 'legislation'. This is certainly a theory of adjudication which undermines some of the assumptions underlying the classical positivist appreciation of law. However, the impact of Dworkin's work upon the central concerns of naturalist theory is rather less obvious.

The introduction of 'standards' into the concept of law and the analysis of the process of adjudication embedded in the 'rights thesis' certainly brings moral issues into the basic model of law. The manner in which this is done tends to limit the actual impact of moral criteria upon the assessment of law. According to Dworkin's analysis the actions of a legislature are properly guided by arguments of 'policy' and thus shaped by what may properly be termed 'political' considerations, whereas the judicial resolution of 'hard cases' is governed by the substantively different arguments of principle which relate to a general communal morality. It is clear also that judicial assessment of the balance between competing 'rights' derived from the communal morality of law involves the comparative consideration of the 'rights' of individuals as against those of the mass of other individuals, which may reasonably be considered to be 'collective rights'. Such an analysis clearly carries the seeds of naturalism within it. Before the 'naturalism' of Dworkin's theory can be accepted, however, the nature of these 'rights' and of the morality which underlies them requires discussion. The morality of Dworkin's concept of law is a communal morality which informs the expectations entertained of the institutional structures of the society concerned. We are told that Hercules, the ideal judge, in making determinations in 'hard cases' balances the available conclusions, one against the other, adopting finally that which best concords with the legal philosophy which underlies the institutions of his society. This philosophy embodies moral perceptions and, in particular, the *rights* which are embedded in the constitutional perceptions of the society concerned. It is time, Dworkin argues, that these moral perceptions are not a populist decibel morality in the sense of being the slave of what may be popular from time to time; they do, however, derive from the moral-constitutional assumptions of the particular society. What follows if in a given society the basic assumptions are objectionable in terms of general morality, a society, for example, which has historically institutionalised genocide as a means of conserving the position of a dominant group?[16] What, in short, is the nature of the 'rights' which are to be protected by Hercules?

Dworkin's response to this is to underline the distinction between those things which a citizen has a 'right' to do and those things which it is merely right for a citizen to do. Clearly there cannot be a jurisprudentially recognisable right to do all those things which it may be commendable for an individual to do. Dworkin himself gives the example of a prisoner of war who may act commendably in attempting to escape but has no basis of justifiable complaint if the detaining power prevents him from doing so.[17] This is actually an example derived from rather extreme and unusual circumstances, but it does serve to demonstrate with clarity the nature of the distinction being made. This is said to be something which it is right to do in the weaker sense of that term. In contrast, a *right*, in the stronger sense of the term, held by an individual means that that person should not be impeded by the state in his exercise of it unless some stronger claim intervenes. This raises, from the point of view of naturalist legal theory, the central issue of legal obligation. What is the position of the citizen whom the law seeks to deprive of a *right*? Dworkin's response to this issue is interesting but not in the end entirely satisfying.

He presents his argument in the context of military conscription in the USA at the time of the Vietnam war and the dissenters who sought illegally to evade the draft. The law of the United States is founded upon certain moral presumptions which are in large measure enshrined in the Constitution and thus guarded by the jurisdiction of the Supreme Court. According to Dworkin the argument that laws must always be obeyed founders upon the fact that the demands of the law, and their limits, are not necessarily certain and where there is dispute upon the constitutional legitimacy of a legal demand, the matter remains an issue for final determination. The dissenter may thus question the obligation purported to be put upon him by the law and the Supreme Court can, in the final analysis, determine the validity of the law concerned in terms of the legal and moral base of the Constitution. If this final determination upholds the constitutionality of the legal provision to which the dissenter objects then his continued refusal to comply with its demands becomes formally illegal. Even at this stage, however, it is argued that the courts should take account of the moral position of the dissident through tolerance and lenience of treatment. If dissent should continue upon a large scale, notwithstanding determination by the Supreme Court and the manifestation of reasonable leniency and tolerance by the courts thereafter, there is obviously a significant dichotomy between law and the social or political expectation of a part of the population. In that event there arises the political issue of the desirability of legislative change to resolve the dichotomy. Where precedent rather than statute is involved in such a dichotomy between law and expectation the courts are of course afforded a greater degree of capacity to take account of *rights* within Dworkin's analysis.

There are a number of important points made here, some of which are of greater general significance than others. In the context of Dworkin's immediate discussion the United States' Constitution is taken as the formal enshrinement of the aims and moral perception of the political community of the United States with the US Supreme Court as its arbiter and guardian. The line of argument based upon the determination of the validity of laws under a Constitution founded upon certain moral perceptions is an important comment upon the institutionalised quasi-naturalism of a legal system such as that of the USA. It is, however, obviously of limited value in the more general context of legal systems which do not operate upon the basis of a written Constitution and machinery for appropriate review of laws. The ultimate argument extending the discussion into the issue of the desirability of legislative change, where there is a gross dichotomy between significant levels of expectation and legal provision, touches upon a most important point. The formal processes of law, as Dworkin cogently argues, take some account of the moral perceptions of the community in their functioning. They can, however, do so only within certain clear limitations. Once the formal limitations of the legal process have been reached in a particular instance the issue of the obligation to obey ceases to be a formal issue for judicial determination and enters into the public and 'political' arena of debate upon the desirability of changing legal provisions in order to meet new or altered expectations. At the level of judicial determination 'standards' in adjudication and the enshrined morality of the Constitution are argued to produce a right answer in terms of the general 'rights' upon the recognition of which constitutional/moral structure of the society rests. The argument for legal change is advanced where in fact the 'wrong' answer seems to have been delivered by the formal legal processes. These arguments raise again the fundamental question of the quality of the morality by reference to which these issues are to be resolved.

The 'morality' in question is the adopted and institutionalised moral and political perceptions of the community concerned; what, again, if the 'morality' so adopted is completely unconscionable? Do we not then return to the basic problems of 'decibel morality', or are there rights capable of advancement even in the absence of an institutional base? This is an important question which divides what may be termed institutionalised naturalism from substantive naturalism. The issue, put shortly, is this: how does the citizen's obligation to obey the law function when the formal processes of the system have confirmed an unconscionable demand made upon him or her and the political system cannot or will not react to that fact? The inherent morality of the system has been exhausted and the personal morality of the dissident remains opposed to the demands of the law. On the face of it one is here left with a choice between unpalatable alternatives by way of conclusion. Either the law's demands are essentially unqualified by the quality of its moral base, or the citizen is under obligation to obey only those laws which, in the ultimate analysis, he or she finds morally congenial. Does Dworkin's argument allow for an escape from this dilemma in the form of a discernible moral limit to the obligation to obey the law. Within the framework of his analysis Dworkin argues that there is indeed such an answer to be found.

In his argument Dworkin centres upon the idea of liberty. He concedes the conventional wisdom that in the broader sense all legal provision is an infringement of liberty in the sense of constraining options in the choice of conduct. The extent to which liberty may properly be restrained, which is the same basic issue as the question of the limitation of obligation, is again founded upon the idea of rights, here in relation to the formulation of policy. He makes a distinction between personal and external preferences in the context of the utilitarian formulation of policy. The former is a preference for the assignment of goods or opportunities to the individual, the latter is the reverse and states a preference for the assignment of goods or opportunities to others. In a truly utilitarian system it is argued that external preferences must be excluded because otherwise individuals will suffer constraint of liberty not only because their personal preferences have suffered in competition with those of others but also possibly because their goals and aspirations are despised by others. In actual practice it is hardly possible to exclude external preferences in this way in any viable process of policy formulation. The only way of avoiding the difficulty is to concede the existence of basic political rights which protect the individual from the undue influences of external preference policies. This is the basis of Dworkin's general theory of political rights, which is stated thus:

> The concept of an individual political right . . . is a response
> to the philosophical defects of a utilitarianism that counts
> external preferences and the practical impossibility of utili-
> tarianism that does not. It allows us to enjoy . . . political

democracy, which enforce[s] . . . unrefined political utilitarianism, and yet protect[s] the fundamental right of citizens to equal concern and respect . . .[18]

This concept of political rights as essentially the definitive limitation upon restraints of individual liberty, which policy formulation through arguments of naked utilitarianism might otherwise demand, is of course important. It is certainly the case that personal and external preferences cannot in practice satisfactorily be isolated one from the other. It is also the case that in a utilitarian policy-forming process some dividing line between proper and improper policies is called for, such as that afforded by the concept of 'rights'. At the same time the notion of a 'fundamental right . . . to equal concern and respect' must surely be taken beyond the role of safety device within a basically well-intentioned utilitarian decision-making process. If policy lines leading to a breach of political rights result from calculation rather than from inadvertences of utilitarian decision-making the question of the obligation to obey law must arise in a specially acute form. No doubt the solution to such problems does ultimately lie in the political rather than the institutional legal sphere but this extreme form of the question of legal obligation does not centrally concern Dworkin's thesis.

What then is the significance of Dworkin's analysis in the context of the development of naturalist legal theory? His contribution is both interesting and important but its significance from the naturalist viewpoint should be neither misunderstood nor over-emphasised. One of the most important aspects of Dworkin's thesis is his convincing demonstration of the non-autonomy of rules even within the operation of a legal system through the introduction of 'standards' into the concept of law. This certainly underlines the restrictions of the classical positivist analysis of law although it does not actually demolish that analysis. It should rather be seen as broadening the analysis of the operation of positive law in an area of jurisprudential study which inevitably rests upon a broadly positivist base. Once the concesssion has been made that standards, and especially principles, play a significant role in legal decision-making, the absolute division between formal rules and moral arguments advanced by the classical positivists seems to crumble. However, it must also be said that the morality which is thereby introduced is very much a formal and institutionalised morality evidenced at the highest level by the constitutional guarantee of 'rights'. It must not be forgotten that a

Constitution, even if it enshrines communal moral perceptions, is itself a positive law and subject to the same moral questions as all other positive laws. In the end Dworkin's account of the role of moral principles and rights in law and law-making, and in particular in adjudication, concerns the particular political and moral assumptions about law of a given society, and does not concern any form of external moral judgement upon the system as a whole.

In this sense Dworkin's thesis is at one remove from the central naturalist concern with the moral and ethical evaluation of positive law since he is concerned more with an institutionalised internal morality within the formal processes of law themselves. The real importance of Dworkin's work lies in the demonstration of the role of a form of moral perception in the practical working of a functioning system and the limitations of a rigid and exclusively positivist analysis. The analysis of the position of the dissident in the context of the obligation to obey relies considerably upon the idea of a Constitution involving powers of judicial review of law-making from a constitutional viewpoint and is perhaps a strong argument for the adoption of this form of arrangement — this being upon the assumption that the defence of the judiciary against the charge of non-democratic judicial law-making is accepted. In legal systems which do not have such a constitutional system the point of exhaustion of formal review processes is reached much more quickly by the dissident and, although the arguments for tolerance and leniency on the part of the courts hold good, the question of the basic political rights of the individual arises therefore much sooner. The idea of these basic rights phrased in terms of 'equal concern and respect' and conceived as an inherent limitation upon the exercise of collective power over individuals is of course very much a naturalist concept and one that is central to the practical importance of naturalism in the modern world. It is notable, however, that these ideas lie outside as a stage beyond the Dworkinian analysis of the legal process as such.

The implications to be derived from this discussion are relatively staightforward. Naturalist thought is essentially concerned with the moral evaluation of positive law and with the quality of the obligation which it imposes upon those subject to it. The basic rights advanced by Dworkin contribute to this area of debate directly. The analysis of the legal process and adjudication is not central to naturalist thought as such, nor properly understood, should it be seen as one of those theories which seeks to approximate naturalist to positivist thought. However, it does supply an important insight into one of the major questions arising from a naturalist analysis — that is, the issue of the practical application of moral evaluations of positive law. What may be termed the internal morality of a legal system, which is the main subject of Dworkin's moral argument, may from an external viewpoint be either 'good' or 'bad'. It is after all perfectly possible to conceive of a system of positive laws founded, *inter alia*, upon the premiss that genocide or some other evil is good and just and true — this would be part of the internal 'morality' of the system but would hardly make the laws 'good' or the source of full moral obligation to the exterior moral analyst. Where, however, a society is in principle committed to a legal order concordant with general morality, Dworkin's analysis, indicates the way in which the moral structure of the law might in practice be maintained.

The basic rights which form the ultimate limitation upon proper formation of policies and development are an inherently naturalistic concept which, like all such, necessarily stand outside the system as a criterion of evaluation. In the end it must seem that the form of moral analysis involved in the basic naturalistic thesis cannot be made a formal part of the positivist legal system but operates rather as a means of analysis of it, independent of the system's own internal structures. From the naturalist viewpoint Dworkin's theory is a valuable insight into the way in which the law uses and incorporates moral perceptions in the search for a right answer within its own terms. It does not, and does not seek to, supply a final answer to the nature of the ultimate moral quality of law. It is, in short, an indication of the way in which naturalist perceptions might be absorbed by a legal system; it is not for the most part a naturalist perception in its own right but an admirable re-analysis of the formal nature of positive laws. The modern development of the overt forms of naturalist analysis are discussed in the next chapter as a properly separate area of consideration.

Notes

1. [1932] A.C. 562.
2. This is especially a feature of the work of the more radical members of the American Realist school represented by, for example Jerome Frank.
3. In his analysis Dworkin breaks down standards into the sub-categories of 'policies' and 'principles'. He also tends to use the word 'principles' as a generic term conterminous with standards except where the context demands the more specific usage. In this chapter the word

'standard' is used generically and the word 'principle' is used specifically except where otherwise indicated.

4. Dworkin, *Taking Rights Seriously*, p. 22.

5. Ibid.

6. The scope of its application may well be subject to development, however, through the operation of the doctrine of precedent, in the process of consideration influenced by standards.

7. This applies of course to the practice of jurisdictions in the common law tradition although there is a parallel but informal process, which may to some extent also be seen in the practice of civilian jurisdictions.

8. Dworkin, *Taking Rights Seriously*, p. 40.

9. See notes 4 and 5, earlier.

10. See Lord Devlin, *The Enforcement of Morals* and H. L. A. Hart's reply in *Law, Liberty and Morality*.

11. Dworkin, *Taking Rights Seriously*, pp. 177 – 8.

12. Dworkin, *Taking Rights Seriously*, p. 100.

13. Where Hercules as the perfect judge is construing a less than perfectly drafted statutory provision he must of course advert to the issues of policy.

14. The particular example selected is the use of 'psychological' facts to disturb an opponent in a game of chess. See Dworkin, *Taking Rights Seriously*, pp. 102 – 5.

15. See earlier.

16. This of course treats the law of the state as a closed system without reference to Public International Law, to which any such system would obviously be contrary.

17. This is indeed the position under the Geneva Conventions. The 1949 Geneva Convention relative to the treatment of prisoners of war provides by Article 91 that a prisoner of war who succeeds in escaping from the territory shall not be liable to punishment upon subsequent recapture. Article 92 restricts penalties for unsuccessful escape to disciplinary sanctions only.

18. Dworkin, *Taking Rights Seriously*, p. 277.

9

Modern Developments in Naturalist Legal Theory

The period from the second quarter of the nineteenth century to the middle of the twentieth century was one in which, at least as far as Anglo-American jurisprudence was concerned, an often rather uncritical positivist consensus predominated in jurisprudential thought. The consensus did not of course go entirely unchallenged during this period but in general it was felt to satisfy admirably the practical requirements of the lawyer's appreciation of the law without need for the introduction of the extraneous elements which naturalism emphasises into any overall concept of law. More recently jurisprudential debate has again widened both in the development of naturalist thought *per se* and also in the working out of innovative modern analysis of law such as Dworkin's 'rights thesis' discussed in the preceding chapter.

A major impetus to the renaissance of naturalist thought in modern jurisprudence was given by the problems associated with the rise of Fascism in Europe in the 1930s and, in particular, with the revelation of the full horror of the abuse of positive law in Germany under the Nazi regime at the end of the Second World War in 1945. To some extent these issues merely raised in a new and more vituperative form the old and rather sterile so-called Naturalist/Positivist debate with each party imputing to the other a jurisprudence conducive to the abuses of Fascism or indeed of Stalinism. However, much of the discussion was upon a much more constructive plane and focused upon issues which are of central importance in the present context. The question of the nature of law and the obligation to obey law generated by the abuse of legal processes in an iniquitous state revived consideration of naturalist principles in Western jurisprudence to an extent which may reasonably be said to justify the use of the phrase 'naturalist revival'. Modern naturalist thought has inevitably pursued a number of different approaches to the central problems. Some have involved a more or less straightforward restatement of classical principles, as with John C. H. Wu's presentation of the Thomist argument.[1] Others have sought to introduce naturalist concepts into a new approach to the understanding of the formal working of laws while some seek to present a more classical naturalist argument in a developed and modern form. In the context of the present discussion two modern theorists are of particular significance, each representing one of these two categories, being Lon L. Fuller and J. M. Finnis.

Lon L. Fuller and procedural natural law

Lon L. Fuller (1902 – 78) was Professor of General Jurisprudence at Harvard from 1948 until his retirement in 1972. He sought a naturalist principle in the procedures of law-making rather than in the substantive content of laws, rejecting the positivist analysis advanced by H. L. A. Hart — but at the same time not seeking to advance claims to the evaluation of law by reference to substantive exterior criteria. This approach led him to advance his theory of 'procedural natural law', which is principally contained in his important work *The Morality of Law*. The content of the book was originally delivered in 1963 as part of the William L. Storr's Lectures at the Yale Law School. The work was published in 1964 and reissued in a revised and extended form in 1969. Fuller commenced from the proposition that debate upon the moral nature of law has commonly been obscured by a failure to make a basic and obvious distinction between two forms of morality, which he termed the moralities of 'aspiration' and 'duty'. The distinction between the two forms of morality is presented as that between a morality which sets out a prescription for the most excellent form of human life and one which lays down the essential basis for a viable social order[2] — the former being strictly an 'aspiration' to maximum moral achievement, the latter a prescription of minimum standards, shortfall from which is actually a delict. Fuller does not claim this to be an original thought but he considered the point to require re-emphasis in order to advance the proposition that law is properly associated with the morality of duty rather than with any morality of aspiration. This is actually rather an obvious point and is essentially related to the ancient question of whether it is a function of law to seek to make people 'good'. As Fuller suggests by implication, it is hardly possible for positive law to prescribe for the actual achievement of moral excellence, but it is arguably a proper legal function to set forth the minimum social order within which aspirations to moral excellence may be pursued.

From the morality of duty Fuller turns to the nature of the law-making enterprise and, in particular, the ways in which that enterprise might be defectively pursued or indeed fail outright. His analysis related to the structure of positive laws and sets out certain minimum standards which must be satisfied if a rule is properly to be considered 'legal' in nature. These are set out in a negative form as a list of eight forms of defect which weaken or even vitiate the claim of a system of government to produce rules entitled to 'legal' status. These are in summary, (i) failure to make rules at all, (ii) failure adequately to promulgate rules to those subject to them, (iii) making rules with retroactive effect, (iv) making incomprehensible rules, (v) making rules which are self-contradictory, (vi) making rules with which compliance is impossible, (vii) amendment of rules upon a scale destructive of certainty of prescription and (viii) contradiction between the stated content of prescription and the practice of implementation. Failure in all these departments or even absolute failure in any of them is argued by Fuller to amount to a failure to produce 'law' at all. This is what is meant by a 'procedural' natural law.

Three comments may immediately be made upon this approach to the assessment of law. In the first place the assumption is made, as it is by many legal theorists, that law can be simply analysed as a system of rules. Rules do of course play a major, even the principal, role in the practical operation of law in most technologically developed societies. Even in such societies, however, as Dworkin has cogently argued,[3] a model of law based exclusively upon rules is not adequate. In so-called 'primitive' societies in which social prescription is largely a matter of custom and consensus, 'rules' in the positive legal sense play a much smaller or even no role, and to exclude such societies from the realm of legal theoretical study may be convenient but is none the less arbitrary and, in the end, unsatisfactory. Secondly, absolute failure in any of the eight categories listed by Fuller seems rather unlikely so long as a viable apparatus subsists — in which case it is difficult to imagine how law-making so defined in practice fails. Thirdly, the eight defects in the law-making process considered by Fuller are all essentially concerned with the clarity and predictive value of the prescription of purported 'legal' rules. The nature of the content of such rules does not enter into consideration so that within the terms of the theory an iniquitous provision conforming with the eight procedural criteria has an unqualified claim to respect as 'law'.

These criticisms are actually somewhat unfair to Fuller, who does take account of the second and third of these points. In reality a legal system is much more liable to manifest radical defects in two or more of Fuller's procedural departments than complete failure in any one of them. This raises the difficult question of relative defectiveness; at what point, if any, do cumulative defects in respect of a number of the eight procedural criteria vitiate the claim of a system to produce 'laws'? Fuller responds to this problem by reference to his original distinction between the moralities of aspiration and duty. At some point upon a moral scale the two moralities meet and the nature of the moral prescription changes at that point from the imposition of minimum standards to the advancement of criteria of excellence. Just as this may be used to distinguish the procedural morality of law from a substantive morality, so, Fuller argues, this is true within the procedural morality. In fact the change from a morality of duty to a morality of aspiration does not occur at a clearly defined point; inevitably the one shades into the other in a 'grey area' in which debate upon the nature of moral propositions, as between duty and aspiration, is possible. This allows for a fairly broad area of discussion in which a legal system may manifest failings in terms of procedural natural law while none the less succeeding in producing 'laws'. It is probably the case that most legal systems actually fall within this grey area of assessment, being neither procedurally excellent nor so defective as to fail to be law-constitutive at all.

It is in practice reasonable to assert that no existing legal system complies with Fuller's procedural criteria in their entirety. If may be that some fail to meet even a minimum standard of compliance as, certainly, some have in the past. Analysis within the grey area involves a delicate judgement of what is permissible by way of derogation from the eight criteria of procedural morality. In some instances practices which are prima facie negative in themselves may actually be necessary for the avoidance of worse evils. To take an obvious example, the third criterion argues against retroactive legislation, the fourth denounces the making of incomprehensible rules, and yet one may readily imagine circumstances in which the distress caused by doubt might properly be alleviated by retro-active legislation without weakening or vitiation of the law-constitutive qualities of the system. It might be, for example, that contracts of marriage entered into bona fide by citizens of state A with citizens of state B under the laws of that state are of doubtful validity under the laws of state A. It would seem unreasonable to object to a retroactive amendment of the laws of state A with the effect of validating such marriages.

The judgement of the levels of flexibility within the procedural structure of a legal system must then be made with care in order to maintain necessary flexibility of response within the system while yet retaining a structure which is procedurally capable of pro-ducing 'law'. That judgements of this type are in fact made, and made with difficulty, may readily be illustrated by reference to English examples. The House of Lords in its judicial capacity is the highest apellate court for both the English and Scottish legal systems, and its decisions therefore constitute binding precedents for all lower courts and represent an element of certainty in the law so far as the exigencies of judicial technique admit. The maximum degree of predictive certainty in precedent is reached if the decisions of the House of Lords are made binding as precedents for the future cases also upon the House itself. This was in practice the effect of the decision of the House of Lords in *London Street Tramways* v *LCC*.[4] This theoretically desirable conclusion, reached in the interests of certainty and in logical pursuit of the doctrine of the supremacy of the Crown in Parliament which alone has 'legislative' capacity, proved in practice to be disastrous. The Parliamentary timetable does not permit the devotion of time to the consideration of the legislative fine-tuning necessary for the changing of detailed points of case law, although legislation obviously is necessary and appropriate where gross or sweeping changes in established case law is called for. The consequence of the *London Street Tramways* decision was thus, not surprisingly, a system of adjudication which tended to be too rigid to take account of new problems or changes in the scope of old ones and this could be to no one's legitimate advantage. Finally the unsatisfactoriness of the situation was recognised by a Practice Direction issued in 1966[5] which declared that thenceforth the House of Lords would have power to set aside the precedents set by its own earlier decisions. The alternative disaster of uncertainty has not followed from this because of the inherent conservatism of superior courts and the House of Lords has been very far from profligate in the use of its power. For those interested in pursuing this example further the subsequent controversy between radical and conservative opinion upon the issue of self-reversal in the Court of Appeal will be of interest — the conservative argument prevailed, quite properly in the context of Fuller's analysis.[6]

Fuller is thus in essence advancing a procedural 'test' for purportedly 'law'-making systems in which there is at some point a 'pass mark' in terms of the level of satisfaction of the eight procedural criteria of evaluation which he sets out. Taking due account of the types of necessary practical compromise suggested above, most advanced legal systems can be seen to fall rather short of the aspirations to procedural excellence required for the highest 'marks' upon the Fuller scale, but on the other hand easily achieve any practical 'pass' standard reasonably required for the demonstration of 'law'-constitutive capacity. In contrast the 'legal' system of a state such as Nazi Germany may be argued to have been so defective upon so many of Fuller's procedural criteria as not to merit the use of the term 'legal' at all.

If Fuller's analysis may thus be defended as an adequate assessment of the procedural necessities of a viable law-constitutive system, there remains the second question: that of the effect of the quality of the substantive content of the rules made by such a system. Fuller deals with this issue quite straightforwardly. He describes his 'naturalism' as procedural in nature and makes a sharp distinction between such an approach and theories of 'substantive' naturalism. In precise terms he relates his procedural natural law to the 'inner morality' of law which may be described as the structural necessities of a viable system of 'legal' rules. He is in short concerned with the making and administration of rules rather than with their substantive content. Thus so long as formal and purportedly 'legal' rules are adequately stated and promulgated in accordance with his eight procedural criteria they will be considered to be 'law' upon Fuller's analysis, however iniquitous their actual content or intention might be. The moral quality of the content of laws is treated by Fuller as an aspect of the morality of aspiration rather than the morality of duty and thus necessarily outside the consideration of a procedural natural law. The maintenance of the moral standard of the content of rules becomes a matter of trust reposing in the sense of propriety of the lawmakers. The reference to the idea of moral trusteeship in the making of positive laws is significant and seems to reach out towards a major strand of what may be called the arguments of 'substantive naturalism'. There is, for example, a clear parallel with the basic Thomist notion of law-making power as one with a moral character which may be either used or abused, producing in the latter case only defective 'laws'. Fuller is not prepared, however, to take the further step of incorporating the idea of such a 'trust power' of law-making into his concept of 'law', leaving it instead as a matter of aspiration rather than duty in the analysis of law-making.

Notwithstanding his refusal to include issues of substantive moral quality into his concept of law, Fuller does not deny that such questions may properly be asked about laws and law-makers. What then is the situation where a legal rule sufficiently satisfies Fuller's procedural criteria but is yet so substantively objectionable as to be morally iniquitous? Fuller simply refers the issue back to individual conscience and declines to admit the possibility of a theory of specific limitation upon the scope of legal obligation by reference to the moral quality of the demands imposed by a law or laws. For the citizen of a state such as Nazi Germany Fuller argues that there is not ultimately any simple criterion of evaluation in the process of decision-making upon the issue of the obligation to obey the law. The issue is ultimately one for the moral perception of the individual citizen, taking care not to confuse inherent respect for the state and its authority with a moral obligation to obey any particular law which it might enact.[7] In short the substantive moral 'goodness' or 'badness' of laws is a question which Fuller's procedural naturalism does not cover because he denies that any satisfactory substantive moral test of validity can be set up and the citizen must thus find his own way through the thickets of moral obligation in relation to positive law. Upon this basis it would therefore seem that, for Fuller, Nazi 'law' was defective because of its massive procedural failings in making, promulgation and implementation, not because of the moral iniquity of substantial parts of its content. Had the same, abhorrent, notions been expressed and applied in accordance with 'proper' procedural criteria then Fuller's tests would fully have been satisfied. This is indeed far removed from the purposive approach to the analysis of law and law-making found in what may be termed 'mainstream' naturalist thought.

Such a conclusion, however, is somewhat unfair to Fuller. He recognised the problem of the procedurally correct but substantively iniquitous law and in the latter part of *The Morality of Law* he sought to take account of the major issue of the substantive moral quality of law. In the first place he argues that the act of making a 'law' as procedurally defined serves to bring the principles upon which legislative (or presumably other law-constitutive) acts are based into the open and thus forces the populace to consider and assess the basis upon which they are being called upon to act or to refrain from acting. To this extent a morality of procedural duty can serve as an encouragement to the pursuit of a morality of aspiration in the forming of substantive legal content — the one is claimed indeed to be a pre-condition of the other. Fuller actually argues that in many parts of the world a procedurally adequate legal framework is a more urgent requisite than the drafting of substantively excellent laws.[8] There is some force to this argument, especially in the specific context of abuses of law-making processes such as those encountered in Nazi Germany. It is certainly true that the Nazi state, although maintaining a façade of legal process, functioned in practice in an almost completely a-legal manner. This almost undisguised arbitrary tyranny wholly failed to meet Fuller's procedural criteria and it is not easy to see how many of its tyrannical measures could have been carried out in a manner which would have satisfied them. The regime of arbitrary arrests, Gestapo terror and genocide could not in fact be so moulded as to conform to any viable system of procedural norms. None the less, the fact that some of the iniquitous features of the practically a-legal Nazi state could not be made realistically to conform to variable procedural norms cannot be taken to mean that much iniquity, including much manifested under the Nazi regime, could not be perpetrated within procedural norms. Fuller's system may obviate 'tyranny' in the sense of arbitrary oppression but it cannot prevent the creation of an iniquitous 'legal' order. Procedural norms prevent procedural abuse; they cannot prevent the 'due' enactment of iniquitous measures.

Fuller concedes that procedural naturalism does not fully address the problem of substantive abuse. He therefore sets out a minimum substantive naturalism in an attempt to close this gap. He claims to find this basic principle in the idea of an aspiration of communication among people.[9] In the broad sense intended by Fuller the idea of the transmission of social and cultural standards and their development thereby is obviously an important aspect of human social life. It is not clear, however, why this admittedly important aspect of human activity should be elevated to a unique eminence as the guarantor of the minimum substantive morality of law. It may reasonably be argued that Fuller's search for principles of substantive naturalism in basic human aspirations is an appropriate method of enquiry. However, the principle which he actually derives from the process actually contains relatively little of substance. It may be that communication of social standards would tend to subject those standards to evaluation by reference to general human aspirations but, even if this were to be the case, it can be no more than a method of evaluation — not a criterion of evaluation. In the end Fuller's minimum substantive naturalism is, oddly, a more limited conception than H. L. A. Hart's 'minimum content of natural law'.[10]

The question then remains as to whether or not Fuller's 'procedural natural law' actually represents a genuinely 'naturalist' approach to legal theory. Fuller, of course, argues that it does, albeit not a 'substantive' naturalism. Fuller's theory does not deny that law-making is a purposive activity which may be well or badly performed and which is open to moral evaluation. However, the nature of the purpose of laws is almost entirely relegated to the morality of aspiration and thus excluded as a criterion of legal identification. None of this sits at all uneasily with the work of an analytical positivist such as Bentham who also accepted, indeed urged, the possibility of moral judgement upon the quality of laws while denying that such judgements could be related to 'law' quality, or form any part of the 'science' of jurisprudence. The procedural criteria of evaluation advanced by Fuller are obviously much closer to a positivist approach emphasising the formalities of law-constitutive processes than to any system for the evaluation of the moral quality of the substance of laws. How wide then is the real gap between the procedural morality of Fuller's thesis and, for example, H. L. A. Hart's union of primary and secondary rules? Fuller seeks to distance himself from the explicit amorality of positivist thought and in particular from that of H. L. A. Hart. He takes as his principal ground of attack the issue of reciprocity which is examined in the context of the famous 'gunman' example given by Hart in *The Concept of Law*[11] to distinguish merely coercive demands from those made with 'legal' authority. Fuller argues that, contrary to Hart's thesis, the mere identification of formally valid legal rules through the agency of a 'rule of recognition' is not sufficient to distinguish rules of law from the demands of a gunman because it fails to import any distinctive idea of reciprocity into the idea of law. By reciprocity is meant a legitimate expectation on the part of the person or persons to whom a demand is addressed that recognition and compliance on their part will be productive of known and predictable consequences, failure in which would in some sense be 'wrong'. In a limited way such reciprocity is actually to be found even in the gunman situation in so far as a demand with menaces implies the lifting of the menace in the event of compliance. 'Give me your money and I will kill you anyway' is not a 'threat' but a statement of murderous intent, whereas 'your money or your life?' implies that the victim's life will be spared as a *quid pro quo* for the handing over of the money — an idea of a certain reciprocity. Law, as distinguished from mere coercive demands, must surely involve at the very least this basic level of reciprocity as between law-maker and subject but Fuller argues that Hart's analysis wholly excludes the idea that the citizen has any legitimate expectation of the law-giver which is capable of violation.[12] This indeed marks the distinction between Fuller's procedural naturalism and Hart's positivism.

Hart is essentially concerned with the clear identification of the law-making process whereas Fuller goes further and insists that the actual form of the exercise of the process should conform with clearly enunciated criteria of statement, presentation and application, failure by reference to which may weaken or even vitiate the law-constitutive capacity of the system concerned. This certainly represents a form of quasi-moral evaluation of the law-making enterprise and to that extent it must be termed 'naturalist'. It is, however, a very minimal form of naturalism. It is in effect almost a 'positivist's naturalism' which sets strict criteria for the statement, promulgation and application of laws but hardly addresses at all the issue of the quality of their content or the nature of the obligation which they impose upon their subjects.

Notwithstanding Fuller's concessions to a minimum substantive naturalism, the theory in the final analysis contains little or nothing of relevance to the limitation of the proper scope of the demands of positive laws once they have been adequately enunciated and administered. Fuller's apparent argument that a procedurally adequate system of law-making is a major step in the direction of the production of 'good' law is not devoid of force but, without careful qualification, it could be a most dangerous over-simplification. It is true that procedural norms can obviate some form of 'bad' law-making, as the Nazi German example demonstrates, but they do not necessarily provide criteria of judgement for the assessment of the 'proper purposes' of law-making. Fuller's approach, in short, leaves unanswered the significant question of the response to be made had Hitler perpetrated some of his enormities in a more 'legalistic' manner; to assume that in all or even most cases he could not have done so is perhaps naïve.[13] In the final analysis Fuller may fairly be said to have contributed an interesting and important critique of positivist formalism from a quasi-naturalist viewpoint but his theory must none the less be considered somewhat peripheral from the viewpoint of the mainstream of naturalist thought.

J. M. Finnis and the theory of natural rights

A markedly different contribution to the development of modern naturalist thought, dealing with substantive rather than procedural issues, has been made by J. M. Finnis. Finnis sets out to represent the classical naturalist case commencing from an essentially Thomist base, not necessarily because Aquinas is assumed to be inherently 'right' in his jurisprudential concepts but rather because the Thomist case is that of paradigmatic classical naturalism.

It is Finnis's contention that many of the 'accepted' modern criticisms of classical naturalism are based upon fundamental misconceptions of the actual nature of the naturalist case. In particular he denies that classical naturalism involves any confusion between 'is' and 'ought' propositions in deriving norms from the observation of human, or general, nature. He argues that this frequently encountered criticism is founded upon grossly simplistic premises and that the claimed confusion of 'is' and 'ought' is not actually to be found in classical naturalist argument. This is an important issue, not because the 'is/ought' argument actually points to any major defect in the generality of naturalist argument but because it has for so long been claimed to do so. Finnis approaches this question in the form in which it was put by Julius Stone[14] and gives a robust answer. As he phrases the issue:

> Have the natural lawyers shown that they can derive ethical norms from facts? . . . They have not, nor do they need to, nor did the classical exponents of the theory dream of attempting any such derivation.[15]

The argument by which Finnis seeks to refute this basic anti-naturalist proposition is interesting. It amounts to the claim that mankind does not frame 'ought' propositions by reference to the observation of the 'is' of human nature as an external observation as, for example, in the proposition that people do drop litter therefore they 'ought' to do so, which is clearly an improper derivation. Instead it is argued that people understand the nature of their own aspirations, necessarily from an 'internal' viewpoint and can see this as a particular instance of the general human aspiration to the 'good' life. Obviously in this understanding not all desires can be aspirations to the 'good' life, either in particular or in general. We are thus speaking of an understanding of a general 'good' through experience of a particular instance of it, which is by no means the same thing as a claim that what men want to do they necessarily 'ought' to do. Finnis denies in particular that St Thomas Aquinas[16] sought to make any improper derivation of 'ought' from 'is'. He interprets Aquinas's position upon this matter thus:

> Aquinas considers that practical reasoning begins not by understanding . . . [human] nature from the outside . . . but by experiencing one's nature . . . from the inside . . . by a simple act of non-inferential understanding one grasps . . . an instance of a general form of good, for oneself (and others like one).[17]

This is not unreasonable, the 'good' of mankind is necessarily related to human nature and can at least in part be deduced from it without falling into any such crass error as imagining that what people desire is *ex hypothesi* 'good'.

From this form of derivation of ideas of human 'good' Finnis sets out to structure his own natural law theory which is very much founded upon a neo-Thomist base. The first step is to examine the range of human value judgements across the broad cross-section of human societies in order to determine what may properly be treated as the basic perceived human 'goods'. The basic 'goods' so derived are said to comprise life, knowledge, play, aesthetic experience, sociability, practical reasonableness and religious experience. It is important to understand that these 'goods' are not set out as being in themselves moral or ethical criteria of evaluation but merely as an observation of near-universal human value judgements upon the basically desirable 'goods' of human social and cultural life. In order to construct moral and ethical criteria of evaluation from these basic 'goods' a framework of assessment and application is necessary in order to determine how the basic 'goods' shall be related to the actual functioning of a society. This structure is imposed upon the 'basic goods' by Finnis in the form of a scheme of tests of 'practical reasonableness'. These are designed to be the means of focusing the aspiration embedded in the basic 'goods' of human life onto specific issues and thus enabling the perceived 'goods' to function as moral propositions for action. The actual tests of 'practical reasonableness' set out by Finnis are really criteria of preference in the application of the principles reflected in the basic social 'goods'. They involve recognition of coherency of life plan, avoidance of arbitrary preferences among both values and people, proper sense of both commitment and detachment in relation to given issues, a concern with 'efficiency' — subject always to the maintenance of principle, respect for all basic values in decision-making and finally acceptance of the dictates of the good of the community at large and of the dictates of conscience. Taken together, these canons of 'practical reasonableness' and the 'basic goods' are set out by Finnis as the basis of a natural law and as the realistic basis for such concepts as 'justice' which many in the positivist and realist schools of jurisprudence have tended to dismiss as chimera. Finnis does not claim that the combination of basic 'goods' and practical reasonableness provides a complete or absolute answer to all social and jurisprudential questions. He does argue, however, that through them one may avert fundamental injustices and also derive certain clear duties and correlative rights.

Finnis advances the case that it is in fact possible to derive absolute human rights from his scheme of basic 'goods' and practical reasonableness. These rights are argued to be derived in particular from the principle of practical reasonableness that '. . . it is always unreasonable to choose directly against any basic value . . . Correlative to the exceptionless duties entailed by this requirement are . . . absolute human claim — rights.'[18] It is in short always 'wrong' to opt directly contrary to any of the basic values and this perception leads to the conclusion that the duty to observe such values generates absolute 'human rights'. The rights said to be so generated are appropriately basic in type and amount, as one would expect, to assertions of minimum legitimate social expectation. The rights advanced are as follows: not to be killed as a means to an end; not deliberately to be deceived where openness would be reasonable; not knowingly to be falsely condemned; not to be rendered incapable of procreation; and positive right to consideration in any assessment of the common good. These are all clearly very important and basic social expectations, the frustration of which might reasonably be considered to be 'wrongful' even if one might make out a case for amendment or extension of the list. There is, for example, no clear reference to access to basic available necessities although the right to consideration in the assessment of the common good might be taken to imply it.

It is certainly the case that these arguments represent a naturalism of substance which seeks to establish substantial criteria for moral action and does so through the perception of principles derived from the understanding of human nature and aspirations. How then is this scheme to be applied as a means of evaluation of the practical process of law-making? Finnis argues that the making of positive law does not generally involve the simple enactment of moral principles but must involve the elaboration of provisions derived from basic moral precepts in the context of a complex system of social relations in order to provide clear normative guidance for citizens. Thus the transmission of moral precept into positive law cannot be a simple direct process. The law relating to unlawful killing, for example, is a reflection of practical reason based upon the most obvious of human 'goods', Life, and right not to be arbitrarily deprived of it. The law, however, does not state simply that 'thou shalt not kill' nor even that 'thou shalt do no murder', at least not without copious definition and qualification of the fatal word in order to take account of such matters as self-defence, reasonable force and so on. This necessary because basic moral principle commonly takes small account of the complex variation of circumstance inherent in social life whereas positive law is necessarily concerned with detailed prescription for precisely such complex varieties of human activity.

Once the correlation of moral principle to positive law has been determined, there remains the issue of the nature of the impact and effect of the practical relationship between natural and positive law. This must be considered from the viewpoint both of the citizen and of the law-maker. Finnis argues that the citizen of a state, the law of which concords with naturalist principle, has need only to consider the basic legal norms, such propositions as 'pacta sunt servanda' (bargains are to be performed), 'crimes are not to be committed' and so on, in order to determine his course of action in matters for which the law makes provision. The reasonable legislator on the other hand must bear in mind not only basic morality and 'rule of law'[19] but also certain general principles in the making of laws. These general principles differ from the 'human rights' described above in that they are not absolute in nature but rather principles of guidance — the weight of which may well vary according to circumstances of time and place. These general principles are clearly not by any means the same thing as Dworkin's 'principles' in the adjudication of 'hard cases'[20] but none the less bear a general relationship to them. Finnis's general principles include such things as the so-called 'principles of natural justice', 'nemo iudex in causa sua' (no man shall be judge in his own cause) and 'audi alteram partem' (hear the other, that is both, side(s)) and also such ideas as the protection of the weak from the oppression of the strong and the vitiating effect of fraud upon agreement. These principles finally represent an attempt to give practical expression to naturalist principles in the context of the operation of real legal systems in a manner not untypical of modern naturalist thought. Finnis himself described the active relationship between natural and positive law as lying in the fact that the naturalist tradition does not

> merely . . . observe the . . . fact that 'morality' . . . affects 'law', but instead seeks to determine what the requirements of practical reasonableness really are, so as to afford a rational basis for the activities of legislators, judges and citizens.[21]

In effect a presumption is made that the rational legislator will act upon the principles of practical reasonableness for the achievement of the concordance between natural and positive law necessary for the facilitation of the effective attainment of the basic 'goods' of social life in the community concerned.

If the mode of the attainment of 'good' law-making is thus set out, what is the situation where legislators are irrational or wayward and act in a manner not calculated to produce concordance between natural and positive law? Finnis considers the nature of the obligation to obey positive laws in some detail. The argument commences from the proposition that a citizen should behave according to prescriptions made for the common good. It follows from this that acts or restraints made compulsory by law should be observed; thus there is an obligation to obey the law. To the charge that this argument is circular — the citizen should obey the law and is therefore under legal obligation — Finnis replies that the reasoning is not circular if the primary assumption is made that the law is in fact made for the common good. It is this which imports the naturalist moral criterion into the assessment of the quality of the obligation to obey the law in Finnis's argument. The argument again parallels the Thomist case which also demands that 'law' should be a prescription made for the good of the community. This issue is one which cannot be raised within the analytical framework of positivism because from the 'internal' legal viewpoint the moral authority of the law is necessarily assumed. The law in fact seeks to impose it own moral framework upon the understanding of the law-abiding citizen so that obedience to the law becomes an unavoidable conclusion. Specifically 'legal' reasoning thus leads to absolute conclusions upon the obligation to obey laws founded upon an unquestioning assumption of the practical reasonableness of positive legal prescription. The rational citizen, however, is not bound by this specifically 'legal' form of limited argument upon obligation and is thus able to examine the crucial assumption that laws are in fact made for the common good. The 'good' citizen may thus reach a conclusion upon the obligation to obey a legal provision which diverges from that reached by formal 'legal' reasoning. A general obligation to obey the law, which is recognised by Aquinas, need not therefore imply any specific obligation to obey each law, be it never so tyrannical or oppressive. This indeed sits easily with the basic Thomist analysis of legal obligation. The general reasoning upon the obligation to obey advanced by Finnis is thus concerned with moral principle and clearly 'naturalist' in form whereas his description of formal 'legal' reasoning is clearly, and properly, 'positivist' in form. This is in effect to make that distinction between the moral and formal ('legal') obligations to obey laws which theorists such as H. L. A. Hart may be argued not, or not sufficiently, to have recognised. Finnis does not linger upon this point but proceeds to the centrally significant issue of the relationship of the moral quality of law to the concept of validity.

Finnis's conclusions upon this issue again have an appropriately Thomist ring. He argues that the moral obligation to obey law is founded upon the assumption outlined above that positive law is in fact made for the common good and varies according to the actual validity in each case of that basic assumption. A law-maker is vested with the authority to make laws for the good of the community and also to enforce such laws. In so far, however, as a ruler makes laws for other purposes not conducive to the common good and outside the scope of that authority, his enactments cannot in their own right impose upon their addressees any moral obligation to obey. Thus the moral obligation imposed by a 'law' may in

Finnis's analysis be vitiated by 'injustice', such as inequitable imposition of burdens, notwithstanding a formally correct pedigree. This argument however, is, made subject to the Thomist caveat that there is a general obligation to obey laws in the interests of the conservation of the legal order of society as a whole, including the concession that, up to a point, this may involve the countenancing of some 'bad' laws. This argument for the assessment of the 'practical reasonableness' of laws by the 'good citizens' does not supply any easy answer to the problem of legal obligation in the face of the 'bad' law, but Finnis argues none the less that in practice these general concepts have to be rationally applied in the face of the wide variety of social and political circumstances with which the citizen might be faced in a complex modern society.[22]

Like its Thomist precursor, Finnis's theory is in the end a presentation of a basic purposive naturalism in that the parameters of practical reasonableness in association with the perceived basic 'goods' set bounds for the proper exercise of the function of law-making, action in excess of which will detract from, and possibly even destroy, the moral obligation to obey imposed by the law concerned. This is a theory very much in the broad Thomist tradition but it is far from being simply a modern re-working of Thomism. The idea of absolute 'rights' derived from basic 'goods' through canons of practical reasonableness is an important one which carries forward the basic classical naturalist argument into a modern context and as such represents an important contribution to the development of modern legal theory.

It is always easy to make criticisms of a substantive theory such as that advanced by Finnis through, for example, the argument that the basic 'goods' as listed constitute either an incomplete or a defective list, or that the 'rights' derived from the methodological requirements of 'practical reasonableness' are of rather variable importance, either too specific or — again — incomplete. The precise content of human 'goods' and 'rights' can, and no doubt will, continue to provide a focus of lively debate, but it is difficult to gainsay the importance of the matters raised in this guise in the course of Finnis's argument. For the development of legal theory the most significant aspect of the theory is the manner of the application of naturalist principle. The relation of a form of human self-perception through methodical reasoning to the practical techniques of law-making represents a form of 'de-mystified' naturalism which is convenient for the discussion of the major issues in a modern context. That the assessment of the morality of laws and law-making becomes a rational process for operation by both the subject and the maker of laws is not a weakness of the theory but a demonstration of a possible mode of operation of essentially classical principle in a modern secular society. Finnis's treatment of the alleged naturalist derivation of 'ought' propositions from 'is' observations is also important as a convincing account of the falsity of this still commonly encountered argument.

In their different ways the theories of both Fuller and Finnis represent reactions to the continuing importance of the essential questions about law and law-making posed within the naturalist tradition of jurisprudence and, as also with the work of R. M. Dworkin, contribute a continuing argument for the inclusion of 'moral' issues within what Bentham was pleased to consider the 'science' of jurisprudence.

To a tentative summing up of the importance of the naturalist case and its potential future value in the development of legal theory in general, and in particular in relation to the concept of legal obligation, we must now proceed.

Notes

1. See Ch. 3, earlier.
2. See Fuller, *The Morality of Law*, pp. 5–6.
3. For discussion of Dworkin's theory see Ch. 8, earlier.
4. [1898] A.C. 375.
5. [1966] 3 All E.R. 77.
6. See originally *Young* v *Bristol Aeroplane Co. Ltd.* [1944] K.B. 718, then the views advanced by Lord Denning, M.R., in (for example) *Gallie* v *Lee* [1969] 2 Ch. 17.
7. See Fuller, *The Morality of Law*, p. 41.
8. Ibid., p. 156.
9. Ibid., p. 185.
10. See Ch. 6, earlier.
11. See Ch. 6, earlier.
12. See Fuller, *The Morality of Law*, p. 140, *et seq.*
13. In fairness to Fuller it should be pointed out that he in fact considered many of the acts of the Nazi regime in Germany to fall outside the concept of 'law'. His disagreement with H. L. A. Hart upon the proper form of response to Nazi legal abuses is of interest here — see Ch. 7, earlier.
14. See J. Stone, *Human Law and Human Justice.*
15. J. M. Finnis, *Natural Law and Natural Rights*, p. 33.
16. See Ch. 3, earlier.
17. J. M. Finnis, *Natural Law and Natural Rights*, p. 34.
18. Ibid., p. 225.

19. Finnis's account of the rule of law (see *Natural Law and Natural Rights*, Ch. X) is in a number of respects convergent with Fuller's 'procedural natural law' (earlier).

20. See Ch. 8, earlier.

21. J. M. Finnis, *Natural Law and Natural Rights*, p. 290.

22. For Finnis's argument upon the impact of the unjust law see, in particular, *Natural Law and Natural Rights*, Ch. XII at pp. 351 – 66.

10

Conclusions

The nature of the obligation to obey law is a complex and important issue which, as even so cursory an exposition of theory as space here permits must indicate, has generated a very broad spectrum of opinion and speculation. It is also unfortunately an issue of which dicussion has been much muddied by basic misunderstandings of the nature and intention of naturalist theory. Clarity of discussion is further hindered by the fact that the very word 'obligation' is ambiguous in its meaning and implication. The word certainly implies an impulsion towards a particular pattern or patterns of conduct. However, such impulsions may take more than one form. There is firstly the distinction drawn by H. L. A. Hart between 'obligation' in the sense of a feeling of 'oughtness' and the situation in which a person is directly 'obliged' to follow a pattern of conduct in the sense of being compelled or coerced into doing so. There is, however, also the rather different distinction drawn by J. M. Finnis between the moral and legal senses of the word 'obligation'. The first refers back to absolute principles upon which conceptions of the common 'good' may be based, the second refers to the formal norms of a legal system which internally presupposes the morality of its premises. In the discussion of the obligation to obey law these different levels of implication and meaning must be borne in mind. Unfortunately, they have all too commonly been either forgotten or lain aside. For the sake of clarity it is thus well to set out the intended significance of the term 'obligation' in the present context. 'Obligation' is taken to have two broad meanings for present purposes — these are:

(i) The 'oughtness' of an action which is, according to an

accepted moral scheme, appropriate in given circumstances. (ii) A formal duty imposed by or through the operation of a positive legal provision.

Thus (i) is the general moral obligation, (ii) is Finnis's 'legal' obligation and also virtually Hart's understanding of the obligation imposed by a primary rule validated by the rule of recognition. For the purposes of this discussion (i) is termed 'moral obligation' and (ii) is termed 'legal obligation'. Hart's category of 'being obliged' is excluded from the category of 'obligation', being actually mere compulsion.

The argument for the obligation to obey law can be addressed upon three broad levels. The first concerns legal obligation and commences from the supposition that either law has all the moral force it requires by virtue of being 'law', or that it requires no moral force since the identifiable 'is' of law is anyway self-sufficient. This approach supplies the method for the positivist 'command' theory and also, paradoxically, the crude quasi-naturalism of Blackstone's approach. This seeming paradox is partially explicable by the fact that this approach lends itself to the lawyer's internal view of law. The second approach relates more to moral obligation and may loosely be termed the 'Social Contractarian' approach. It represents the classic argument for general obedience to legal norms from Plato's *Crito* onwards. The argument is in essence this: a citizen by living in a social order accepts both its benefits and its burdens, *qui sentit commodum, sentire debet et onus*. Such a one who finds the laws' demands unconscionable has the option (i) of urging change through the established channels, if any; (ii) of removing himself to a more congenial social order. Upon this reasoning the citizen does not have the option of arguing that the law or some laws exercise no claim to obedience upon him. This is really an argument for social order and its force is recognised in varying degrees by most of the classical naturalist thinkers. Aquinas recognised that some 'bad' law is a small price to pay for the avoidance of anarchy, and this point should be borne in mind when naturalist principle is taken as an inflexible counsel of perfection. At the same time it must also be remembered that the argument is not necessarily one for unreasoning obedience. Plato himself did not so treat it in his *Crito*, although the form of his exception was perhaps rather bleak. In the *Crito* Socrates is made to argue that the laws can never force a man to do evil and if they essay to do so then they themselves stand thereby condemned.

However, once arguments for change have failed, if the 'good' citizen remains obdurate in the face of 'bad' laws then for the sake of social order he must take the consequences. The implications of this argument have been considered in Chapter II above. In a later form the social contractarian approach takes on a more substantive form. In the view of Locke and Rousseau, although to a lesser extent in that of Hobbes, the 'contract' involves clear requirements of performance by the political power and failure in this regard may abrogate the 'contract' through breach and undermine or even destroy the claim to obedience.

The third level of argument is that of substantive morality and is that correctly termed 'naturalist' in the fullest sense of the term. It is this argument which deals most extensively with the nature and limits of the moral obligation to obey law. The argument in its simplest form is that positive law imposes 'obligation' upon its subjects by virtue of its informing morality, including the moral desirability of *some* social order as opposed to none, and is otherwise dependent upon mere coercion for its effectiveness. This argument is frequently, even conventionally, presented in a crudely misleading guise in the form 'lex iniusta non est lex' — the unjust law is no law. If this is taken, as it often is, to mean that an unjust or 'bad' law is ineffective then it is merely fatuous, as generations of positivist writers have pointed out. However, this was not in fact the naturalist argument. St Augustine himself, in many ways the most absolute of the classical naturalists, did not make this claim. His claim that 'lex esse non videbitur quae justa non fuerit' — no 'law' was ever seen which was not just — refers to 'law' in a very specialist sense. Positive 'law' in the proper sense is here taken as the human statement of a norm derived from a clear moral base made with moral ends in view. Like some later theorists, including thinkers as apparently remote as Karl Marx, St Augustine identified positive law with the coercive imposition of values upon the refractory or otherwise unwilling. It was recognised that such a process is almost peculiarly capable of abuse. Such an abuse of process would produce 'bad' law which might indeed be effective but which was none the less an abuse and had no claim to obedience beyond what force could extract. Once the narrow confines of this link with coercion are shaken off and the formal enunciation of norms is accepted as a 'normal' human activity the way is open to a fully purposive analysis of the exercise of law-making. This was the step taken by Aristotle, as distinguished from Plato, and St Thomas Aquinas, as distinguished from St Augustine. The degree of difference between the conventional caricature of the unelaborated 'lex iniusta non est lex' and the classic naturalist position indicated by the Thomist assertion that 'Lex tyrannica cum non sit secundum rationem non est simpliciter lex sed magis est quaedam perversitas legis', which is to say that the tyrannical law made contrary to reason is not properly 'law' but rather an abuse of law, is considerable. This statement is highly significant and contains all the basic elements necessary for what has been termed in this discussion a 'purposive' naturalist approach. The elements of the statement are three in number: (i) a 'tyrannical' law which is, (ii) contrary to reason is, (iii) perversion of law. Note that the claim is that the defective law is an abuse or perversion, not that it is necessarily ineffective. Before proceeding further it is necessary to clarify this basic proposition further. The first point is the idea of a 'tyrannical' law. Like many quasi-political terms, the words 'tyrant' and 'tyranny' are used very loosely but they are in fact capable of precise use. The Thomist use of the word centres upon arbitrariness, the enunciation of rules based upon nothing but the coercive capacity to impose the demands made thereby — in short the simplest 'command' model of law. The second point is the relationship of law-making to reason. This is the purposive element. Law, as Aquinas states elsewhere, is properly a 'rational ordinance' which is made for the good of the community and this applies to the law of man as to the law of God. In short, law should not be a mere arbitrary imposition but a means of securing the rationally determined 'good' of the community of individuals which make up human societies. The ultimate bedrock of this proposition is the simple idea that governmental power is designed for the good of the governed and not vice versa — an idea to be found expressed or implied in such diverse sources as the work of Aristotle, Aquinas, Mencius, Locke and Rousseau, to list but a selection. The third point raises the all-important question of the status of a 'law' made in pursuit of some goal other than the rationally determined 'good' of the community. The statement is simply that the making of a tyrannical 'law' contrary to reason is an abuse of the law-making process and that the product is a perverted 'law', a flawed norm. In what sense flawed is the obvious next question. The answer lies in the distinction drawn by Finnis between the legal self-assumption of morality and the substantive moral base upon which laws are based. As Finnis concludes the equal duty to obey the laws is not necessarily an equal duty to obey *each* law. Thus a 'bad' law is simply a coercive imposition and lacks moral suasion according to the degree of its 'badness'. This is not to deny that positive law has a coercive dimension, merely that a description of law as a purely coercive mechanism ignores dimensions of its actual working.

It is now possible to outline the basis of a purposive naturalist theory of the obligation to obey the law. Positive law-making is a means of stating formal norms for the conduct of individuals within a society and for the conduct of the society *vis-à-vis* its members. The purpose for which such norms are enunciated is the facilitation of the attainment of the 'good' of the members of society, both individually and collectively. A law rationally calculated to that end is made for a proper purpose and imposes an obligation to obey upon its addressees derived from the basic morality of the social order. Such a law may also have a coercive dimension which 'obliges', in the Hartian sense, a dissident to obey but none the less imposes 'obligation' upon all subject to it. A legal enactment which is framed upon some basis other than the social 'good' is made in pursuit of an improper purpose and imposes no 'obligation' to obey upon its addressees although it may coercively 'oblige' citizens to obedience. This is a bare outline of the form of a purposive naturalist theory of law but one which does set out the basic nature of the enterprise in a way which one may hope to be free from the traditional misconceptions.

A bare outline of theory calls for elaboration if the theory is to be maintained. In this instance three issues in particular call for clarification: (i) the nature of the social 'good' which defines the proper purpose of law-making; (ii) the means by which the validity of purpose of an exercise in law-making shall be determined; and (iii) the status of law determined to have been improperly made. A purposive naturalism must obviously disclose some substantive criterion of judgement of purpose if it is to have any real value. Any such criterion must equally obviously represent something more than the subjective preferences of the theorist if it is to gain any measure of acceptance. Many attempts have been made to define the content of natural law as a superior prescription by reference to which the content of positive law may be evaluated. Their very diversity is on occasion pointed out as a weakness of the naturalist approach. For all the diversity of detailed conclusion there are in fact only two broad means of derivation of principles of natural law, that is — derivation from absolute prescription or from rational perception. The two differ radically but are not necessarily mutually exclusive or in conflict. The absolute derivation essentially involves reference to a specific extrinsic pre-scription such as the will of God and to that extent must find its ultimate roots in the perceptions of faith. This is the ultimate base of the substantive principles adduced by such writers as St Augustine and St Thomas Aquinas. Derivation from rational per-ception has taken a number of forms and was the method of the classical Hellenistic thinkers and later of the Social Contractarians, among many others. It normally involves a consideration of the nature of man and of human society from which the basic aspira-tions of man in society may be determined. This may or may not relate directly to the absolute approach. To take the example of the Thomist approach, the will of God, the Lex Aeterna, is related to human law through the twin media of the revelatory Lex Divina and the perception of human reason through the Lex Naturae. Thus an ultimately absolute naturalism is perceived and derived partly upon an absolute basis and partly upon the basis of rational perception, thus combining both approaches within a single scheme — the point being that behind the rational perception of phenomena there always lies the imponderance of ultimate cause. None the less, the perceptions of faith being inherently undebat-able, a general argument for a substantive naturalism must be pre-sented in the context of rational argument, keeping in mind the ultimate non-conflict of absolute and rational derivations upon the scheme suggested.

An initial difficulty with the derivation of naturalist principle from rational observation is the apparent derivation of an 'ought' from an 'is'. It is of course almost platitudinous to say that no such derivation may properly he made and this is frequently urged as a major weakness of the naturalist case. This claim is fallacious, however. Finnis effectively disputes this conventional argument upon the basis of derivation of norms from non-inferential self-perceptions. It is also, upon a more general level, possible to argue that the idea of a confusion between 'ought' and 'is' perceptions in naturalist theory is founded upon a basic misunderstanding of the nature of the naturalist enterprise. Naturalist legal theory is ulti-mately concerned with the moral nature of law, both generally and in terms of its claim to be obeyed. Morality itself is ultimately a perception of 'rightness' in human behaviour and relationships. In short a series of value judgements upon forms of human living and associations. Such value judgements can only relate in one way or another to perceptions of human nature and aspirations. That nature of course is something which 'is' and it would obviously not be legitimate to argue that as such it is necessarily as it 'ought' to be. That, however, is not the claim of the naturalist argument. Law, as a social regulator, must obviously take account of the nature of its subjects, which is to say human nature. There are many value judgements to be made about human nature and human aspirations; thus co-operation and oppression both stem in their different ways from aspects of human nature and a judgement is readily made that the one is 'good' whereas the other is 'bad'. Such common value judgements form part of a general perception of the proprieties of human life. This may be indeed a form of self-perception, but is anyway in the end a product of the 'is' of human nature — whatever the ultimate cause or source of the form of that nature. The basic argument that law should be moulded to serve and facilitate human aspirations to a 'good' life is not, however, a crude elevation of an 'is' observation into an 'ought' proposition. The 'ought' proposition is independent of the 'is' of human nature in that what is being argued is that the 'is' of law 'ought' to conform to the purpose of the facilitation of the basic value judgements upon individual and collective human 'good'. The perception of that 'good' clearly relates to human nature and could not well do otherwise; the two are not identical, however, because the former is an aspiration, the latter is a fact and neither are the same as the 'is' of positive law which is simply a formal prescription which may or may not be morally 'good'. Thus the purpose of law-making can quite properly be defined in terms of externally derived 'ought' propositions without in any way falling foul of the basic methodological proposition that an 'ought' may not be derived from an 'is'.

The concern of naturalist theory is not then to assert that law 'is' calculated to the 'good' of mankind in the sense that rules otherwise calculated are ineffective, but that law-making 'ought' properly to be calculated to that end. In whatever form this concern is presented two fundamental questions arise: firstly, what is the purposive 'good' to which law-making should properly be calculated and, secondly, what is the status of 'law' made in pursuit of some other and 'bad' purpose?

Many ideas of the proper content and purposes of law have been set out in the course of jurisprudential speculation. The concerns of these various theses have varied. Some have sought to set out an absolute content for natural law, usually based upon some form of higher prescription, others have sought naturalist principle in basic human aspiration, yet others have sought to define law in procedural terms while others, like Nozick, have sought merely to justify the *status quo*. The degree of apparent merit of these many approaches varies; some have much to recommend them, some are too closely bound to the concerns of their time and place of origin to be of much general application, probably some had little merit even to start with. The concerns of basic natural law, however, are necessarily universal in their application to the human condition. A postulated content of substantive naturalism which reflects too closely immediate temporal and cultural concerns cannot in fact be more than a specific and local application of more general principles. The substantive naturalism itself must seek to enunciate the guidelines from which such specific applications to particular cases may be derived.

An attempt to outline the proper purposes of law-making must commence with the basic PURPOSE of law in the sense of the point of the generation of such an institution. If positive law is taken as a set of formal rules with a penumbra of principles, concepts and administrative sub-rules which shape their application and development, the question of the function of such a system can actually be answered quite simply. It is an answer which is to be found at least implicitly in the social contractarian method. An individual who lived free from any association and who therefore affected no other individuals whether for good or ill might be subject to absolute moral principles but could hardly have any use for positive law. If legal principles are examined they are found, almost without exception, to concern relations in social structures, between individuals, between groups and between individuals and groups. For the castaway alone upon a desert island such concepts as 'property', 'contract', 'tort', 'crime', 'dispute resolution' and so on are irrelevant. The appearance of another castaway, or a group of castaways, upon the island immediately generates issues to which some such concepts are a form of answer. The freedom from restraint enjoyed by an isolated and asocial individual cannot be enjoyed by individuals within a group for the simple reason that the free expression of each individual impinges upon the freedom of each other individual and thus unrestrained action itself serves as a potentially severe limitation upon the actual freedom of each individual. A social order thus involves the development of ways of doing things which represent compromises between the conflicting desires to be unrestrained and not to be protected from undue impingement by the lack of restraint of others. This is not to suggest conscious decision-making upon a need to 'invent' law, but that the pragmatic development of rules and standards which become 'legal' is a response to that category of need. To reformulate this basic purpose of law-making, it may be said that law is a formal normative structure which defines the minimum balance in a given society between the individual claims of each member and the collective claims of the society as a whole upon its members. This is true of obvious areas such as the rules of contract — which sets out the formal framework of bargain and exchange within which social economic activity takes place. Examples could be extended but for the sake of brevity the general point is that law is concerned with the minimum formal regulation of social relationships, protecting both individual and collective claims to their proper extents and maintaining an appropriate balance between the two aspects.

If this balance between collective and individual demands is the root cause of positive law, the proper purpose of positive law-making is to maintain that balance so far as possible to an equitable equilibrium. This inevitably leads to a discussion of 'rights' in the sense of proper claims made by individuals and by societies as collective entities. Denying the Hegelian proposition that the state (as the continuing symbol of social organisation) is greater than the sum of its parts, with the reservation only that a society must be considered as an entity in which future generations also have an interest, legislative purposes must be referred to the claims of the individual members of society both singly and in groups and not to the demands of 'the state' as an independent entity as against the people.

Discussion of the claims of the individual and of society leads one into the quagmire of detail associated with the concepts of liberalism, moralism and authoritarianism; this, however, is not necessary for present purposes. If society is taken as an association the aim of which is the facilitation of the 'good' of its members, all that is needed is to outline the general nature of that 'good'. Many methods have been adopted in efforts to solve this problem. Rawls in *A Theory of Justice* advanced the idea of a distribution of equal basic liberties upon a 'maximum' approach and subject to a 'just savings' principle, the latter being essentially a recognition of social claims in the continuum. Methodologically this is a useful approach, however the emphasis upon 'liberties' is perhaps misleading in the immediate context of the present discussion. 'Liberty' implies a guarantee of freedom from restraint, even conceding that an isolated liberty is functionally distinguishable from licence. In fact this represents only one side of the jurisprudential coin. The purposive concern of law-making is formally to define the boundaries of minimum claims in society, both individual and collective, and not, as such, either to guarantee or to restrain 'freedoms'. It must also be stressed that law is concerned with MINIMUM rather than with MAXIMUM norms. It lays down the basic tolerances for social living, it does not map out the ideal pattern of human relationships. No serious naturalist has claimed otherwise. Thinkers in the traditions of Plato, St Augustine, Confucius or Marx would have thought the idea quite bizarre. Those in the broader perspective of Aristotle, St Thomas Aquinas, Rousseau *et al.* do not claim that law *per se* makes men 'good', merely that it can be a formal expression of 'goodness' and can maintain the circumstances in which further 'improvement' is possible. What then are those proper purposes of law-making? As many writers have in various ways suggested they must clearly relate to basic human expectations of social life. This, however, is not sufficient — it involves no value judgement and cannot really be termed an 'ought' proposition or propositions. A desire ruthlessly to exploit others in the cause of personal gain may be an expectation, even a fairly common one, yet it falls foul of precisely that equitable balance of claims which it is suggested that law is functionally expected to maintain. Herein lies the answer. The proper purpose of law-making is to facilitate the achievement, so far as circumstances permit, of those basic human expectations which may be attained by the individual, while restraining the due expectations of all other individuals subsumed in the collective claims of society as an entity.

For reasons outlined above, the precise and detailed listing of particular 'proper' expectations can play no part in the formulation of a general theoretical exposition. Such particularisation is in the main an exercise in the APPLICATION of theory and not a statement of the basic theory as such. The statement of purposes must thus be general in nature and capable of specific application in the broadest possible spectrum of social structures. In particular it should be free, so far as possible, of subjective desiderata which are specific to any particular culture. There is in short no point in formulating a theory which may be reduced to the proposition that 'all human beings ought to want those things which are regarded as desirable in the culture within which the author of the theory lives', at least if the theory concerned purports to be general in

197

application. In fact there are certain broad ethical propositions which are to be found across a very wide spectrum of thought — abstract, religious and humanist. For the present purpose a broadly Kantian form of statement seems most effective. The basic ideas of the Categorical Imperative and the Principle of Right afford the best starting point. These may be expressed for present purposes in the form that (i) all actions should be capable of forming the basis of a rule for general action and (ii) an action should tend to confirm and enhance the humanity of its subjects rather than to diminish it. These are essentially ideas of equity and respect which can be found in very far removed systems of ideas. Essentially similar concepts may be discerned behind the religious propositions that 'Thou shalt love the Lord thy GOD' and 'Thou shalt love thy neighbour as thyself'; the general and neutral Kantian formula serves best in this context, however.

Translating these ideas into the realm of legal theory, the nature of the specific exercise of law-making involves a reversal of order and we emerge with the propositions that a properly conceived positive law will (a) *recognise the equal humanity of all its subjects and will be calculated to the maintenance or enhancement of that quality*, and (b) *form a prescription equally applicable for all persons engaging in the category of action envisaged and not make arbitrary discriminations among persons.* These may for convenience be considered to be principles of HUMANITY and EQUITABLE APPLICATION. The second principle is fairly simple and amounts to a rule against arbitrary infliction, the first needs further elaboration as it is the parent of a number of basic propositions which, for want of a better term, may be called 'Human Rights'. Many lists of 'human rights' have been produced. Some of these, especially those listed in international conventions, are immensely elaborate and are perhaps more properly to be regarded as *applications* of human rights to particular situations or cases. The same is true of a number of jurisprudential essays in this field. The 'goods' of Rawls's theory of justice are an example of this although, to be fair, Rawls does not claim that his scheme is applicable to all social conditions. The concern at the level of general theory must be one of basic human expectation not linked to specific social or economic conditions. This is a need for basic propositions about general human expectations which embody the general value judgements which lie at the roots of human association.

The basic principles of 'Humanity' and 'Equitable Application' set out the optimum mode of performance of the basic legal purpose of achieving the best balance of individual and collective claims within the social framework. They suggest that properly made laws will in the first place not be arbitrary or discriminatory upon grounds of age, sex, race, religion, ethical or political belief except in so far as such discrimination is justified by the maintenance or enhancement of the humanity of the subjects of the law. Thus a law providing for an age of retirement and for the payment of old age pensions is discriminatory upon grounds of age, but hardly objectionable. Genocide laws in contrast are also discriminatory but highly objectionable. It is not sufficient, however, to say merely that discriminatory laws are acceptable only if they are for the benefit of those who are thus selected for discrimination. This issue is resolved by the primary principle of Humanity. The humanity of the subjects of law is an overriding consideration which can be used also to resolve issues of doubt as in the case of old age pensions. The principle of humanity demands that laws affecting individuals should respect the humanity of each person and should treat people as worthy of consideration in their own right and not simply as means to ends. This is of course a case against arbitrary totalitarianism and subjective ideological tyranny; it is also a case, however, against some expressions of liberalism or at least libertarianism. In his classic exposition of liberal theory, *On Liberty*, John Stuart Mill asserted a 'very simple principle'; that the only cause for which a civilised community might interfere with the liberty of one of its members against his will is the prevention of harm to others. The idea that mere disapproval or prejudice is not a valid ground for imposed restraint is surely unexceptionable, indeed respect for humanity dictates such a principle. It does not by any means follow, however, that 'anything goes' or that judgements upon conduct or even inclinations as such necessarily fall within that stigmatised modern category of 'moralism'. The source of obscurity in this area is the term 'harm'. When is conduct 'harmful' to others? Some categories, like physical violence, are self-evidently harmful, others are more debatable. What, for example, of the production and dissemination of pornographic literature? That pornography is shocking or disgusting to many perhaps does not constitute a ground for repression; such shock or digust is after all readily avoidable by not seeking out such materials. The *a priori* argument of 'immorality' is again perhaps more a case for argument and persuasion than for coercive prevention.

There is a deeper argument to be advanced, however, against

the dissemination or production of pornographic material and it is derived from the basic principle of humanity. It is the nature of pornographic publications to treat their subjects, usually women, as objects rather than people. Their humanity is thereby by implication diminished if not actually denied and, in case consent of the particular subjects be argued, an attitude of such diminution or denial is engendered towards women in general and indeed to all people. This may quite properly be considered 'harmful' even in Millsian terms and a legitimate case for restraint. Thus the principle of humanity may resolve some of the major difficulties of control in a 'liberal society', as well as setting the bounds of action in a more authoritarian one.

Such matters are of course highly specific applications of general principles. There are, however, certain specific matters which can be advanced as being of general application. These approximate to the idea of 'human rights'. Such rights are those expectations which are general and reasonable as part of the basic human condition in ANY form of society. It is suggested that these include expectations (i) not to be arbitrarily killed, (ii) not to be tortured or in any way unwarrantably maltreated, (iii) to be allowed an equitable share of available basic resources and a fair opportunity to participate in any available surplus, (iv) an expectation that all, including the subject, will make such contribution to the general well-being as is most reasonable and that full respect will be accorded to each such contribution, (v) an expectation that within the context of social order each person shall be afforded the opportunity to develop his or her potential without restraint upon arbitrary or illegitimately discriminatory grounds. These specific principles are attached to the two basic principles which themselves inform the specific and local applications appropriate to specific times and places. A tentative formulation of an outline substantive modern naturalism may now be essayed. This is not intended, however, as a complete or definitive statement, merely as a suggestion of possible FORM.

The following propositions are advanced: (1) The purpose of positive law is to provide the minimum formal norms balancing individual and collective claims in a rational social order. (2) The form of that balance in any given case is determined by reference to two fundamental principles: (a) the principle informing a legal norm should be capable of general application, (b) the effect of a legal norm should be to conserve or to enhance the humanity of its addressees, not to diminish or to deny it. (3) From, and subject to, the above, certain universal specifics may be derived, including, but not exclusively, the following expectations: (i) not arbitrarily to be deprived of life, (ii) not to be tortured or otherwise unwarrantably maltreated, (iii) to have fair access to the available necessities for the maintenance of life, (iv) to have equitable opportunities for access to the benefit of any available surplus, and (v) that all, including the subject, will make the contribution for which they are best fitted and will receive fair and proper respect therefore. Specific applications in particular economic and social circumstances may then be devised. Multiplication of examples would serve little useful purpose; however, some discussion of 'problem' cases is necessary in an effort to ward off inevitable accusation of concealed subjectivity in any suggested naturalist scheme. How can one be sure that the key concept of 'humanity' is not merely a cloak for the theorist's personal view of what the life of man 'ought' to be?

A 'problem case' may be found, for example, in a religious or cultural practice which seems odious to an external observer but desirable or even 'necessary' from an internal viewpoint. The guideline in decision-making in such an instance must clearly be the principle of the maintenance or enhancement of humanity. This dictates at the least that no person should be compelled by law or be legally permitted to be otherwise compelled to submit him or herself to any such practice. For that to occur would reduce the person concerned to a mere ritual object without choice, in a fundamental breach of the basic principle of humanity. If, however, a person chooses to submit to a practice which appears from an external view to be detrimental then perhaps that choice should not be denied provided that it is a free choice made by a person capable of rational decision. It may indeed be that from the internal view the practice concerned actually enhances the humanity of the subject and that to deny the capacity of choice would actually be wrongful. To this must be added the rider that a practice which is destructive of social life for others, such as human sacrifice, may indeed be impugned upon the grounds of the general purpose of law-making in the first place. There is also a general need to protect children and others who are not capable of independent decision-making for whom in the last resort society as a whole must be considered to be *in loco parentis*.

It is obvious that a perfect answer to all such problems is difficult, if not impossible, to devise. By the nature of complex modern societies it cannot be anticipated that clear ready-made answers will always present themselves. In many cases compromises must be reached in order to achieve the best practicable result which the circumstances of a given instance permit. In many, even most, cases of doubt a substantive naturalism cannot be expected to do more than suggest directions of approach to appropriate decision-making.

An outline naturalism of this form does not conflict with the basic tenets of the principal traditions of classical naturalism. Almost all the classical theories involve an insight based upon rational perception of the human condition. This is true even where the approach, as in the case of Thomism, is based ultimately upon the absolute dictates of religion which add a revelatory element defining the basis of the insight. Those theories which limit positive law to a narrowly coercive role would limit the scope of theory; this, however, is an issue of the placing of moral judgement, not in the end the form of its making. There remains the crucial issue of the effect of naturalist doctrine as a criterion of evaluation of positive law.

It has already been suggested that the crude and ridiculous claim 'lex iniusta non est lex', the unjust law is no (that is, a completely ineffectual) law, is not actually made by any serious naturalist thinker. A 'purposive' naturalism *ex hypothesi* posits a 'proper purpose' in law-making and the criterion of judgement of legal quality becomes one of analysis of purpose. What then of the positive law judged to have been made in pursuance of an 'improper' purpose? The broad answer is that such a law becomes defective in the MORAL, but not the FORMAL, obligation it imposes. From a social contractarian viewpoint it is a more or less serious 'breach of contract'; upon a Thomist perspective it is a 'perversion' or abuse of law-making powers. In short, such a misuse of law-making powers produces a formal norm having positive legal quality but depending upon actual or potential coercion for its effectiveness, having no moral suasion. Granted that perfection is in fact as rare in positive law-making as in any other human activity, it must now be asked how 'bad' a law must be before moral suasion is entirely lost. This question can be answered by reference to the suggested basic purpose of law — the maintenance of equitable equilibrium between individual and collective claims in a social order.

Among the values which the concept of an equitable social equilibrium embodies one of the most important is that of social order itself. As St Thomas Aquinas pointed out *some* price in imperfect law must be paid for the avoidance of anarchy in any real society — this is not to argue, however, that iniquity must or should be accepted. The line may be suggested to be drawn at the point of clear inequity of purpose or disrespect for the humanity of subjects — the breach, in other words, of the two broad principles of substantive naturalism suggested above: the point in short at which the society so signally departs from its basic purpose as to cease to be worth the price in compliance claimed. This is not an assertion of an outright social catastrophe theory. The choice of options is not restricted to unreserved obedience or absolute disobedience. The scale of response to questionable law covers a wide range of debate, argument, protest, civil disobedience and so on. Acceptance and outright withdrawal of obedience are simply the extremes of the scale. It is of course a truism that the worse or more iniquitous a regime is, the shorter the practical range of responses becomes until the range of options indeed shortens to the two extremes.

There remains the question of the mode of effect of naturalist principle. An institutional naturalism in a full sense is not readily conceivable in the modern world. In the high Middle Ages the 'doctrine of the two powers' purportedly set out such a system attributing spiritual power, including that of releasing subjects from obedience to iniquitous government, to the universal (Western) Church and secular, including positive law-making, power to earthly governments with the Holy Roman Emperor at their head. However, whatever the idealism of such a scheme in the first place, the idea as a practical expedient foundered upon the inappropriate ambitions and pretentions of popes as well as kings and emperors. Naturalist principle, it is suggested, in fact operates as a structure of value judgements which underlies the exercise of law-making. The way in which laws are so evaluated will of course vary widely from society to society. At the most institutional level the basic values may be incorporated in some form of written Constitution. This is what underlies Dworkin's institutional naturalism. The value of written Constitutions is currently (1985) a matter of academic dissension in the United Kingdom. On the one hand it is argued that a Constitution defines and therefore limits 'rights', on the other that it gives formal voice to those 'rights' which are stated rather than leaving them to convention and political understanding. The Dworkin thesis asserts the value of a written Constitution or Basic Law, even if the concession is made that the quality of any system depends upon that of those who administer it. It may reasonably be added that there is no reason to assume that a written Constitution necessarily excludes recognition of other basic principles. In general, however, a Constitution may REFLECT naturalist principle but cannot be regarded as a substitute therefore. Such a Constitution is in fact simply an especially fundamental form of positive law which is ultimately subject to the same principles of external evaluation as any other positive law — a point which Dworkin in essence concedes.

A written Constitution is of course only the most formal expression of the value judgements upon which the positive law-making of a given system is based. The role of the standards and principles discussed by Dworkin also reflects those value judgements but here fitted into the interstices of a formal structure of legal rules and informing their application and implementation. All such incorporations of naturalist or quasi-naturalist principle within a system are by definition internalisations of value judgements and thus not an extrinsic judgement upon the quality or content of the system itself. In short, such institutions are a method which may well be of value but should not be confused with substantive principle as such.

The basic judgements of naturalism must clearly also function in a manner independent of the system itself if they are to represent a genuine assessment of the practice of law-making. In the end such judgements form the criteria of evaluation of policy and law in a much broader sphere than the narrowly judicial. Naturalist principle at this basic level operates as a judgement upon the correlation between positive law-making and its purposive moral base. This is not a subjective judgement by the observer in terms of his liking for the laws made but a comparison of positive law to certain basic human social principles, an outline content of which has been suggested above. Such principle operates through a climate of ethical opinion informing both the principles and standards referred to by Dworkin and the political debates and discussions which form the background to the practical exercise of law-making.

So far as the determinedly 'bad' law is concerned the subject is forced back upon personal judgement which must still follow in broad outline the scheme set out in Plato's *Crito*, making due and considerable allowance for the marked distinctions between the form and organisation of ancient Greek city-states and modern national states. Ultimately this raises the issue of legal obligation in its sharpest form. How much may the state, as the expression of collective social being, properly demand of the citizen within the terms of its moral purpose and authority before moral suasion is lost and the descent to reliance upon coercion alone is made? As most major theorists have conceded, the individual member of a society does not have a 'right' to claim all the benefits of social life while renouncing the concomitant burdens. A measure of 'bad' law is part of the 'price' to be paid for the avoidance of the much greater horrors of anarchy in any, necessarily imperfect, human social order. That 'price' is not susceptible, however, to infinite inflation. We may agree with Plato, speaking through Socrates, that the law may not force men to do evil, but in a modern context we must surely also argue that where such demands are made the citizen is not under a moral obligation to submit, being subjected merely to force by a government which thus destroys any meaningful distinction between itself and St Augustine's pirate or H. L. A. Hart's gunman. In a telling phrase in his master work *The Rise and Fall of the Third Reich* Wilhelm Shirer described the German Third Reich as a 'gangster state', making in effect exactly this point. The point of nullity of moral claim, and possibly of generation of countervailing moral duty, is set out by the tenets of the basic purposive naturalism already outlined.

Initially such judgements *in extremis* must be personal in nature and it may fairly be presumed in such an extreme case that useful public discussion or debate is precluded. However, there may even so be a wider and more general implication to be derived from such decision-making. There is of course the general possibility of a social value judgement in rejection of an iniquitous rule or system of rules. This supposes, however, a historical neatness which is in reality rarely, if ever, encountered. More usually such general value judgements will be made *ex post facto* following the fall or overthrow of the regime or state concerned. Such questions bring to mind again the 'grudge cases' brought to light following the collapse of the Nazi government in Germany. Upon a purposive view many of the provisions upon which such cases were brought were blatant abuses of 'law'-making which indeed, as many Germans and non-Germans under Nazi rule recognised, derived their effect solely from force or the fear of force — being, as it was said, 'terror laws'. Once the terror is lifted the only claim to effectiveness which such 'laws' ever had is lost and those who *imposed* or *voluntarily used* such rules become answerable for their abuse of power. This approach is perhaps the most reasonable basis for the subsequent decisions upon some of the 'grudge cases' themselves and also for the more publicly dramatic proceedings after the Second World War at Nuremberg and Tokyo, as also for German 'de-Nazification' proceedings.

There remains the important question of the practical value of purposive naturalism in the real modern world. Fortunately the extreme cases of iniquity which wholly negate the conscientious claim to obedience of positive law are far from being the general experience of mankind. Much more common is the experience of legal structures which combine both 'good' and bad' aspects, in which neither the ideal nor an abomination is achieved — in short, the common product of the human mind with its combination of altruism and self-centredness, idealism and calculation. In this 'normal' case naturalism does not invite drastic assertions of validity or invalidity, indeed generally it counsels obedience upon more or less Platonic lines. Its importance lies in the informing moral and ethical climate within which law-making and legal implementation takes place. In one way or another all concerned with law, legislators, judges, lawyers in general and the people as a whole conceive of law as a phenomenon about which value judgements may be made which are distinct from the pragmatic issue of effectiveness. It is the role of naturalist principle to inform those value judgements and to set positive law-making in a rationally maintainable ethical and purposive light. Thus law-making may be judged in the light of its purpose and effect and in the light of such judgement argument for maintenance or change may be advanced. There is no conflict here with the positivist or realist analyses of law. The positivist asks what is identifiable as a formally applicable norm, the realist enquires into how such a norm takes effect upon its administrators and subjects, the naturalist is concerned with the fundamental claim of the law to be obeyed and into the wider propriety of its making and functioning. These are vital questions which cannot be excluded from the spectrum of jurisprudential study without its dangerous impoverishment.

Index

Index